NEW RELIGIONS & MENTAL HEALTH:

Understanding The Issues

Edited with an Introduction by
HERBERT RICHARDSON

THE EDWIN MELLEN PRESS
NEW YORK AND TORONTO

Symposium Series, Volume Five

New Material © The Edwin Mellen Press 1980
"Who Shall Define Reality for Us?" © Richard L. Rubenstein 1980
Excerpts from *Study of Mind Development Groups, Sects and Cults in Ontario*
© The Queen's Printer 1980

THE EDWIN MELLEN PRESS
Sales Office
P.O. Box 450
Lewiston, New York 14092

ISBN 0-88946-910-5

Symposium Series ISBN 0-88946-989-X

Printed in the United States of America

For
John Calvin Richardson
counselor, critic, comrade, son

PREFACE

Richard Ottinger, member of the United States Congress, wishes to introduce legislation to require medical treatment for persons who join certain religious groups. This legislation, formulated in New York as the Lasher Amendment, states that certain religions are so bad that no one could freely choose to belong to them. Therefore, membership in these groups should be regarded as "psychological slavery," i.e., the loss of free will. The proposed legislation contends that only by requiring persons who belong to such religions to give up their faith, through a pseudo-medical process called "deprogramming," can their free will be restored.

During the past decade the practice of "deprogramming" has grown from an occasional criminal activity to a practice now commended by legislatures as medically required. In the past, Rabbi Maurice Davis, whose congressional district Ottinger represents, has arranged for Ted Patrick, who has now been sentenced for kidnapping, to assault and lock-up members of religious groups. Patrick's victims have included Catholics and Episcopalians, as well as Hare Krishnas and Unificationists. Were Rabbi Davis only an isolated anti-cultist, he would be no more important than the isolated Christian anti-Semite. But, Rabbi Davis is not such an isolated exception. On this issue, he is a spokesman for his Rabbinical Association and for the Union of American Hebrew Congregations. Davis' initiative has also received support from many evangelical Christians of the "new right." For example, Davis' associate in establishing the New York deprogramming organization called CERF is George Swope, an evangelical Baptist minister.

Already this coalition of Jews and new right evangelicals has managed to win the passage in New York State of the "Lasher Amendment," which would require that persons who convert to religious groups be forced to undergo a medical treatment to give up their faith. Such a political initiative could not proceed without the support of certain psychiatrists, who seek to promote themselves as professionally competent to diagnose and cure a new illness: "faith sickness." For example, at a conference convened by Wayne State University School of Medicine, the New York legislator Howard Lasher was billed as a co-speaker with the psychiatrist Margaret Singer, both advocating enforced medical treatment of persons who experienced religious conversion. For attending this conference, Wayne State University awarded physicians "six hours of continuing education category II credit." In this way, a pseudo-medicine is created and given professional sanction.

One of the reasons why people are hesitant to say that Wayne State's pseudo-medicine resembles the German creation of a pseudo-science to justify the extermination of non-Aryans is that so many American Jews are actively promoting "deprogramming." "How could I, who belong to a persecuted people, persecute someone else for his religion?" asked an amazed rabbi. But having been persecuted does not guarantee that one does not become a persecutor.

It is a tragic irony that so many rabbis today fan the flames of religious bigotry. It is also a tragic irony that so many evangelical Christians, who believe that conversion is central to religion, should crusade against those whose conversion is to a religion other than their own orthodoxy. Certainly, evangelicals have also suffered from the liberal mockery of their religion. But the anger of evangelicals, as they gain increasing political influence, is now turned against groups whose zeal and practices resemble their own.

The irony is doubled when we see how many of the chief defenders of the new religious groups originate from those constituencies from which the "anti-cultists" also come. For example, no persons have been more instrumental in the present fight against religious bigotry than Jeremiah Gutman of the ACLU and Distinguished Professor Richard Rubenstein of Florida State University, both Jews. No persons have been more important in the struggle to maintain religious liberty than the evangelicals James Wood, of the Baptist Joint Committee on Public Affairs, and Dean Kelley, of the National Council of Churches. Kelley has written to Ottinger: "You must be under tremendous pressure from some of your constituents to 'do something' about 'cults,' and, having met some of them, I can sympathize with their concern and your plight, but the effort to 'go after' such groups can only be pernicious for religious liberty in this country."

This book seeks to present a range of issues involved in evaluating the legislative proposals of Ottinger, Lasher and others who seek to involve the government in evaluating and regulating religious practices. Many of the contributions to this book have been developed from recent conferences: the American Civil Liberties Conference on Religious Deprogramming, the University of Toronto Conference on Deprogramming, the University of Ottawa Conference on New Religions and the Toronto School of Theology Seminar on Media Ethics. It has been impossible to include all the papers which were presented at these conferences. But here is the proper place to thank all the participants. Their contributions to my own understanding of the issues have shaped the introductory essay in this volume.

There are, however, several persons whose support has been so crucial that, without it, the conferences would not have taken place nor this volume prepared. I wish, therefore, especially to thank Douglas Jay, Warren Jevons, Joseph O'Connell, Will Oxtoby, Aryeh Neier, Jeremiah Gutman, Dean Kelley, Anne Pritchard and Susan Reinbold.

Herbert Richardson
New York City
October, 1980

CONTENTS

PART IV   CONVERSION: A THEOLOGICAL VIEW

MENTAL HEALTH, CONVERSION, AND THE LAW

HERBERT RICHARDSON

PART I: DEFINING THE PROBLEM

This book gathers together a variety of documents and essays which help clarify the status of religious conversion in relation to the law. At the present time there are efforts being made, in several legislatures, to prohibit persons from changing their religious affiliation or from joining a different religion from that to which their family belongs. The general charge is that religious conversion, or even first-time adherence to certain religions, is a *prima facie* evidence of mental illness. A small group of psychiatrists have chosen to play the role of "expert witnesses" in testifying to courts and to legislators that religious conversion, or certain forms of religious belief, is an evidence of incompetence. They believe that persons who hold such belief, or who join certain religions, should be required to undergo involuntary treatment at their hands for the cure of such "illness."

In 1980, both houses of the New York State legislature passed a "mental health" bill which allows the state to appoint "conservators" to take physical custody of adults who have converted to, or otherwise joined, various religions and require them to suffer "medical attention for the proposed temporary conservatee as is necessary."[1] The legislation specifies that a criterion of the incompetence of the proposed conservatee is that the person's "judgment has become impaired to the extent that he is unable to understand the need for such care."[2] In other words, if a person should try to argue that he or she is healthy, reasonable, and voluntarily choosing to belong to a particular religion, this would constitute evidence that that person must be given medical treatment to "cure" this disease.

If this account sounds exaggerated, then the reader is urged to read the entire text of this New York State "Lasher Amendment," which appears in full in this volume. It should be noted that New York Governor Carey did veto the bill because "it places in jeopardy constitutionally guaranteed rights and raises false hopes by appearing to create an acceptable procedure — but one which would ultimately prove to be both unworkable and unconstitutional."[3] But, Carey continued, "I have asked my Counsel to work with the sponsors of this

---

Herbert Richardson is Professor of Religious Studies at the University of Toronto

bill in order to determine whether constitutionally acceptable legislation can be developed in this difficult area."[4]

The question whether, and what kind of, constitutionally acceptable legislation can be developed in order to control religious conversion 'or religious adherence is today being widely discussed. The major legal advocate for such legislation is Richard Delgado, assistant professor of law at the University of California. Delgado argues that some religious proselytizing is essentially "mental kidnapping." He argues that unless a person is given "full information about the cult and his future life in it should he choose to join" *before* he begins to get involved in it, then he has not joined the group voluntarily, but has been "mentally kidnapped."[5] Under such circumstances, argues Delgado, the state should be empowered to intervene in order to liberate the church member from his "mental kidnappers." This liberation from mental kidnapping will involve, necessarily, a mental therapy which will free the convert from his (supposedly involuntarily held) beliefs.

Another form of this argument is made by David Weisstub, a professor of law at York University in Canada. Weisstub criticizes Delgado for suggesting that "because the cults have an aura of deviancy about them, their members are to be viewed *prima facie* as corrupt citizens."[6] Weisstub rejects Delgado's view altogether ("He seems to be arguing that they are a threat to our social democracy, but more than that, that they induce psychoses.") He also rejects Delgado's proposal that the state intervene by means of conservatorships to liberate mentally kidnapped people from their religious groups. But Weisstub does argue that an alternative way for dealing with cult groups would be to invoke the law of "false imprisonment" or "mental restraint." Says Weisstub:

> The matter of mere mental restraint is more difficult. There has not been a case in false imprisonment with respect to cult behavior which has been grounded on mind coercion. However, there is some jurisprudence which suggests that such parameters could be built where as a secondary manifestation of mental fear or embarrassment, a plaintiff would find his movements restricted."[7]

One of the relative strengths of Weisstub's proposal — as opposed to Delgado's — is that it is at least religiously neutral. If one focuses on the act of religious proselytizing and conversion, then one is specially biased against religions that evangelize. But if one focuses on the conditions of adherence to a religion — any religion— then it is just as likely that someone born and raised a Catholic or a Jew is as likely to feel "mentally imprisoned" in his or her religion as someone who, later in life, converts to a group like the Baptists or the Hare Krishnas. These considerations help us see why all religions, and not just evangelical or new religions, have a special stake in the present efforts to create new legislation which seeks to determine allowable forms of religious life.

The legislative initiative in New York State, discussed above, is not an isolated incident. In many places there is an organized movement seeking to establish a foothold, or precedent, which can serve as the base for a broader attack against religion. For example, in Pennsylvania, State Legislator Goebel introduced a bill to investigate whether various churches "recruit and/or retain their membership by way of techniques which undermine voluntary consent, involve the use of duress, interfere with free will or otherwise involve improper mind control practices."[8] In Ontario, Provincial Legislator Sweeney introduced a bill which would establish a government commission "to investigate and report on any cult or mind development group, adherence to which is alleged to constitute a danger to the mental health of any person . . ."9 Note that the operative category in both these bills is "mental health." Such proposed legislation is the beginning of the effort by the state to define and to control the "mental health" of its citizens through empowering medical psychiatry to impose therapy on involuntary subjects.

That the supposed objects of such treatment are deserving "cultists" is not at all as clear as the proponents of such legislation claim. Again and again it is pointed out that the wording of their proposed legislation includes all religion. For example, in the Ontario legislature debate on the Sweeney bill, Legislator Breaugh spoke in opposition, saying:

> I do understand the problems parents go through when their children grow up and don't do the right thing in the parents' terms. That's been going on since man began. I don't know how you deal with that.
>
> I know people, friends of mine, who did what I thought were irrational acts when they were 16 and 17 years of age. They went off to convents and seminaries. They renounced worldly goods. They took a vow of poverty. They gave up the automobiles and the hockey sticks and the football games that I wanted and thought were important. They didn't want to go out with girls. They wanted to go into a seminary. How strange, I thought. How can they do that?
>
> They wore funny clothes. They had values the rest of the society didn't have. Were they a cult? No, they were Jesuits. I think, quite frankly, the Jesuit order in Canada and in the world has proved its value to our society.
>
> It's simply a matter of who's calling the shots. Who are the good guys? Who are the bad guys? It's incredibly difficult to do that.
>
> There are a couple of points in the principle of the bill I do find more than disturbing. One is the proposition that a commission be set up to do this.
>
> I would have hoped that in our free society, where our brothers and sisters have died in two world wars and in a police action in Korea to retain the rights of freedom that we have, we would not ever establish inquisitions or commissions or whatever name you would care to give them to provide that kind of activity.
>
> Secondly, nowhere in here does it say what is a cult and what is a mind development group. I listened very carefully to the arguments put forward this afternoon. I sympathize to some degree with them. But it's like saying that in here in this bill we decide the bad guys are going to get monitored and regulated and later on we'll tell who the bad guys are.10

The problem "Just what is a cult?" — is one of the basic stumbling blocks to the proposal to legislate against them. For example, within this volume the case of a Jewish attack on a Hebrew Christian cult is presented. In this incident, Rabbi J. Emmanuel Schochet led his group of Hassidic followers in an attack on a Messianic Jewish congregation. According to a document prepared and distributed by the Union of American Hebrew Congregations, such Hebrew Christians and Jews for Jesus constitute one of the two most dangerous cults. Marcia Rudin, a Jewish authority on cults, attacks them for deception: "The Hebrew Christians are not selling an honest product."[11] Rabbi Schochet, who led the attack, says "the Jews for Jesus missionaries invariably approach people who are under emotional stress, who have various problems, are lonely, perhaps alienated, looking for answers."[12] The Union of American Hebrew Congregations advises Jewish parents to consider deprogramming family members from their Messianic Jewish groups "only *after* your Rabbi has consulted with Rabbi Maurice Davis (his address appears under III above); and only after you have counselled with a psychologist or psychiatrist."[13] In this way, it involves the religious leadership of the Jewish community in the sanctioning and carrying out of kidnapping attacks.

However, although the Union of American Hebrew Congregations defines Hebrew Christian groups as dangerous "cults", anti-cult evangelicals — whose hostility to new religious movements equals that of the rabbis — deny this altogether. Brooks Alexander, a leader of the anti-cult "Spiritual Counterfeits" project located in Berkeley, California, writes:

> In the first place the concept of "cult" should not be equated with the intensity of commitment or involvement which is characteristic of the so called high demand groups, religious or secular. Nor is aggressiveness or proselytizing cultish in itself. Both of these qualities — in one form or another — are basic to authentic Christianity . . . .

> These two qualities in particular are worth singling out because they have apparently been the basis for *mis*labeling some groups as cults. Two groups which have occasionally been the target for such mistaken identification are "Jews for Jesus" and Campus Crusade for Christ.[14]

If the anti-cult Union of American Hebrew Congregations cannot agree with the anti-cult Spiritual Counterfeits project on the definition of a cult, then what hope is there that non-experts can agree? Rabbi Maurice Davis, the Union's authority on such matters, is said to have deprogrammed over 100 persons from various "cults." Brooks Alexander of the Spiritual Counterfeits project is no less active. But what is a cult for Rabbi Davis is not always a cult for Brooks Alexander. In Alexander's view, Davis might be deprogramming people from "real religions."

To make the situation even more confused, Rabbi Schochet and his Hassidic followers who attacked a Hebrew-Christian congregation for being a "cult" were themselves attacked as a cult by Rabbi Levyveld, the president of the Central Conference of American Rabbis. According to the *Jewish Post,* Rabbi Levyveld "compared the Lubavitch Hasidim as being in the 'cult' category along with the Moon Church, Scientology, and the Children of God."[15] Levyveld stated "that similarities of cults (including the Hasidim) are (a) authority of a charismatic leader; (b) the irrationality and mediaevalism of their stance; c) the deliberate driving of a wedge between parents and children; and d) the removal of the cult followers from society's mainstream."16

The *Jewish Post* went on to report that the local Hassidic rabbi Alevsky found it "incredible that a rabbi would make such a statement about an authentic Jewish movement, international in scope, and supported in its activities by the state of Israel, the Joint Distribution Committee and other Jewish groups in the U.S."17

So what is a cult? A Jewish rabbinical association, involved in deprogramming, says that the Jews for Jesus is a cult; the evangelical Spiritual Counterfeits project says that the Jews for Jesus is not a cult; a Hassidic rabbi and group which attacks a Hebrew Christian group for being a cult is itself called a cult by the president of yet another rabbinical conference. Anson Shupe, a University of Texas sociologist, notes that all three of these groups are "anti-cult cultists." And the Hare Krishnas go around to legislative hearings passing out pamphlets which say "Don't lump us in with *everyone else!*"18

Daniel Hill, the director of a one and a half year research study of "Mind Development Groups, Sects, and Cults" undertaken by the Ontario government, sees the key idea in "The Case Against the Cults" as "the brainwashing concept." The concept of "brainwashing," Hill notes, was developed in the 1950's by the Yale psychiatrist Robert Lifton.19 At this time, Lifton attempted to study the propaganda techniques used by the Communists on American prisoners during the Korean war and he created during the study the concept of "brainwashing." Although Lifton has not carried on research into the new religious groups, he has analogized about them on the basis of his earlier work. Hill says that "Lifton and advocates of his position claim that messianic leaders have developed techniques of thought reform, which do not require bodily restraint or physical coercion of subjects."20 These techniques involve the minimization of external influences, the development of a special language, and the manipulation of the recruit's sense of guilt. "Inner doubts about even the most bizarre cult doctrine and practice," says Lifton, "are then attributed to one's own evil, the influence of the devil, as represented by society outside, or in some cases specifically by one's own parents. Control over individual guilt is perpetuated by a variety of small and large group meetings, stressing criticism, self-criticism, continuous confession — and, at times, public humiliation of those who appear to deviate."21

By stressing the originality of Lifton's "brainwashing concept," Hill has located what is most interesting and critical to the present debate. The claim is being made, by Lifton and others, that they have discovered *a new form of mental illness.* For example, Dr. John Clark — an associate of Professor Lifton in the brainwashing controversy — claims that ordinary methods of psychiatric diagnosis cannot adequately diagnose the condition of "brainwashing."22 The mental illness of being brainwashed is so subtle, claims Clark, that it can elude an ordinary diagnosis. Hence, says Clark, a brainwashed person may appear, to the ordinary psychiatrist, as perfectly normal and healthy. This only shows, Clark argues, the depth and dangerousness of the condition — for the brainwashed person can actually fool an ordinary psychiatrist into thinking he is normal. Hence, Clark argues, only someone specially trained in the techniques of cult indoctrination is able to diagnose the brainwashed mental condition — for it is the essence of the brainwashed mental condition to appear normal and healthy, but "involuntary." Clark claims that he is one of the few psychiatrists competent to diagnose this new and dangerous mental condition.[23]

Because they contend that brainwashing is a new disease which eludes ordinary psychiatric diagnosis, Clark, Lifton, and other anti-religious psychiatrists, discount the reports and scientific studies carried on by "ordinary psychiatrists" which conclude that the claim of mental danger is exaggerated. For example, Dr. Saul Levine, in conjunction with the Hill study, made personal interviews with over 100 persons who had been members of allegedly dangerous religious groups. He also consulted with more than 20 clinical psychiatrists who claimed to have had direct experience with "cultists." (Those psychiatrists he interviewed included John Clark, Margaret Singer, and Susan Shulman — all psychiatrists active in the anti-cult deprogramming movement.)[24] From his entire sample, he received reports on only "25 individuals who were described as having had difficulties possibly relating to a cult of mind-bending groups.... [and that] Clinicians admitted that traditional and 'acceptable' religions and psychotherapies have also engaged in practices attacked in the groups under discussion."[25] However, Levine found that his interviewees seriously disagreed concerning "whether an over-age-of-majority adult enters a group freely or is duped, mentally coerced or hypnotized into sinking into the whole program, including time, energy, and money."[26] That is, although they had no significant *clinical* evidence that there was any damage to persons from new religions, many of the psychiatrists still entertained the idea that these people were not "freely" and "rationally" holding their beliefs.

The *problem* which Levine's interviews uncovered was not that members of new religious groups behave in unhealthy ways. Levine's research found that members of new religious groups, like members of traditional religious groups, appear generally normal. There are some who have symptoms of psychological illness, but, notes Levine, this condition frequently antedates membership in their religious group. The problem, Levine discovered was that many of the psychiatrists he interviewed *did* believe that persons who exhibited no empirical symptoms of any mental dysfunction were still "mentally coerced" and not voluntarily doing what they freely chose to do. The psychiatrists tended to view these religious persons as "brainwashed" and "self-deceived." These believers did not know they were acting involuntarily — and there was no behavioral abnormality to corroborate that claim. The only symptom of their sickness was that they belonged to a religious group with which the psychiatrist disagreed! That is the problem which Levine's research discovered, a problem with the psychiatrists!

Note how this argument, as advanced especially by Lifton and Clark, disqualifies an adult person from being able to claim that he or she is a trustworthy witness about the state of his or her own mental condition. A "brainwashed" person is someone who, when they do what they feel they freely choose, is actually acting unfreely. Evidence that they are acting freely is for them to choose what their deprogramming psychiatrist choose that they do. He knows the deeper springs of free action — and only he is in a condition to diagnose whether or not they are "mentally controlled" or "free."

Of course, society has come to accept the idea that there are some adult persons who feel they are acting freely and rationally, but are actually mentally ill.

Persons who are senile or schizophrenic often do not realize their condition and are taken into involuntary custody for prescribed medical treatment. However, in these cases, there is always some corroborating behavioral evidence which can be used to judge that a person is acting in a way which is dangerous to himself or herself. Does belonging to a religion belong in that class of deleterious self-injuring actions?

Though some anti-religionists argue that membership in a religious group is precisely such a self-injuring form of activity, the more fundamental argument — advanced by Clark, Lifton, Delgado, and others — is not that particular religious believers are self-injuring, but that the very act of religious faith and adherence is itself an involuntary and mentally coerced act. A free person, so their argument goes, would *never* convert to, or adhere to, a religion. Therefore, not the religious behavior, but the antecedent act of converting to or affiliating with a religion itself is the *prima facie* evidence of the loss of free choice. It is this act — conversion! — which should move the state to therapeutic intervention, argue Clark, Delgado, and their friends.

Of course, the continuing anti-religion tradition since Voltaire — or Rabelais or Lucretius — has repeatedly asserted that religious adherence is an irrational and unfree act of persons who are manipulated by priests who prey on their guilt and fear. The founder of modern psychiatry, Sigmund Freud, explained religious belief as a neurosis — a form of mental illness, though he was not sure it could ever be "cured." Much of the argument advanced by Lifton, Clark, Delgado and others is not new. What is new, however, is the creation of "the brainwashing concept" *as the name of a disease* and *the existence of a group of medical professionals* who seek to be empowered to treat it.

Of course, one might ask why, if the condition of religious superstition and irrationality has been so long in existence, we have come so recently to recognize it as a serious disease. It has been suggested that this is only the consequence of an ever-increasing secularization of a society that seeks to medicalize all human life and see everything therapeutically.[27] In such a secular society, the ancient charge that religion is superstition and never the voluntary act of a rational person begins to be reformulated as the charge that religion results from "brainwashing" and this condition can be reversed by medical intervention.

In fact, Lifton, Clark, and the other anti-religion psychiatrists do not believe that the present forms of religious conversion or adherence they denounce are like the older "neuroses" and "superstitions" which were denounced in earlier times. Lifton and Clark both believe that present day conversion is a *new* type of mental illness. It never existed before their time. That is why it was never discovered before. It never existed before. How could this be true?

On Lifton's account, the reason why the condition of "brainwashing" never existed before is that it was the communists, in their thought reform programs, who created the techniques of brainwashing. They have discovered how to effect mental control over even the free will of their victims. Such dangerous mind control techniques never existed before this generation because, argues Lifton, systematically totalitarian societies never existed before the present day.

Clark's argument, differs from Lifton's but resembles it in trying to account for the fact that "brainwashing" is a totally new emergence in human history. Clark claims that brainwashing derives from psychiatry — for it is psychiatry which has learned how to control human behavior. Speaking to a conference of predominantly anti-religious psychiatrists in Hanover, Germany, Clark said:

> As physicians and scientists, we have to recognize that "the cat is out of the bag." Popular religious leaders are seducing and manipulating people by using many of *our own discoveries. (Wir, as Aerzte und Wissenschaftler muessen erkennen, dass in dieser Kulterfahrung "die Katze aud dem Sack" ist. Die Volkskunst der Verfuehrung und zwingenden Ueberredung benutzt viele unserer Entdeckungen.)*[28]

Lifton and Clark argue, therefore, that brainwashing has only recently been discovered as a mental illness because brainwashing did not exist before our time. It came into existence only when people of a scientific cast of mind began to employ the techniques of psychological manipulation to deprive people of their free will *without their knowing it.* Because this new psychological illness is caused by the use of psychological tricks, it takes — so their argument goes — enforced psychiatric treatment to reverse the condition.

The use of medical labeling to "qualify" certain persons for medical "treatment" is a well-advanced development in our time. Professor Richard Rubenstein, in his essay appearing in this book, reminds us that in the Soviet Union political dissidents are certified as "insane" and placed in mental institutions:

> There is an institution near Moscow, the Serbsky Institute of Forensic Psychiatry, whose fundamental purpose is to convey to the dissident the message, "Your way of seeing things is madness . . . . We can certify with all the authority of scientific psychiatry that you are an outcast from normal society. No one will have to deal with the issues you raise.[29]

Similarly, Stephen Chorover, professor of brain science at the Massachusetts Institute of Technology, provides another example of "medical labeling" as a way of coping with unpopular social behavior. He reminds us, in his essay in this volume, that the American Medical Association discovered — in the nineteenth century — a new mental ilness: *drapetomania.*[30] The symptom of this disease, noted the physicians who diagnosed it, was a person's being overcome by an uncontrollable desire to run away. It was black slaves, they noted, who were most likely to be afflicted by it. When afflicted by drapetomania, the slaves would run away from their masters and seek freedom in the northern states. No healthy slave — so the doctors' argument went — could conceivably prefer "a new condition" to his loving plantation family. Those who ran away, they presumed, had to be afflicted by a disease.

The argument about *drapetomania,* like the argument of Lifton and Clark about "brainwashing," seeks to justify the status quo by labeling those who choose something new as "sick." What is the difference, we should ask ourselves, between the medical discovery of *drapetomania* in the nineteenth century and the medical discovery of "brainwashing" in our time. The nineteenth century took its social problems with the same degree of medical seriousness as we take ours.

Another newly discovered and diagnosed mental illness, appearing at yet an earlier time, is that of "witchcraft." Today people are "brainwashed"; an earlier century said they were "bewitched." The illness of "being bewitched" was actually discovered — or created — by scientific specialists living in the fourteenth to the seventeenth century. In America, the most learned man of his age — Cotton Mather — carried out witchcraft investigations. Here is part of his summary of the Trial of Martha Carrier, held in Salem on August 2, 1692:

> Martha Carrier was indicted for the bewitching of certain persons, according to the Form usual in such Cases, pleading NOT GUILTY to her Indictment; there were first brought in a considerable number of the bewitched persons who not only made the court sensible of a horrid Witchcraft committed upon them, but also deposed that it was Martha Carrier, or her Shape, that grievously tormented them by Biting, Pricking, Pinching, and Choking of them . . . . Moreover, the look of Carrier laid the Afflicted People for dead; and her Touch, if her Eye at the same time were off them, raised them again . . . .
>
> 2. Before the Tryal of this prisoner, several of her own children had frankly and fully confessed, not only that they were Witches themselves, but that their Mother had made them so . . . .
>
> 3. Benjamin Abbot gave his testimony, that last March this Carrier was very angry with him upon laying out some Land near her Husband's: her expression in this anger were "That she would stick as close to Abbot as the Bark stuck to the Tree; and that he should repent of it afore seven years came to an end, so as Doctor Prescott should never cure him . . . ."
>
> 4. Allin Toothaker testified that Richard, the son of Martha Carrier, having some difference with Him, pulled him down by the hair of the head. When he rose again, he was going to strike at Richard Carrier, but fell down flat on His back to the ground and had not the power to stir hand or foot until he told Carrier that he yielded; and then he saw the shape of Martha Carrier go off his breast . . . .
>
> 5. John Rogger also testified that upon the threatening words of this malicious Carrier, his cattle would be stranglely bewitched . . . .
>
> 6. Samuel Preston testified that about two years ago, having some difference with Martha Carrier, he lost a Cow in a strange Praeternatural unusual manner . . . .
>
> 7. Phebe Chandler testified that about a Fortnight before the apprehension of Martha Carrier, on a Lord's Day while the Psalm was singing in the Church, this Carrier then took her by the shoulder and, shaking her, asked her where she lived. She made no answer, although Carrier, who lived next door to her Father's house, could not in reason but know who she was . . . ."[31]

After several more evidences of witchcraft similar to the above, the court concluded that Martha Carrier was a witch and burned her to death. Cotton Mather added to his court record the following memorandum: "This rampant Hag, Martha Carrier, was the person of whom the Confessions of theWitches, and of her own children among the rest, agreed That the Devil had promised her she should be *Queen of Hag.*"[32]

Of course, many persons will see no resemblance at all between Cotton Mather's self-assured diagnosis of "bewitching" based on the testimony of children about the strange behavior of their mother and Robert Lifton's self-assured diagnosis of "brainwashing" based on the testimony of parents about the strange behavior of their children. Many will see no similarity between the medical diagnosis of *drapetomania* to account for slaves running away to new lives and the medical diagnosis of *brainwashing* to account for young adults joining new religions as a way of trying to create new lives. Every age tends to judge past science as silliness and to judge present science as indubitable truth. But the ancient charge of "bewitching" seems strangly akin to the modern charge of "brainwashing." It appeals to the same emotions and confusions. The only difference is that, in an earlier century, the theologians thought themselves able to distinguish normal psychological behavior from "bewitched" behavior while, today, psychiatrists think themselves able to distinguish normal religious behavior from the "brainwashed" kind.

PART II: SPECIAL INTEREST GROUPS

The debate about healthy and unhealthy religion would not have moved into legislative chambers were it not for the fact that there are self-interested constituencies who are seeking to have legislation created which will either prevent certain religious conversions from taking place or, if they do take place, have them reversed. Proposed legislation in Pennsylvania, Ontario, and elsewhere (included in this volume) seeks to limit the religious evangelism of specific groups. Proposed Legislation in New York State (the Lasher Amendment) seeks to require persons who have converted to certain religions to undergo an enforced psychiatric reversal of that condition, restoring them to their "families, prior religions, education, and society and its viable values."[33]

It is clear, as we have seen, that the special interest groups seeking to limit *conversion* are generally those defending the established *status quo*. "Prior religions" do not like to lose their members to "new religions." "Families" do not like to lose their children to "new families." "Society with its viable values" does not like to have people reject these values as unviable. Yet it is never the case that political initiative arises from such highly generalized concerns. Political initiative arises when there are organized and self-interested pressure groups at work, groups who have something to gain from the creation of new laws.

The anti-religion movement has been relatively successful in persuading the public that it is acting in the general interest. Yet even were this the case, the groups active in the anti-religion movement are still seeking to promote special interests of their own. Were we to see these special interests, we might evaluate the anti-religion initiative somewhat differently. What do these self-interested groups seek to gain for themselves from such legislation?

There are at least four special interest groups presently active in the anti-religion movement. They do not all agree all the time. We have, for example, already seen that what the rabbinical associations call a "cult" is denied to be a "cult" by evangelicals. Yet, Jewish anti-conversionists have been active in promoting their special interests in conjunction with their war against the cults - while evangelical heresy hunters, although cooperating, have sought their quite different goals. In addition to Jewish anti-conversionists and evangelical heresy hunters there are two other special interest groups who have promoted the attack on new religions for their own ends: psychiatrists concerned with behavior control and the popular media. All four of these special groups seek to advance their particular interests in conjunction with their attacks on religion — although their particular interests are not at all overlapping. These four groups are a coalition; they will all profit in different ways if their anti-religion crusade suceeds. Yet they have all failed to be "up front" about their purposes. They all claim to be acting only in the public interest — in the name of "normalcy" and "health." In order better to understand what each of these groups has to gain from anti-conversion legislation, we must consider them one by one.

The Jewish Anti-Conversionists

Judaism differs from Christianity by regarding birth, rather than choice, the basis of identity. A Jew is one who is born of a Jewish mother. For this reason, Judaism — unlike Christianity — does not actively evangelize or seek to convert non-Jews to Judaism. Sometimes it is said that Judaism's not seeking converts, or not evangelizing, is a sign of moral superiority or religious tolerance. But this is not the case. Judaism does not proselytize because of moral reasons, but because it determines Jewish identity on the basis of birth rather than voluntary choice.

It is neither more moral nor less moral to define religious identity on the basis of birth rather than conversion, or choice. The familistic, or birth-determined, character of Jewish identity has been attacked by some as "racism" or "tribalism." Such attacks are either ignorant or else malicious misrepresentation. But they point out that far more critical than any theological difference between Judaism and Christianity is the fact that these two religions are also different kinds of religion sociologically. For Christianity, birth (race and family) does not determine religious identity. Religious identity, in Christianity, is determined by a decision and an affiliation. Birth is, for the issue of identity, *irrelevant*. This is why St. Paul says, "In Christ, there is neither Greek nor Jew."

From the perspective of Judaism, the conversion of a Jew to another religion is a contradiction in terms. To be a Jew is to have an identity from birth; it is not possible to choose not to have that birth. Hence, for a Jew to convert is not merely for him or her to choose his or her own religion; rather, it is for that person to choose his own non-existence. Hence, within Judaism there is a prayer which expresses that — for Jews — a Jew who has converted to another religion has ceased to exist.

The Jewish theory of religious identity, together with its in principle rejection of the very possibility of conversion, is a consistent and meaningful theological idea. It is not, as some argue, merely a practical strategy arising primarily out of the Jewish struggle to survive. Jews have always been, so this argument goes, a small group within a larger culture. They are zealously evangelized and always in danger of assimilation. Hence, the argument continues, Jews must oppose all conversion attempts if they are to survive. More recently, this point of view adopts holocaust rhetoric, as when Rabbi Immanuel Schochet says that "in the past where Nazis were successful in taking our Jewish bodies, Jews for Jesus missionaries are now working to take Jewish souls."[34] Evangelizers, in his view, are spiritual Nazis — and every Jewish convert to Christianity has been gassed to death in a spiritual Auschwitz.

That the "small Jewish community" is in danger of being engulfed by a larger world is NOT the essential reason behind Judaism's opposition to conversion. The ideas of Judaism are perfectly able to commend and sustain themselves by their intrinsic dignity and claim to truth. Abraham Heshel and Martin Buber present Judaism in a way that wins the assent of heart and mind. Yet in Israel, where Jews are not an endangered minority, the state has passed anti-conversion laws. These Israeli laws are hardly needed to protect a small Jewish minority from being assimilated in a larger population. They were passed because of the strong feeling among Jews that conversion is something wrong *in principle*, since it logically contradicts the idea that Jewish identity is a matter of *birth*.

The Israeli anti-conversion laws were also passed, it should be noted, at exactly the same time as Rabbi Maurice Davis and the Union of American Hebrew Congregations began using the brainwashing charge in order to discredit evangelism and conversion in America. Rabbi Davis and his rabbinical association have sought to legitimate the practice of "deprogramming," or reversing the conversion of persons to other religions. Should we believe that, behind their attacks, there is only animosity toward "cults" and not also a concern to discredit the idea of conversion *per se* and to make normative, as an alternative, the Jewish idea that religious identity should be determined by family membership rather than (the Christian idea) that religious identity should be determined by decision and an act of affiliation.

But, one might object, Rabbi Davis and his rabbinical association are not opposing *all* evangelism and conversion. They only oppose the new religions that "brainwash" and do harm to people's mental health. In reply, it should certainly be acknowledged that this is the *professed* goal of Rabbi Davis and his associates. But the New York State legislation promoted by Rabbi Davis and others in the Jewish community does not limit its applicability to specifically named "cults." The Lasher Amendment says that if the behavior of anyone changes while he or she is in close contact with *any group whatsoever* which might influence, in various ways, his or her behavior, then any spouse, parent, grandparent, child or (under certain circumstances) appropriate state official may seek to be established as that person's conservator and require him or her to undergo treatment to change that condition.[35] The legislation, as drafted, is aimed to prevent *all* conversion to *any* religious group. When one hears that "This is not the *intention* of the legislation," then one must ask why not write what is intended more precisely in words!

There is a close relation between the anti-conversion legislation in Israel and the anti-religious activity of many Jews in the United States and Canada. The special interest sought by these Jews is to discredit the general idea of *conversion*. Behind their professed concern for "mental health" is their own vested religious interest: in defining religious identity in terms of birth and family. They seek to discredit the idea that voluntary religious affiliation (as the basis of identity) is mentally healthy. Their effort to establish anti-conversion legislation is an effort by these Jewish anti-conversionists to establish *their own* form of religion as normative for society at large. This interest is legitimate, just as the Christian interest in maintaining the conditions of religious voluntariness is a legitimate one. But neither interest, in the present debate, should hide itself behind the mask of "mental health."

The Evangelical Heresy Hunters

A second active interest group promoting anti-religious legislation is composed of evangelical heresy hunters. This may seem an anomaly, since evangelical Christianity bases its idea of true religion directly on *conversion*. One would think, therefore, that evangelicals would be most active in the general defense of the right of persons to evangelize and to convert. Yet, although there are many individual evangelicals who are active in opposing legislative initiatives to limit evangelism and conversion, the weight of the evangelical opinion today seems to support the anti-cult crusade.

Historically, it was the evangelicals who created the pejorative use of the word "cult." "Cultists" were those whom evangelicals found as their direct competition in their door-to-door and street corner preaching. In earlier decades, the most important "cultists" attacked by evangelicals were Christian Scientists, Seventh Day Adventists, Mormons, and Jehovah's Witnesses. Even today evangelically inspired deprogrammers "snatch" members of these groups to destroy their heretical beliefs and restore them to the true gospel faith. For example, Pam Fanshier — a young woman who was deprogrammed by Joe Alexander — says that "Mr. Alexander informed me that not only all 'cult' members would have to be deprogrammed, but eventually all Mormons, Jews, Jehovah's Witnesses, people who meditated and members of all groups who did not accept Jesus . . . ."[36] Even Billy Graham, well known Baptist evangelist, in an article headlined "It's Dangerous to Practice Transcendental Meditation," says:

> These millions of people don't know what they are letting themselves in for. If a person meditates without religious content — leaving himself with an empty and susceptible mind — there is a great danger that satanic influences will take over . . . . The only lasting effects of mediation, in my belief, occur with it takes the form of a service prayer in the name of Jesus Christ and the Holy Spirit.[37]

More recently, evangelical heresy hunters have targeted their "cult" rhetoric on the new religions. According to Brooks Alexander of the Spiritual Counterfeits project, the especially dangerous cults today are not the Mormons and the Christian Scientists; today they are the Moonies, Scientologists, and Hare Krishnas.[38] Alexander, because he is an evangelical, does not agree with Rabbi Davis in regarding heavy evangelizing and conversion as the mark of a cult. Rather, for Alexander, the primary mark of a cult is that it teaches a non-Scriptural doctrine. Says Alexander, "Qualities which can be recognized as cultic in terms of a *theological* definition (i.e., constituting deviations from orthodoxy) would include the following:

> 1. *A false or inadequate basis of salvation.* The apostle Paul drew a distinction that is utterly basic to our understanding of truth when he said, "By grace are you saved through faith; and that not of yourselves; it is the gift of God: not of works, lest any man should boast" (Eph. 2: 8-9). Inasmuch as *the* central doctrine of biblical Christianity is the sacrificial death of Christ for our sin, all cultic deviations tend to downplay the finished work of Christ and emphasize the importance of earning moral acceptance before God through our own righteous works as *the basis for salvation.*

2. *A false basis of authority.* Biblical Christianity by definition takes the Bible as its yardstick of the true, the false, the necessary, the permitted, the forbidden, and the irrelevant. Cults, on the other hand, commonly resort to extrabiblical documents or contemporary "revelation" as the substantial basis of their theology (e.g., Mormons). While some cult groups go through the motions of accepting the authority of Scripture, they actually honor the group's or the leader's novel *interpretation* of Scripture as normative (e.g., Jehovah's Witnesses, The Way International).[39]

Of course, we have read and heard this kind of argument about theological orthodoxy all our lives. But the factor that makes things different this time is that many evangelicals are crusading politically to legislate their conception of religious orthodoxy for everyone else in society. These evangelicals not only promote such anti-cult legislation as the Lasher Amendment, they also seek to legislate other things which would force people who do not agree with them to act in violation of their consciences: legally enforced prayers in schools, legally enforced confessions of belief in Christ for holders of public office, legally enforced censorship of books and programs deemed offensive to biblical morality, legally enforced heterosexuality. The political efforts of an organized group of evangelicals to impose their particular conceptions of religious and moral orthodoxy upon society at large is one of the major political factors in America today. This political effort has also found a cause in promoting such anti-cult legislation as the Lasher Amendment in New York State.

However, it may be objected that if the Lasher Amendment is anti-conversion, then it would seem that the evangelicals — who evangelize and seek to convert — would oppose it. This objection misunderstands, however, the essential interests of the evangelical community. The essential interest of the evangelical heresy hunters is for religious and moral orthodoxy — as it defines orthodoxy — rather than for pluralistic freedom. Orthodoxy stands first in the scale of values.

It is God's Scriptural revelation which is the foundation of the evangelical movement. Hence, the evangelical is interested in freedom as the right of people to preach and to accept THIS revelation. Freedom in general, or freedom to belong to a different kind of religion or no religion at all, is not rigorously defended by most evangelicals today as true freedom. Rather, it is called "license" and "sin." For this reason, many evangelicals seek today to impose their orthodoxy on others.

Of course, the evangelical community — like the Jewish community — also provides strong defenders of pluralistic freedom. William Willoughby, an evangelical journalist, is also a chief defender of religious freedom for Scientologists. Moreover, the Unification Church has been accepted as a dialogue partner by many evangelicals who, in this way, both defend the religious freedom of the Moonies while vigorously seeking to persuade them they are wrong. But such cases seem to be the exception. The evangelical community originally generated the language of "cult" and actively promotes its conception of religious orthodoxy throughout the land.

It is ironic that many of those same legislators who would vote in favor of laws against some religious groups would be the first to be dismissed when they refused to take the "faith in Christ" oath of office other religious groups would require of them by law. People seem not to understand that the involvement of the state in religion can eventually become an involvement to be used against *them*. If evangelicals can persuade legislators to outlaw certain kinds of religion, they can — and soon will — require legislators to enforce other kinds. One must see that the evangelical support for legislation to control new religions is part of its larger effort to create a Christian America. These evangelicals comprise the second special interest group in the anti-cult coalition.

Anti-Religious Psychiatrists

We have already considered the role of the psychiatric profession in creating the concept of "brainwashing" as a kind of illness. Robert Lifton, Margaret Singer, John Clark, William Sargant are all psychiatrists who have played a key role in the construction of this concept and its legal defense. They speak in professional societies, write papers, appear as expert witnesses in legal cases, testify before legislatures. Some of them work in close relation to the various deprogramming organizations. For example, one of the issues of the newsletter of CERF, the deprogramming organization established by Rabbi Maurice Davis and the evangelical clergyman George Swope, contains the information that "There has been a confusing report that we cancelled the meeting between U.S. Attorney General (AG) Levi and Dr. Lifton, which is not true. His office did tentatively agree to let Dr. Lifton and Professor Delgado meet with the Chief of the Criminal Division, Mr. Keetch . . . ."[40]

However, we have not yet considered the specific personal gain that psychiatrists stand to gain from legislation such as the Lasher Amendment. Of course, some psychiatrists are strongly opposed to involuntary psychiatric treatment. For example, Dr. Thomas Szasz has the utmost contempt for Lifton's "concept of brainwashing." He asks:

> What is brainwashing? Are there, as the term implies, two kinds of brains: washed and unwashed? How do we know which is which? Actually, it is all quite simple. Like many dramatic terms, brainwashing is a metaphor. A person can no more wash another's brain with coercion or conversation than he can make him bleed with a cutting remark. If there is no such thing as brainwashing, what does this metaphor stand for? It stands for one of the most universal human experiences and events, namely, for one person influencing another. However, we do not call all types of personal or psychological influences "brainwashing." We reserve this term for influences of which we disapprove.[41]

However, mere dislike of new religious groups is not sufficient to explain the personal interest of many psychiatrists in "brainwashing," nor is this sufficient to account for their support of legislation that would make them state-appointed custodians of the mental health of members of these religions. The personal interest of many psychiatrists in such legislation is that they will profit by providing treatment for this new clientele. Legislation such as the Lasher Amendment increases the psychiatrists' "market share."

One problem with psychiatrists' diagnosing conversion or religious faith is that an anti-religious bias is built into the very foundations and history of the psychoanalytic movement itself. Freud claimed religion was a "neurosis." Few psychiatrists are religiously neutral. In fact, for reasons well understood, psychiatry and religion are competitors, for both claim to provide effective knowledge about the life of the soul. How, then, can it be presumed that psychiatrists do not have a stake in excluding religious leaders from "the care of souls" in order to increase their own share of the business?

Professors Thomas Robbins and Dick Anthony point out, in their study "Cults versus Shrinks: Psychiatry and the Control of Religious Movements" that

> 1. "Cults" and "shrinks" are competitors, i.e., many persons attempt to improve themselves or resolve their difficulties with the assistance of Scientology or gurus instead of employing "legitimate" therapists;

> 2. Religious "deprogramming" and auxiliary services for the "rehabilitation" of cultists and ex-cultists expand vocational opportunities for psychiatrists and psychologists as well as for social workers, lawyers, detectives, clergy, and ex-devotees.[42]

If it can be presumed that the size of the market for "legitimate" deprogramming of persons by professional psychiatrists is roughly equivalent to that developed by undercover Ted Patrick-types, then it amounts to over $4,000,000 a year. (This is the ACLU estimate of monies spent on deprogramming in the year 1977.)[43] If one adds to this income from the involuntary deprogramming of converted persons the still larger market arising from people who come for "psychiatric counseling" because they have been inhibited from seeking religious help from gurus or person-developing spiritual groups, then there is an even larger clientele and income created for the psychiatric profession.

It is amusing that, however angrily people protest about religious converts engaging in fund raising, no convert has ever been accused of raising even 1/5 as much in a single hour as a typical psychiatrist charges for an hour of treatment. When we ask how the selfish interests of psychiatrists are served by anti-conversion legislation, the answer is obvious. It gives them more dollars and cents. Can anyone, therefore, take seriously the claims of psychiatrists to be scientifically disinterested when they, more than any other group, stand to profit financially from the proposed changes in the law? Moreover, since psychiatrists specialize in adjusting people to the *status quo,* "society and its viable values,"rather than changing it, they are the perfect therapists to set in opposition to religious prophets who seek to change the world.

Another paper in this volume "Professional versus Traditional," compares psychiatrists and religious leaders in terms of their different ways of influencing behavior. We have already seen how Dr. John Clark warns, with great concern, that "the cat is out of the bag": religious leaders are using the same seductive and manipulative methods that psychiatrists have been using all along. Actually, according to Professor Richard Weisman, Clark's fear is only Clark's own bad conscience. Weisman shows that religious leaders and psychiatrists are both engaged in a struggle to find "consumers to whom to offer their services." But their strategies and techniques differ. Psychiatrists, says Weisman, attempt to gain and securely possess their clientele through the device of "professionalization." "Professionalization may be viewed as a collective strategy for transforming skills into scarce resources and, in turn, for transforming those scarce resources into . . . money."[44]

Religious leaders, Weisman points out, cannot gain their clientele in this way, i.e., by persuading the state to license and thereby artificially to make their services scarce. "Religious leaders must promote their services in full view of the public . . . . Their strategy of proselytization bears the character of groups who must compete on a relatively open market, and who must therefore occasionally appear in the somewhat undignified posture of helpers who need clients."[45]

If a legislator were to make a plea for the passage of a law whose effect would be to profit him financially, this would be regarded as a serious breach of political morality. When, however, psychiatrists (such as John Clark and Margaret Singer) actively promote before legislative committees the passage of anti-religious legislation which would have the effect of benefiting them financially, we are not so quick to charge a conflict of interest. But conflict of interest there is — and it is precisely because anti-conversion legislation would be so especially profitable for psychiatrists that their political interest in it cannot be explained as merely benevolent concern for the public at large.

The Media

The special interest of the media is to sell newspapers and to attract viewers. The "cult-story" has all the drama needed: religion, money, sex, family, exotic races, strange cultures, supposed conspiracies, white-hatted vigilantes, and resonances with America's Asian wars.

The press plays the "cult story" for all the papers it can sell. The press has always done this, and always will. For example, in the 19th century, Harper Brothers (now New York's Harper and Row) set up a dummy publishing company to sell and promote Maria Monk's "Awful Disclosures of the Hotel Dieu Nunnery of Montreal." According to Maria Monk, who was an ex-member of the group she was then exposing, Catholic nuns in her convent were "executed for refusing to obey the lustful will of priests and the strangling of two small babies."[46] Maria claimed that she had become pregnant by one of the priests whose lust she was obligated to serve, and fled the nunnery because she would have been required to strangle her own infant at birth.

Maria's story, loudly vented in the public press, appealed to the increasing anti-Catholic feeling in the America of the 1840s. Journals sought to outdo themselves in reporting Catholic atrocities. The public was enraged and, in certain cases, broke into religious houses in order to liberate the young novices who were held there captive. A perverse power to enslave the young was attributed to the Catholic clergy — especially Jesuits — who were accused of playing on the superstitutions and credulity of the young.

Why is it the argument and rhetoric directed against the new religions so resembles the rhetoric of earlier anti-Catholicism and anti-Semitism. Compare for example, the earlier claims of anti-Catholicism and anti-Semitism with today's anti-cultism.

Anti-Catholicism	*Anti-Semitism*	*Anti-Cultism*
The pope is seeking to take over the world.	The Jews are seeking to take over the world. (The Protocols of the Elders of Zion)	Moon is seeking to take over the world.
Catholicism is not a true religion, but a political system.	Judaism is not a religion, but a political system.	The Unification Church is not a church but a political front group.
Catholics aren't loyal Americans, but are really loyal to Rome — a foreign power.	Jews aren't loyal Americans, but are really loyal to Israel.	Moon teachs Americans to fight for Korea.
The Catholic church exploits the poor in order to build rich churches and buy land.	Jews are really only after money.	Moon claims to be a prophet, but is really only after profit.
The priests enslave the minds of young people, inculcating irrational superstitution.	Judaism is a legalistic, tribalistic system, ritualistic and anti-rational.	Moon brainwashes his converts.
Catholics control their young people's lives by teaching that sex is evil.	Jews control their young people's lives by making them feel guilty about marrying a non-Jew.	Moon controls young people's lives by making them remain chaste and then arranging their marriages.
Catholics justify lying by "mental reservation."	Jews always lie.	Moonies don't tell the truth but practice "heavenly deception."
Catholics entice children, while too young to decide for themselves, to become nuns and priests.	Jews kidnap gentile children for vile purposes.	Moon entices the young to leave their families.
Catholics are swarthy (Latin) and have too many children.	Jews have crooked noses and are verminous.	Moonies have glazed-eyes and are under-nourished.

Why is it that all three of these anti-religious rhetorics play on the same themes? Does not the very similarity of pattern in these three anti-religious rhetorics make us suspect that they are based more on primitive hatred than on empirical analysis? When I hear the Catholic Father LeBar vilifying "cultists," I am always reminded that I, when young, heard a protestant fundamentalist describe Catholics in the same way. There was even a "converted Catholic priest" who, coming on a regular lecture circuit, would describe how horribly the Catholic church had held him by the mental chains of "superstitution" until he escaped. Today, "ex-cultists" travel the same circuit telling how they were "mentally imprisoned" by Sun Myung Moon. Again, when I hear Rabbi Maurice Davis or Rabbi James Rudin vilifying the Moonies, I am struck by the fact that what they are saying is exactly what Hitler said about the Jews.

Anti-cultism is the anti-Semitism of the Jews; anti-cultism is the anti-Catholicism of the Catholics. Anti-cultism exploits these two older forms of anti-religious rhetoric and makes possible an ecumenical chorus of primitive Protestant-Catholic-Jewish hate. In reply, Rev. Moon once laughingly remarked — "I have managed to achieve my greatest goal. I have united all religions."[47]

The press today, like the press in earlier generations, fans the popular passions. It fans these passions not merely by reporting what is going on, but by creating the sense that something is going on — when not much is. The press creates pseudo-events and invents pseudo-threats and dangers to "your child" in order to sell papers.

For example, according to Marcia Rudin — an intemperate opponent of the "cults" — Moon's Unification Church has "7000 hardcore members."[48] (Ms. Rudin believes that the Unification Church is a great danger and therefore her estimate of its membership is surely not understated.) If, now, we accept her figure, we might ask how a group which has only as many members as, say, a small college has students can manage to be under constant discussion in the press? Hardly a day goes by without some press coverage on Moon. Are the cults *really* an event of this magnitude? Or is their magnitude really the creation of the press?

For almost a decade now the membership of Moon's Church has remained a stable 5000-7000. But the press, by constantly discussing the Moonies, makes us believe they are everywhere. By its stories, the press creates our sense that the Unification Church is a vital growing movement — one to concern us and about which we should think.

This is probably nonsense. The cults are so small they are no problem. But making them appear big in order to justify, and create a claim for, new laws *is* a problem.

Anti-cultism sells papers. But by creating stories about "cults" out of all proportion to their actual magnitude, the American press has promoted anti-cultism just as German papers once promoted the anti-Semitic frame of mind. Once these anti-religious feelings have been created, there can be a public pressure to pass laws against cultists and laws against Jews. The press here — as once in Germany — makes everyone feel that there is a conspiracy afoot and that dangerous members of alien religious groups are everywhere.

Marcia Rudin's American membership figures for the largest new religions, are:[49]

Hebrew Christians	10,000
Unification Church	7000
Church of Scientology	5000-10,000
Children of God	5000 (Worldwide)
Hare Krishna	1500

Can we really believe that this number of people constitutes such a danger, that we should urge our legislators to modify, for 250,000,000 citizens, their national Constitution and Bill of Rights? This is what is urged by the anti-cultists and what is promoted by much of the press?

PART III

JUDICIAL DECISIONS & GOVERNMENTAL STUDIES

Of the vast number of judicial decisions relating to new religions that have been made in the last decade, the one selected for inclusion in this volume is the Queens County decision in the Hare Krishna/Angus Murphy case. This decision relates directly to the charge that "brainwashing" or improper "mental contraint" is exercised by the new religious groups over their members.

The case is also interesting because it reveals something of the complex personal and family strains that must, inevitably, lie behind the action of a parent seeking to bring his adult son or daughter to court. In this case, we see a family conflict that has overflowed into the public sphere, where parents are seeking to use the courts to compel their adult children to do what the parents want. This legal intervention is sought in the name of "family unity." But it is questionable whether family unity can ever be achieved this way. The Queens County case shows clearly that the disruption of love and trust between parents and their offspring often *antedates* the young adult's involvement in a new religion. The subsequent attempt by the parent to *blame* the religion for this separation is clearly false.

The Queens County Case

The background to the Queens County case is as follows: A young college age woman named Merylee Kreshour joined the New York Hare Krishna community in 1974. Two years later, her mother arranged with a New York private detective named Galen Kelly to kidnap and confine her until she had given up her religious beliefs and practices. Hence, in the words of the Queens court judgment, "The uncontradicted testimony adduced in respect thereto shows that Merylee Kreshour (who at the time was and to the present day remains a member of Iskcon, Inc.) was forcibly taken from a street in Queens County on August 3, 1976 by her mother and others and for a period of four days was subjected to a treatment referred to as "deprogramming." This treatment, the mother testified, was administered in order to liberate her daughter's mind and to restore her "free will." The mother testified further that her daughter was a victim of "mental kidnapping" by the defendant Iskcon, Inc. (Hare Krishna Group) and that by physically taking her daughter into custody she was "rescuing her."[50]

When Merylee Kreshour was released from her deprogrammers, she sought to bring a legal suit against them for her kidnapping. To do this, an account of what happened to her had to be presented to the Grand Jury. Not only did the Grand Jury refuse to accept her plea, but it turned around and laid counter charges against the Hare Krishnas and their leader, Angus Murphy. These were charged with engaging in the "unlawful imprisonment" of the Hare Krishna members. The method of this unlawful imprisonment, it was acknowledged, was not by physical force, but "mental." The Grand Jury's charge was that Hare Krishna members

> Were deceived or inveigled into submitting themselves "unknowingly to techniques intended to subject their will to that of the defendants . . ." and that the same resulted in ". . .an evil consequence . . . ." The entire argument propounded by the People is that through "mind control," "brainwashing," and/or "manipulation of mental processes" the defendants destroyed the free will of the alleged victims, obtaining over them mind control to the point of absolute dominion and thereby coming within the purview of the issue of unlawful imprisonment.[51]

In its charge against the Hare Krishna group (and its leader, Angus Murphy), the Grand Jury named as "victims" Merylee Kreshour and a second Hare Krishna member, Ed Shapiro. Shapiro had joined the group while at Brandeis University and had a pilgrimage to India where he discovered, much to his delight, that practically everyone there was a Hare Krishna and it was "normal" to be one. When Ed Shapiro returned to New York, he was pursued by his angry father and named, by the Queens County Grand Jury, as one of the brainwashed victims of the cult.

In his evaluation of the Grand Jury's charge, Judge Leahy of the Queens County Court decided that "as to the premise posed by the People that the religious rituals, daily activities and teaching of the Hare Krishna religion constitute a form of intimidation to maintain restraint over the two alleged victims, the court finds no legal foundation or precedent for the same but a concept that is fraught with danger in its potential for utilization in the suppression — if not the outright destruction — of our citizens' right to pursue, join and practice the religion of their choice, free from a government created, controlled, or dominated religion . . . ."[52] Judge Leahy went on to sound "the dire caveat to prosecutional agencies throughout the length and breadth of our great nation that *all* of the rights of *all* our people so dearly gained and provided for, under the Constitution of the United States and the Constitutions of all the States of our Nation, shall be zealously protected to the full extent of the law."[53]

In his decision, Judge Leahy recognized that not only had the Grand Jury failed to protect the rights of Merylee Kreshour, but that there was a general reluctance in America to prosecute the kidnappers and deprogrammers of members of new religious groups.

The legislators of New York State, faced with Judge Leahy's decision, have therefore now sought to change the law of the state to allow the very kind of deprogramming which his Queens County decision had disallowed. This change was to take the form of an amendment to the Mental Health Act (the "Lasher Amendment") and it was approved by both houses of the New York State legislature by large majorities. Only the veto of Governor Carey, citing its unconstitutionality, prevented the Lasher Amendment from becoming law.

But, together with his veto, Governor Carey also proposed the establishment of a joint committee to find constitutional means to achieve the same end.

Part of the downright absurdity of the Queens County decision — an aspect that reveals the utter irrationality of the public state of mind — is that the leader of the New York Hare Krishna Temple, who was accused of exerting mind control over the 24 year old Ed Shapiro was Angus Murphy, 23 years old and Shapiro's close friend in high school. In commenting later on the absurdity of the situation, Murphy said:

> My reaction to this case is one of shock. The fact is that the person I'm supposed to have under the control of my mind is twenty-four years old and I'm twenty-three years old. This person is a personal friend of mine. He was a friend of mine in high school, and his father, Dr. Eli Shapiro, used to chase after us when we were sneaking off to the Cape, cutting school and going to hockey games, because his son wanted to avoid the regimen his father was trying to impose on him. So I think there has been a longstanding animosity between Ed and his father. Second, it was Ed Shapiro who introduced *me* to Krishna Consciousnes. I didn't introduce him to it. In high school, he used to visit the Hare Krishna temple. His friends thought that he was a little insane; why didn't he just go and play hockey with the rest of us? He just seemed to be interested in going to the Hare Krishna temple, and his father was always trying to stop him. There was always a battle between him and his father. He didn't like his father. His father's first wife had died, and his father had married his secretary. Ed always resented that. Ed's animosity was based on that, and was compounded by his father's attempts to control his life. I watched Dr.Shapiro develop — I would even term it though I'm no professional — a kind of mental disease, as he pursued his son all over the countryside, from San Francisco to Boston to New York, to India. Ed's father was always trying to find out where he was. I was usually with Ed, and therefore gradually there began a fixation in Dr. Shapiro's mind about me.
>
> It seems to me that a phobia grows within the mind due to fears or misgivings so that people are willing to ascribe to others strange powers and capabilities. I'm astonished to hear, for instance, that others think I have emanations coming out of my fingertips and that you can't look into my eyes or you'll become hypnotised. (When I told these things to my spiritual master in India he just laughed.) . . . The fear in this instance led to my indictment for mind control by the same man whom I've known for seven or eight years, and whom I can remember from my high school years as an oppressive father. That same person was indicting me, or rather through the agency of the State I was being indicted for a crime of controlling his son's mind. But it seems to me that I was indicted because of the failure of the relationship between a father and a son. That's all.[54]

The Goelters Report

One of the consequences of the strict separation of church and state which characterizes America is that the government has, at least until recently, sought to avoid becoming entangled with religion. That principle of separation is under attack in America today. Some groups seek tax support for religious schools; other groups seek to require prayers in public schools; still other groups seek to make laws to investigate or otherwise harass particular religions. As Judge Leahy, in his Queens County Hare Krishna decision says, "Neither congress nor the states may establish a religion or compel individuals to favor one religion over the other."[55] He might have said "*disfavor* one religion over another."

In Germany, however, there is no such separation of church and state as is found in America. The Lutheran and Catholic churches have an "established" status and are financially supported by tax funds collected by the government. This system is so deeply rooted that even in East Germany the Communist government, though opposed to religion, has continued to collect and dispense the "church tax." The German government, unlike the American government, does, therefore, claim a right to favor some religions and to disfavor others. It does seek to guarantee to its citizens the right to have the religious affiliations they prefer. But Germany does not accept, at the same time, the absolute separation of church and state that is characteristic of America. In Germany, therefore, the government can and does label some religious groups as good and others as bad; it does favor some religions *qua* religions and disfavor other religions *qua* religions. This is one consequence of having an "established religion" — and it partly explains why in Germany the government could undertake a study which labels some religious groups as "destructive" (*Juegendliche in destructiven religioesen Gruppen*).

In America, notes Dean Kelly of the National Council of Churches, it is not the business of government to decide what is true or false, constructive or destructive in *religion*. What is good judgment, according to some people, is bad religion according to others. But in Germany things are different — and worse. This is because the "scientific" basis for the German government's evaluation of religions in the Goelters report is a *public opinion poll*! (See my longer essay in this volume.)

The Hill Report

A second government study of new religions is also included in this volume. It comes from another country where there is also no sharp separation of church and state. In Canada, as in Germany, there is a degree of establishment of religion. For example, in Canada tax funds are used to support religious schools, prayers and creeds are required by public school boards, and the clergy of certain religions are not legally entitled to perform marriages. These seemingly small things are but symptoms of the larger fact that the various governments (federal and provincial) within Canada have not been bound to remain absolutely neutral towards religion and towards various church groups. Rather, in Canada, as in Germany, the government has frequently acted to disfavor and constrain certain religions — while favoring others. Hence, the government of Ontario was free — in a way that an American government would not be free — to commission and fund a lengthy "Study of Mind Development Groups, Sects and Cults." The central researcher for this study,

Dr. Daniel Hill, noted that he added a further *religious* specification saying "The study of new religions, cults, sects, and mind development groups was conducted over an 18 month period."[56] The Hill study of new *religions* was commissioned, funded, and published by the government itself.

This is not the place to debate whether the strict separation of church and state, as practiced in America, is better or worse than the kinds of establishment of religion found in Germany and Canada. In both Germany and Canada, there exist a variety of religions and people have the freedom to belong to the groups they choose. There is "freedom of religion," therefore, in nations that do not observe a sharp separation of church and state. A state does not have to stay completely outside all religions in order to allow its citizens a freedom of religion.

In fact, many people would argue that the sharp separation of church and state, as practiced in America, does not promote freedom of religion, but rather allows charlatans and pseudo-religious promoters to prey on credulous and weak people. In America today the present attack on the First Amendment "Freedom of Religion" clause is led by those who claim that the separation of church and state does not protect religious freedom, but allows the *abuse* of religion in order to take peoples' religious freedom away. Cults, so their opponents argue, violate the First Amendment by taking away the freedom of people to believe in the religions they choose — since they didn't freely choose to belong to the cults, but were coerced into them. The proponents of this argument urge, therefore, that the government violate the separation of church and state by legislating against "pseudo-religious groups" which destroy free will by promoting conversion, thereby taking peoples' freedom of religion away. The anti-cultists prefer a situation closer to that which obtains in Germany or Canada than in the United States.

The purpose of these considerations is not to defend nor to oppose the American practice of separation of church and state. In fact, by seeing the difference between the American way of defending religious freedom and the alternative ways used by other nations, we can become better sensitized to the advantages and the disadvantages involved in different social arrangements. The author of this essay was born in America but now lives in Canada. He knows that there is freedom of religion in both countries, though it is protected in different ways. He knows that in Canada the government could undertake a study which could not constitutionally be undertaken by a government in the United States — a study of fourteen specifically named new religions, including the Hare Krishnas, the Church of Scientology, the Unification Church, and other groups charged with being "cults." This study was commissioned by the Attorney General of Ontario and directed by Dr. Daniel Hill, a sociologist who had previously worked for the government on issues relating to human rights. Dr. Hill worked closely with a number of government agencies during his study; he employed a large number of outside consultants from various fields. He commissioned special further studies by Dr. Saul Levine, a psychiatrist. Levine then interviewed all the clinical psychiatrists in North America who were known to have worked with "cultists." After 18 months of study, Hill published a 773 page study, whose central conclusions are exerpted in this volume. He answered the question raised by the Attorney General as to whether there should be a formal public inquiry into "mind development groups, sects, and cults" by saying: "In response to that request, the study first offers its only recommendation: *it is recommended that* no public inquiry be held regarding the issues arising out of the activities of cults, sects, mind development groups, new religions or deprogrammers."[57]

The rationale for this conclusion is contained within Hill's entire lengthy study. But what is significant is that, although Hill acknowledged that he and his researchers found many problems, much confusion and argument, and many issues which require further research, they did *not* find any evidence which would support the contention that the government should begin "implementing new legislative measures to control or otherwise affect the activities of cults, sects, mind development groups, new religions or deprogrammers." Rather, Hill contended, "To the extent that the movements and deprogrammers foster problems that are susceptible to legal resolution, the criminal and civil law appear already to afford sufficient avenues of punishment and redress."[58]

It might be suggested that American legislators — although inhibited from commissioning such a study by that strict separation of church and state required by their constitution — obtain and read the Hill "Study of Mind Development Groups, Sects and Cults in Ontario: A Report to the Ontario Government." It is available, as a government document, from the Queens Printer in Toronto. Since Hill's study covers all North America (recognizing that the fountain of new religions seems to be in the United States), its content and conclusions will be as applicable to New York and California as to Ontario. In fact, one of Hill's suggestions is that what Ontario needs is something like the Berkeley (California) Interfaith Council which includes, alongside the traditional religions, representatives from all the new religious groups. Hill observed that:

> The Berkeley Council has also been successful in finding members of religious groups for their families. The council, it seems, can employ conflict resolution strategies that neither families nor anti-cult organizations can command, largely because it has members from both traditional and new groups and therefore is to be trusted.[59]

The Congressional Hearings of Senator Dole

In spite of the fact that the American Government is required, by the Constitution, to remain religiously neutral, the anti-religion movement has managed to gain, within the government, support for its ideas. On the national level, the major promoters of the anti-religion movement are Senator Dole and Representative Ottinger. Senator Dole has taken the initiative in organizing two congressional hearings where he has given his sponsorship to the charges of various deprogramming organizations.

The first of these hearings took place in 1976. In planning this hearing Dole worked closely with Rabbi Davis, the evangelical clergyman George Swope, and their CERF deprogramming organization. The text of the planning letter for this session reads as follows:

> The date is WEDNESDAY, FEBRUARY 18. Senator Bob Dole of Kansas has obtained the Caucus Room, Room 1202, Dirksen Office

Building, on the corner of First and Constitution Avenue, N.E. for us from 1:30 p.m. to 3:30 p.m. He is contacting the I.R.S., the Immigration Bureau, and the Justice Department to have representatives present. He is also contacting all Senators and Congressmen to have their aides present as monitors.

No speeches will be made by our group. Our National Committee and others will sit at a table with government officials and address questions with factual information. The officials will reply to these questions. Out of this conference, enough material may be brought forth to stimulate a Congressional investigation.

The group as a whole will sit in an observer's area. Because Moonites and other cultists will infiltrate our group and cannot be denied the right of joining us, we are establishing a ground rule that no questions or statements will be accepted from the audience.[60]

Senator Dole worked closely with various anti-religion groups to set up a hearing which was supposedly to gather information, but which was arranged to make it impossible for a variety of viewpoints to be presented. The "Moonites" and — as one will see — spokespersons for freedom of religion were not to be allowed to speak in the hearing. Their very attendance was described as an "infiltration" even though, it was acknowledged, they had every right to be present. The proceedings from this "hearing" were then published and widely distributed by the deprogramming groups, who sought, in this way, support for a congressional investigation into the new religions. But this first attempt was unsuccessful. So, Senator Dole tried again.

In January, 1979, Senator Dole made plans with the anti-religion leaders to organize a second congressional hearing. Once again Dole's group of witnesses were the leaders of the deprogramming movement: Richard Delgado, Rabbi Maurice Davis, Ted Patrick, Joe Alexander, Dr. John Clark, Father James Labar, Rev. George Swope, Daphne Green, Flo Conway and Jim Siegelman. This time, however, Washington Church leaders began to realize that the Dole attack on the "cults" was, in fact, an attack on the freedom of religion for all Americans. Rev. Barry Lynn, Legislative Counsel for the United Church of Christ, took the initiative in organizing church resistance to what Dole was doing. Religious leaders from nine national church and synagogue offices joined together in releasing a public letter attacking Dole's procedures.

Dear Senator Dole:

We were distressed to learn today of your forthcoming February 5, 1979 'independent hearing' on the issues related to so-called 'religious cults.' We fully accept your desire to educate members of Congress about the broad range of issues surrounding such groups. We are concerned that all of the witnesses you have scheduled appear to have definite positions in support of regulation of 'cult' activity or efforts to 'deprogram' members of such groups. No strong advocates for religious liberty are represented, yet vital First Amendment concerns are at the very heart of the debate about the so-called 'cults.[61]

The letter continued with an appeal to make the panel of witnesses more representative, noting that "we have seen increasing regulation and surveillance of religious activities by all kinds of government agencies, and are not pleased to find a potentially flamboyant hearing become the vehicle for the genesis of new regulatory effects." The signers of the letter were:

Robert Z. Alpern
Director
Washington Office of
Social Concern
Unitarian Universalist Association

Dr. J. Elliott Corbett
Director
Department of Church/
Government Relations
Board of Church and Society
United Methodist Church

Paul Kittlaus
Director, Washington Office
Office of Church in Society
United Church of Christ

Dr. James E. Wood, Jr.
Executive Director
Baptist Joint Committee
  on Public Affairs

James A. Hamilton
Director
National Council of Churches
  of Christ
Washington Office

Ruby Rhoades
Washington Representative
Church of the Brethren

Mary Jane Patterson
Washington Office
United Presbyterian Church

Dr. Charles V. Bergstrom
Executive Director
Office of Governmental Affairs
Lutheran Council, U.S.A.

Rabbi Daniel Polish
Director
Synagogue Council of America

The consequence of this protest was that Senator Dole added four new witnesses to speak in behalf of religious liberty and the rights of new religious groups. These included the Rev. Dean Kelley of the National Council of Churches (on behalf of the ACLU) and the Rev. Barry Lynn of the United Church of Christ. Lynn's statement at that hearing appears within this volume. He reminded Dole that his own church, the Congregational Church, "was the established church in Salem, Massachusetts in 1692, and a Congregational elder presided at the infamous witchcraft trials. With that sense of history, we are particularly troubled at any hint of governmental scrutiny of religious faith."[62] The rest of Lynn's statement contained a succinct, but thorough, analysis of the issues at stake. Perhaps the most interesting, in relation to our present concerns, is Lynn's contention that "Once it is determined that an individual legitimately holds a religious belief, it is not proper for the government to evaluate the *origin* of that belief" (emphasis mine).[63]

It is worth noting that whenever the traditional churches have taken the time to study the issues involved in the attack on new religions, they have concluded that their own practices are also under attack. Again and again, the similarity of the evangelism of evangelicals with that of the new religions has been noted (so much so that the Campus Crusade for Christ and various Baptist groups have frequently been labeled "cults."[64]) Again, the methods of spiritual discipline within the so-called cults has been seen to be identical with methods of discipline within the Catholic Church. For example, Father Joseph Fichter, S.J., has noted that:

The process of becoming a full-fledged member of the Unification Church is in some ways similar to that which the Catholic experiences on entering the novitiate of a religious order. Life there is regulated, disciplined, and goal oriented. You give up your worldly aspirations and your worldly goods and commit yourself to the ideals of the organization. No drugs, no alcohol, no sex, no money, few decisions and few worries. You put yourself under spiritual direction and you develop a loyalty to your religious congregation, its philosophy, its program, its leaders.[65]

It is these kinds of similarity that lead so many to ask whether the present attack on conversion and religious discipline would not include the Catholic religious orders, too. One must note that once the law is there, we cannot decide to apply it to some groups and not to others. If it is to be illegal for the Unification Church to have strict rules for their religious novices, then it will also be illegal for Catholics, too.

Even on such a difficult and painful issue as the relation of members of new religious groups to their families, the resemblance to practices within traditional religions has also been noted. Commenting on this fact, Professor Richard DeMaria has written:

What marriage counselor would not advise a young man or woman whose parents consistently berate or humilate his new wife or her new husband to limit these contacts, because one's first duty is to his or her new life, new partner, and new vocation? For centuries, the religious orders of the Christian Church have acted in much the same way: efforts are made to help family and friends to accept and support the decision of the member involved to embrace the communal vocation. But if parents' letters consist of little more than pleas to the son or daughter to return home, if the visits amount to little more than attacks by the family upon the theology, lifestyle, mission of the novice, leaving him or her shaken and torn with grief, there is not a novice master or mistress who would not discourage any further communication, unless the family changes its posture.[66]

When Dr. Daniel Hill prepared his study on new religious groups for the government of Ontario, he requested all of the religious bodies (or individual clergy) to comment on the situation. Their responses were unanimously to oppose the creation of laws or government agencies to regulate, or otherwise control, the "cults." Here is a sampling from their responses:

"We believe that he present law is sufficient to protect ' the general public,' " — Ontario Conference of Catholic Bishops[67]

"Historically speaking, one has always to fear that the state could regulate religion to such an extent that we may again see the repeat of manipulation of religion as in the Third Reich." - a minister of the Presbyterian Church[68]

"The religious liberty of a person or group may be limited by government only on the basis of an important and compelling public interest." — Canadian section of the Lutheran Church in America[69]

"The question of legislation, as you have raised it, is nevertheless, in our view fraught with problems, to say the least. There is a large difference between physical or external forms of coercion, and the 'inner' types, those for example of psychological or philosophical persuasion.'' -- Fellowship of Evangelical Baptist Churches[70]

"Where no force is used and there is no detainment against one's will, who decides that it is really brainwashing? Of course, if force is used in any way, we repeat, laws exist to cope with that situation." — Watchtower and Tract Society (Jehovah's Witnesses)[71]

"Although Mr. Dean Kelley is not a Christian Scientist, his statement expresses so well the position and concern of our own church in regard to this subject.

'Should the government inspect and certify religion as it does meat? Should it send infiltrators to join the groups to seek informers in it to keep the government apprised of its activities (as was done with supposedly subversive political organizations in recent years)? To some of us that cure would be worse than the complaint as well as violating the First Amendment's protection of the free exercise of religion.' "
—Committee on Publication for the Christian Science Church[72]

PART IV:

CONVERSION: A THEOLOGICAL VIEW

Conversion as Life Process

The legacy of revival preaching has led many to imagine that conversion is a sudden moment of crisis when a person, surrounded by external persuading influences, breaks through to a new faith. Our sense of the suddenness of this experience is reinforced by our hearing those archetypal conversion stories: Paul's sudden conversion on the Damascus road; Augustine's sudden conversion when hearing *tolle lege*; Wesley's sudden experience of grace.[73]

That this conception of conversion as a sudden event, involving a transition from one form of life to another, is also accepted by those who seek to forge legal weapons to oppose it is shown by their claims that it involves "*sudden* personality change" and a crisis within "a closed environment." The evangelical account of conversion typically says that a person is turned around and begins moving in an opposite direction, as St. Paul did when he changed from persecuting Christians to preaching Christ.

Without at all denying that there may be such moments of experienced religious intensity, or that there may even by moments when a person *suddenly becomes aware* and *suddenly chooses fully* his or her new direction, I shall here argue a different viewpoint: conversion is *not* sudden; rather, it is a gradual process of growth and change. Conversion is not unrelated to the process of personal growth; rather, it is deeply embedded within that process. Conversion is not one, big dramatic change; rather, it is little undramatic changes. Conversion involves both new experiences and the harmonization of these new experiences with old. Conversion involves both learning through failure and learning through process. Conversion involves both leaving some things behind and persevering with others. Conversion involves both appropriating some traditional symbols and creating some new symbols. That is, conversion involves all the elements of the human life process. In conversion, all these elements come together and find unity in a "moment," a "spiritual birthday," or a "rebirth." But that moment is not the person's conversion. The "*moment of conversion*," if it is even experienced or recognized at all, is when a person chooses fully to accept the process of conversion that has been going on throughout his or her life.

How can this process of conversion be described if it is so diffuse that it is identical with the tendency of a single person's whole life process? If a person's conversion is inseparable from the story of his or her whole life, then conversions are as different as there are individual persons. Conversions are as unique as persons' lives are unique. But if conversions are so unique, how can we recognize or understand them at all?

On the deepest level, in fact, a particular conversion *cannot* be understood by any outsider. This is not because it is supernatural, but because it is unique. A particular conversion, as the development of meaning of an individual person's life, is unique. One person's conversion is not like the life story of any other person — less because of different external circumstances than because of the many acts of internal free choice by which a person constitutes his or her life. There are, therefore, no scientific explanations of an individual conversion. Hence, the attack by scientific psychologists on conversion is really an attack on the integrity of individuality and the right of persons to define their own lives.

However, we can understand a person's conversion if we will allow him or her to explain how he/she understands it as the meaning of his/her life process. When we do this, we let the particular language that a person uses to explain his/her life history also be the norm for interpreting his/her account of what happened in "the moment" when he/she consciously appropriated the new way.

A Case of Conversion

A conversion must be explained as an event within a particular life story, ideally an autobiography. Therefore, it is wrong to seize upon "the moment" or upon some isolated experiences that seem extraordinary and then judge them in terms of a theory that is extrinsic to that person's life. This does not help us understand what the conversion means *for the person involved.*

When we listen to "stories of conversion," then we do discover that there are certain analogies among some life stories. Here, for the sake of concreteness, we shall consider one case: the autobiography of a young man who joined the Unification Church. What we shall see is that his story involves events from his entire life. (1) He describes various problems, influences, or predispositions in childhood. (2) He describes his adolescent exploration of a range of meaning-possibilities. (3) He describes how he, at the end of adolescence, consciously chose to make a voyage in order to attain an adult identity and task (the archetypal *hero's* journey). (4) He describes how the adulthood he found was not different from, but something that was a *ratification* of, what he had already come to believe as true.

This story is unique, but it resonates analogically with many other conversion accounts. Here is a summary taken from his 20 page autobiography.[74]

1. He was born in New York state in 1950, the oldest of three children. His father was a retail jeweler; his mother "spends her time at the golf course and the tennis court."

2. He was very bright and competitive in grade school where he won the regional science fair and, beginning with 5th grade, he began studying college-level chemistry and bio-chemistry under a (parent-provided) tutor.

3. "My family was reformed Jewish, but religion never really played a deep part in my life."

4. "When I was fourteen, my parents, sensing my potential genius, sent me away to private school, not just any school but the best — Phillips Andover . . . . I didn't make friends easily . . . . As a senior I went through an entire term when my roomate wouldn't speak to me."

5. "Andover was very stimulating academically, and that is where I excelled . . . . Also at Andover I was exposed to Protestantism, since we all had to attend chapel services and study the Bible. This didn't seem too important at the time, but now [at age 26] I can see how God was preparing me even then to accept a Christian ideology."

6. "I entered Harvard in 1968 [age 18], the year of the great campus revolution and takeover by the radicals . . . . The talk of a new 'relevant' university and participatory democracy was all very exciting. I could plainly see that we could go beyond the shortcomings of an impersonal society . . . . When everything was at its height, the radicals wasted their energy fighting among themselves, and the outcome of it all left me empty."

7. "So I began to seek after the 'cultural revolution,' which was expressing itself in the Hippie movement and ecology and life styles more harmonious with nature. I sought a revolution of human behavior . . . love and brotherhood and reverence for the environment instead of the system's values: money and power . . . . One summer I worked with an environmental action group to fight against the hazards of a nuclear power plant in southern Vermont. Four of us lived in an old farm house and went around visiting families and talking about ecology [age 20]."

8. "But my first love was still science and I spent [other] fruitful summers studying brain physiology and bio-electricity back in my home town."

9. "Sophomore year was my time of initiation into drugs, and Junior year, my initiation into sex [age 19-20] . . . . I could never feel that sexual love was a totally honest and giving relationship, free from selfish and egoistic lust. My conscience taught me what I was later to re-learn in the *Divine Principle* [the teaching of the Unification Church] . . . ."

10. "My investigation of the youth culture led me to 'neo-Hinduism,' those cults of yoga, meditation, health foods, and mysticism that flourished around Cambridge. I tried out Sufism with its mystical dancing, encounter groups . . . . I read books by

Castenada and Yogananda and Wilhelm Reich that convinced me of the reality of the spiritual world . . . . When I finally graduated from Harvard in the spring of 1972 [age 21], my degree was in biochemistry but my mind was busy searching out these various spiritual and religious ideas.''

11. "After graduation, I hitchhiked out West . . . . I took a backpack and $150 in traveler's checks and trusted myself to my wits and to fate (which may be a purposeful force, so I thought) . . . . I determined to try by myself to find a better way, and I set off with that hope.''

12. "[Two] experiences illustrate my spiritual development during my travels. In Boulder, Colorado, I met some born again Christians . . . was impressed by their sincerity and agreed to pray with them to receive Jesus, but I don't believe my prayer was very sincere, being a Jew . . . .''

13. "A month later, there was a festival in the mountains called the"Strawberry Lake Festival'' . . . 20,000 people came . . . . The site was compared to the 'new Jerusalem' and we were celebrating the fulfillment of an American Indian prophecy that in the last days a White Buffalo would come down from the skies . . . . At the climax, we worshipped God together and in the prayer and chanting I could hear praises to God in all the different religions and languages chiming at once.''

14. "I reached Berkeley six months from the time I left Cambridge, having a depressing sense of disappointment about the hippie movement . . . . I knew that in that city there might be a spiritual group that I had not met, but that I was destined to encounter. That group found me in a few days. It was the Unification Church.''

15. "I saw in the [Unification] church the unity and brotherhood I had seen at that festival in Colorado. I saw a commitment to changing society into a forum that can survive . . . . I met, for the first time since I began studying mystical philosophy at school, a life that combined the spiritual with the physical, the ideal with the practical, the religious with the scientific . . . . Since the *Divine Principle* was very close to what I already believed, it was not difficult to accept the teachings in their most simplified form . . . .''

16. "But the true measure of its teachings had to be in how they could contribute to raising my spiritual life. My very first lesson at my first workshop was that I had to change myself to place the needs of others ahead of my own desires; only in this way can we create unity and harmony in human society. That was just a beginning . . . .''

17. "On Monday morning, November 6, 1972, I walked to the Oakland center and said I wanted to join, to move in. There were some brothers working to clean out the garage, as they were opening a new branch center, so I joined them and worked." [just before 22nd birthday]

Evaluating the Story

This person's autobiography, or personal story of his own conversion, ends with a decisive act, which he dates: November 6, 1972. This act was not a religious confession nor was it an act in a religious context. He joined a group of other persons and began cleaning out a garage. This is the act which he describes as so decisive that he remembers the date, the act when his new life began. For some people the decisive act takes place like this: a non-religious act in a non-religious context. For other people, the act of decision or "joining" takes place in a church or at a revival meeting, while surrounded with religious symbols and spiritual persuaders. But, as the above personal narrative shows, the "conversion" is not the moment of decision or faith. It is rather, the entire process of growing and searching which leads to this outcome. In fact, most of the influences, experiences, and choices within this life chain of events that lead to the "*moment* of conversion" are not even recognized as more than momentarily significant when they occur. Only later is their providential importance seen. ("This didn't seem too important at the time, but *now* I can see how God was preparing me even then to accept a Christian ideology.")

But, someone might object, it is not this kind of conversion to which we object. This conversion is obviously one which has resulted from the gradual unfolding of life, or through the searchings and choosings of this person. What we object to are conversions where someone is taken away, almost forcibly, from their own life context and surrounded by people who seek to break down their ego and take their freedom away from them. To which objection, let us first note that Rabbi Maurice Davis and the evangelical Rev. George Swope, together with the young man's parents, decided that he had been brainwashed and forcibly initiated into the Unification Church. So here is what happened:

> When my parents knew I was in the Unification Church, they became very upset, being that they were Jewish, and alarmed by the bad press which the church had been receiving. They contacted Rabbi Davis and soon they were in touch with the deprogrammers. . . . On June 12, 1975 [24 years old] . . . I was grabbed from behind by two men and thrown into the back of my mother's car. We left for Connecticut, to a house owned by Mr. Gervasoni, where I was deprogrammed for five days. My deprogrammers included Ted Patrick, Joe Alexander, Jr., and Dr. George Swope....
> [N.B. — all the chief witnesses for Senator Dole's hearings!]75.

After an intensive five day "treatment" in Connecticut, the young man was taken to Canada and confined in another home for 28 more days before being able to escape and return to his church.

If, now, it is objected that this case is unusual or that Rabbi Davis and those who wished to "treat" the young man for his conversion made a mistake, then the reply is to consider any of dozens of other autobiographies of such conversions to see whether or not this one is typical. Not typical in the sense that any other life story is the same, but typical in the sense that all life stories are authentic, genuine, and unique. They do not lie!

The anti-conversionists and heresy hunters do not take such personal narratives into account. They will not listen to their victims. The "Lasher Amendment" would make the claim (by some outside person) that someone's behavior has changed while he/she was associating with some religious group to be the *criterion* of mental illness. There is no suggestion at all that the anti-conversionists and heresy hunters are interested in the integrity of a person's life story. The anti-religionists are not interested in *conversion* itself or in the process by which a person's soul grows and takes form. Or if they are, what is their alternative account of *spiritual* growth?

Mysticism or Hallucination?

The essay by Professor Thomas McGowan, included in this volume, explains the concept of "conversion as process" by showing its relation to the contemporary developmental theories of Piaget, Erikson, and Maslow. The developmental approach allows us to understand why *change in behavior* is normal and why this change requires periods that one *pass* through, crises of breakdown and reconstruction, exploring possibilities and rejecting possibilities, and — what is most important for young adults — the determination of a personal vocation in the context of an ideological vision of the world. Of course, there are young adults (probably most) who do not undergo a crisis of identity and vocation. They just leave college, get married, and get a job. But the *inauthenticity* of this process reveals itself in the discontent of middle age: alcoholism, divorce, job boredom, anger at youth.

McGowan's *process* theory of conversion, he acknowledges, is essentially Catholic. (That is, it regards the processes of nature as ordered to the processes of grace.) The Protestant theory of conversion, McGowan acknowledges, has been more focused on the moment of crisis and radical life reversal ("I used to be natural, now I'm spiritual.") Charles Colson is McGowan's example of this Protestant way.

McGowan points out, however, that the best American exponent of the *process* theory of conversion was Horace Bushnell and that, today, the leading Protestant religious educators, such as Professors James Fowler and Robin Lovin, accept, drawing on developmental psychology, the Bushnell-Catholic *process* point of view.

To accept the process theory of conversion, notes McGowan, does not involve rejecting the traditional Protestant focus on the *moment of crisis* and the particular act of consciously choosing rebirth (e.g., November 6, 1972). Rather, it only means seeing that moment of crisis as part of the process itself instead of analyzing it in isolation. If anything, the process view of conversion allows us to see even more meaning in the moment of crisis because it allows the description to have an historical-horizontal as well as an eternal-vertical referent.

For example, consider the case of a girl who felt that, in the "moment of her conversion," she heard the voice of God. Her way of describing her experience utilizes "vertical" symbolism. God speaks from "on high." Suppose, however, I also told you that this girl had been — since early childhood — fascinated by the story of Joan of Arc, who also heard "voices" and whose faith in her "voices" was the redoubt of her resistance to the attempt to make her "recant." Suppose I also told you that less than a year before her hearing "the voice of God," the girl had made a trip to Domremy (the birthplace of Joan of Arc) and that, after that trip, wore on her finger a Joan of Arc ring. Then would it not seem that the symbolic form of her conversion experience drew on, and was consistent with, the intrinsic development of her past life?

Since that girl was my own daughter, I can now go on to say that when she told those around her about her experiences, she was told she was heretical or insane. The group of evangelical Christians, with whom she was living, told her that God doesn't speak directly to people anymore, but only in His *written* Word! They said, "Ruth, how can you be so stupid?" "But Dad," she wrote in a letter, "I became a Christian that day and totally accepted the Holy Trinity into my heart and suddenly the Bible has become a living book."

While the evangelicals were rejecting the "authenticity" of her "voices" because the voices didn't agree with *their* orthodoxy, the local physician regarded the voices as symptoms of illnesss which required psychiatric treatment. Voices? According to psychiatric orthodoxy, voices mean mental illness! The psychiatrist wanted me to authorize *deprogramming* my daughter out of her "delusion."

Neither the evangelicals nor the psychiatrists understood the continuity of the "voices" with the earlier and continuing symbols of her life. They have their orthodoxies. They selected out, from what she said, a few behaviors and words. They ran on her tests of their *own* invention, i.e., they didn't want to try and understand the meaning of *her* language. They wanted to make her give it up and understand herself through *their* language. They wanted her to use *their* language to explain the meaning of what had happened to *her*!

When I received the psychiatrist's letter and compared it with my daughter's (two versions of the same event, they arrived the same day), I didn't make a hasty decision. I hopped on a plane and went to talk with my daughter. Her letter described her living situation as follows:

> I am now living with a fine group of young Christians, and I know you will love them. Many of the people in the house are doing voluntary social work in the hospital, bringing the patients flowers, etc. and generally cheering them up. All of us are doing handicrafts and every Wednesday afternoon from 1:00-4:00, I take batik lessons. Our schedule is like this:
>
> 7:30 — family prayer meeting

8:30 — tea
9:00 — assigned work (dishes, etc.)
9:30 — free
10:00 — brunch
11:15 — we hear tapes from ministers and theologians and do Bible study (at the moment I am studying Luke). I haven't heard many tapes yet, but I'll tell you more about them soon. They are so interesting . . . .

I am still not ready to accept Joan of Arc and am still pondering writing a book about her. ["Her story sounds believable, but I sometimes wonder how God could order someone to kill. Doesn't it say in the Bible, "Thou shalt not kill?"] But before I do that I want to understand every word that has been said in the Bible. Believe me, the Dilaram House (which is also a mission house, in case you didn't catch on) is my school.

So what did I think about that?

Human Growth and the Soul

The argument between Plato and Aristotle is basically an argument about the nature of the soul. According to Plato, the soul is like a "spiritual eye." We develop our soul by learning to experience eternal and unchanging realities ("Ideas"). We can *increase* our power to perceive the eternal as we "look through" the changing to the unchanging structures and principles that are beyond every changing thing. So, for example, there is an unchanging musical form we can learn to perceive "within" the succession of notes that constitute music; and there is an unchanging mathematical form within every changing physical thing. For Plato, conversion is the training and turning of mind to the *experience of the unchanging* which lies beyond time and change. This also involves a *turning away* from the temporal. Plato's theory provides the structure for the older Protestant account of conversion ("Augustinian").

Aristotle's concept of the soul is different from Plato's. For Plato, the soul sees truth and the form of things *beyond time*; for Aristotle, the soul sees truth and the form of things *within time*. For Plato, time and change were less important than the timeless and unchanging. For Aristotle, time and change are more important than timelessness and the unchanging. But this, for Aristotle, is only true if one understands the *real meaning of time*. To do this is the work of the soul.

According to Aristotle, every growing thing has a soul. For a flower, the soul is that invisible "green fuse" which unfolds the seed into a stem and then a blossom. At no moment of time is the flower *all* the flower is. The real flower is the *whole* flower, says Aristotle. The *whole* flower is the flower in *all* the moments of its growth from seed to stem to blossom. We can't experience the *whole* flower in any moment with our physical eyes. We can only experience the whole flower by an act of understanding whereby we hold together, in one act, all the different stages in the life of the flower. When we understand the wholeness, or the unity of the flower in this way, we have discovered its "soul."

Notice that what Aristotle is describing as the "soul" is not something beyond time, but something that is the very truth and meaning of time. This "Idea" of time which we know, is not something that makes time worthless, but something that makes time *worthwhile*. This is Aristotle's idea of the soul. The soul is, according to Aristotle, the truth of time itself — and the truth of time itself is the process of *growth*. This is also the Catholic position (Thomism), as presented in the essay by McGowan in this volume.

For Aristotle, of course, the *soul* of a human being is not like the soul of a flower. There is a soul, according to Aristotle, in all *growing and developing* things (since the soul is the principle of growth, i.e., wholeness). But human beings change and grow in time primarily through their purposing and choosing and then persevering in their choices. It is by purpose, choice, and perseverance that we knit the single times of our lives into a continuity that has pattern and meaning. For example, in the autobiography we considered above, the young man's growth took place by his deciding to go to two schools, deciding to read certain books, deciding to join certain groups, deciding to take a trip west, and so forth. The unity of the events in the story is created in large part through the purposes and acts of the person whose autobiography this is. The *unity* of all the single moments of this life is the *whole* of that life. This unity, or *whole*, is constituted by that person's power to reflect and act, and his purposings and choosings. This power, and its acts, which create the wholeness of the person's life in time is the *soul*. In other words, the soul is the power by which a person seeks to create a meaningful wholeness in his or her life — which wholeness can only be expressed as a *story* because it describes a person's growth and change in time.

To focus on the strivings of individual people for wholeness and meaning is what many psychiatrists fail to do. Rather, they work with abstract ideas about how "normal people" should behave. This leads to the situation where, today, we think that people who have *no* meaning in their lives are normal; they are soul-less. The person who has a soul which leads him or her to act unusually is an affront to the person who has no soul and who tries to act normally. As Scripture says, "The spiritual man is the judge of all things."

The critical rule for trying to understand any person's conversion is to allow that person to explain the meaning of that event (his or her religion) in his/her own words, i.e., as an event whose sense is seen only as part of the story in which it appears. When a person is allowed to explain his/her conversion (both process and crisis) in his/her words, then we see why it is true in the only sense that it should be true, namely, as the *truth* of his/her own life. One person's conversion does not need to be the truth, or untruth, of any other person's life. But that is exactly what the psychiatrists, anti-conversionists, and heresy hunters do affirm. *They* are trying to make their meaning, or denial of meaning, into the meaning of my life. This can never succeed, for the deepest truth of life is only known through my own act of self-appropriation — an insight that the theologian Bernard Lonergan has well explained. For those who are interested, a bibliography of theological writing on conversion, with some special attention to Lonergan's undertanding of conversion as insight, is included in the fourth section of this volume.

Conclusion

The understanding of conversion as the essential element within the life process, which I have presented, does not deny the legitimacy of the older understanding of conversion as a moment of crisis where a new meaning for life is consciously appropriated. Though the idea of conversion as process is the traditional Catholic view, it is understood that this process includes moments of crisis. In fact, as I have argued above, the symbols used in describing the moment of conversion are typically drawn from the earlier life process. For example, a young girl who in the moment of her conversion hears God's voice is also one who, in the process of her own life, has been fascinated by the story of Joan of Arc's voices. In this case, the symbol in the moment of conversion is derived, at least partly, from the earlier process of conversion. Similarly, many people who were told, while younger, the story of St. Paul's conversion will utilize the symbols from that conversion to describe what happened later in their own moment of conversion.

This partly explains why even the strongest evangelical proponents of the moment of conversion theory fully understand that this moment comes after a person has first heard or read stories from the Bible. These stories give a person, in the moment of his or her conversion, a way to describe what has happened to him or her. Hence, the process theory of conversion helps also to explain and validate the moment theory of conversion.

The understanding of conversion which I have presented above is a theory which, is Catholic and Protestant, but also it is consistent with contemporary psychological studies into the life development process. Professor McGowan's paper in this volume presents several of those theories at length. However, I have come to believe in the adequacy of this understanding of conversion primarily because of my own struggles to understand my daughter's conversion and to try to deal fairly with her rather than to discredit her story. I was struck by the fact that boththe religious and the medical authorities around her were so insistent that her way of explaining her conversion was wrong or, still worse, that what she decribed simply hadn't occurred. When I heard her story, I didn't know what to make of it, but it seemed to me at least I should credit what she said enough to try to understand it rather than, by discrediting it, to try to evade that task.

She wanted to tell me what had happened, perhaps to convert me and perhaps to test my reaction in order to better measure her own conversion. Who knows? But the beginning of understanding anyone is to credit their story and their sanity at least long enough to listen. That is what many parents, clergy, and psychiatrists are unwilling to do.

Of course, I was concerned when my daughter told me about her conversion and about the new community where she was living. Better than any attempt now to recollect and explain my reactions, will be to present a part of the letter I wrote to my wife soon after I arrived in Kathmandu to visit my daughter Ruth.

"Kathmandu
"May 20, 1974

"Dear Dorothy,

"Ruth is well, though pretty thin. I like the Dilaram people very much. They are a diverse group: from Germany, Australia, Finland, France, the U.S., Canada, etc. Each one has a story of how he or she got here that is as unique as Ruth's. A little monastery in the foot-hills of the Himalayas! It is amazing to me that such people still decide to 'serve Christ.'

"That's what Ruth seems to have come to. She said to me, quite insistently, that being a Christian doesn't mean being 'saved,' but following God's will and being his minister. It means living for God. So her conversion seems to be primarily a moral thing. It involves a new and specific idea of who she is and what she should be doing with her life. It is her committing herself to an ideal of life and life's purpose so that she can begin to move in a specific direction. Con-cretely, this means that she now wants to learn some skills so that she will be able to do a serviceable work. (She has an idea that she'd like to try working with the deaf.) This Fall she plans to return to school.

"How does one know whether this is just another teen-age trip like the Children of God episode or whether it is an authentic conversion? Do I believe in conversions? God's so entering the life of a person that it is totally turned around? Yes I do. And I believe that such conversions mark the beginning of someone's becoming what they are meant by God to be. As Ruth said, 'My first baptism was for you, but this second one's for *me.*'

"But how do we tell a true conversion from just a transient 'high'? Are the unusual experiences, voices, Scripture texts, and visions the real sign? Or is it that the changes in Ruth have been pre-ceded by and spring from suffering? Or is it the emergence in her of a moral will, a sense of vocation, and a commitment to serve God with her life? I think that all these things are important and, in Ruth's case, equally essential. Why? Because it seems to me that the truth of her conversion doesn't hang on one or another factor alone, but on the integrity of the whole story. Her conversion is true because it is the fitting outcome to a long odyssey which has been moved throughout by the providence of God.

"How does one discern this providence? (Here I find the life of my own daughter presents me with all the hardest questions I have ever sought to understand.) I think the providence of God can be dis-covered by looking back over the events of Ruth's life — the acci-dental, trivial, and unintended — in order to uncover there the hidden will that was making of these adventitious meanderings an actual progress towards a higher goal. No less important, I believe, are the mysterious criss-crossings between her life and that of others as part of God's plan. When we discern a pattern in this way, we also discover the constant leading of God in the formation of her soul.

"The test of true conversion, I'd say, is that it makes us realize that everything that happened took place through the providence of God. It is the realization that all that occurs (whether by our choice or against it) is done by God's will. His will is right and it alone is really done. I think this realization — that God alone is 'sovereign' — is the foundation of the moral change in Ruth, the willingness in her now to serve Him. And I think the coming to this realization ("nevertheless, not my will but thine . . .") is part of the suffering that she endured.

"I'm glad now that last summer I urged Ruth to write the story of her journeyings before she started off to Kathmandu. Autobiography. Confessions. That's the way we uncover the progress of the pilgrim. We can see in what Ruth wrote, I think, a truthful preparation for this final act. The outcome of her journey is no absurd reversal or *deus ex machina*, but a fitting culmination by the God whose providence was throughout the author of the plot.

"If one wants, then, to judge whether Ruth's extraordinary experiences, voices, and strange transactions are true, one has to take them as part of the whole story rather than lifting them out and looking at them alone. One can't just say, "Hmmm, she says her Gramma entered her soul and strengthened her . . . ." or "Aha, here's a girl who heard voices tell her to give her money and identification papers away . . . ." One can't just lift extraordinary experiences out of a total story and judge them separately (by reinserting them into a story or framework of one's own!). The psychiatrists who laugh at stories of voices (lifted out of context) are as silly as the enthusiastical religious who praise them (also lifted out of context). The integrity of each thing that happened rests upon the integrity of the total story and what it means in her life. The world Ruth travelled through and looked at and talked about is the measure of her language — not the world of the 'medical clinic' or 'local church' or 'middle class family.' Those worlds are not the measure of her words; the sole measure is her own story.

"For this reason, Ruth's experiences have to be read as part of Ruth's autobiography, which means keeping them in her own language. For this reason, I've urged her to hold fast to her own version of what happened. Specifically, she's been attacked by both her Christian friends at Dilaram and also the medical authorities for saying that voices ("God, Jesus, or angels") told her to give away her identification and money. But Ruth must stick to her story because it's her conversion and not theirs. If she accepts their version of what happened (and abandons her story and her language), then the person she'll become through *their* version is someone else than who she truly is.

"Ruth's new self and her story of how she became that self are not separable, but one and the same. Her soul is in her story, in her own words. These are holy and she must not be taught to distrust them or find them strange. ''

NOTES

[1]See proposed New York state legislation in this volume.

[2]*Ibid.*

[3]Veto message of Governor Carey, July 8, 1980.

[4]*Ibid.*

[5]Cited in Daniel Hill, *Study of Mind Development Groups, Sects and Cults in Ontario: A Report to the Ontario Government* (Toronto: The Queen's Printer, 1980) 164.

[6]David Weisstub, "The Legal Regulation of Cults," in Hill, 644.

[7]*Ibid..,* 652.

[8]See proposed Pennsylvania legislation in this volume.

[9]See proposed Ontario legislation in this volume.

[10]*Legislature of Ontario Debates: Official Report* (Hansard), Fourth Session, 31st Parliament (Thursday, March 27, 1980, After Sitting), 284.

[11]Marcia Rudin, "The New Religious Cults and the Jewish Community," *Religious Education,* 73 (May-June, 1978) 354.

12Cited from Barb Silverman, "Rabbi says missionaries trying to outdo Hitler's destruction," *Canadian Jewish News,* May 10, 1979.

13*Adult Jewish Studies* (New York: Union of American Hebrew Congregatior..) Fall, 1977, 8.

14Brooks Alexander, "What is a Cult," *Spiritual Counterfeits Newsletter,* V/1 (Jan.-Feb., 1979).

15"Lubavitch a Cult Not Unlike Moon," *Jewish Post* (Cleveland, Ohio), April 1, 1977.

16*Ibid.*

17*Ibid.*

18Hill, 165.

19*Ibid.*

20*Ibid.*

21Cited in Hill, 166.

22Hearing of the Vermont State Committee for the Investigation of Alleged Deceptive, Fraudulent and Criminal Practices of Various Organizations in the State, August 18, 1976.

23*Ibid.*

24Hill, 621, 625.

25Saul Levine, "Report on Physical and Mental Health Aspects of Religious Cults and Mind Bending Groups," Hill, 703.

26*Ibid.*

27Even more important than Philip Rieff's *The Triumph of the Therapeutic: Uses of Faith after Freud* (New York: Harper and Row, 1968) is, in my judgment, Ivan Illich's *Limits to Medicine* (London: Marion Boyers, 1976).

28John Clark, "*Die Manipulation des Wahnsinns.*" (Unpublished paper)

29See Rubenstein essay in this volume.

30See Chorover essay in this volume.

31Cotton Mather, *On Witchcraft* (New York: Bell, 1974) 125-127.

32*Ibid.,* 128.

33*Deprogramming: Documenting the Issue* (Documents collected for the American Civil Liberties Union and the Toronto School of Theology Conferences on Religious Deprogramming, 1977), ed. Herbert Richardson, 172.

34Cited from Silverman.

35See text of proposed New York state legislation in this volume.

36*Deprogramming,* 110f.

37*Ibid.,* 33.

38Alexander.

39*Ibid.*

40*Deprogramming,* 30.

41*Deprogramming,* 182.

42See Robbins and Anthony essay in this volume.

43Unpublished proceedings of the American Civil Liberty Conference on Deprogramming, Feb. 5, 1977.

44See Weisman essay in this volume.

45*Ibid.*

46Ray Billington, *The Protestant Crusade* 1800-1860 (Gloucester, Mass.: Peter Smith, 1963), 100.

47A joking comment made by Moon to friends in Tarrytown, 1977.

48Rudin, 353.

49*Ibid.,* 351-353.

50See Queens County decision in this volume.

51*Ibid.*

52*Ibid.*

53*Ibid.*

54Unpublished proceedings of the Toronto School of Theology Conference on Deprogramming, March 18-20, 1977.

55See Queens County decision in this volume.

56Hill, xi.

57*Ibid.,* 596.

58*Ibid.,* 588f.

59*Ibid.*

60*Deprogramming,* 173.

61Letter of January 30, 1979. (Unpublished)

62See Lynn statement in this volume.

63*Ibid.*

64Alexander.

65Joseph Fichter, "Marriage, Family and Sun Myung Moon," *A Time for Consideration,* 2nd ed., edited by M. Darrol Bryant and Herbert Richardson (New York: The Edwin Mellen Press, 1978) 132.

66Richard DeMaria, "A Psycho-Social Analysis of Conversion," *A Time for Consideration,* 96.

67Hill, 436.

68*Ibid.,* 437.

69*Ibid.,* 439f.

70*Ibid.,* 440.

71*Ibid.,* 441.

72*Ibid.,* 441f.

73The extent to which Augustine's conversion is a process of several conversions over time rather than a single sudden reversal has been studied by Judith Mazlack, *Three Disputed Questions regarding Augustine's Conversion in the "Confessions"* (M.A.thesis, University of St. Michael's College, 1978). Her work considers the following three disputed questions regarding Augustine's conversion in the *Confessions*:
1. Does Augustine's adhesion to Manicheanism immediately after reading Hortensius indicate that Cicero's work effected his conversion?
2. Was Augustine's response to the Hortensius also a philosophical and religious conversion?
3. Was his conversion in the garden at Milan a conversion to peace or hope? (pp. 2f)

74*Religious Autobiographies,* ed. Tyler Hendricks (Barrytown: Unification Theological Seminary, 1977), 164-174.

75*Ibid.,* 179. Statement by Rabbi Marc Tanenbaum describing the deprogramming referral system: "I met yesterday morning with a Jewish father whose daughter was a member of the [Unification] movement. He was desperate. She couldn't get to see him. He sought out Patrick by contacting Rabbi Maurice Davis." *Deprogramming,* 18.

PART I

DEFINING THE PROBLEM

THE CASE AGAINST THE GROUPS

DANIEL G. HILL

Some critics say there are no essential differences among the groups that come within the confines of this study or other movements of their ilk. When shed of the stubborn diversities typologists may find, they are all cults. Moreover, these critics' definition of the term "cult" signifies an elitist group that engages in deceitful recruiting and mind control, isolates its members from society, severs their relationships with family and friends, and has as its central function the satisfaction of its leader's desire for money, power, or some other form of aggrandisement. To achieve these ends, movements need members with a level of devotion pitched so high that they are prepared to direct every energy to the service of their leaders. It is in the recruiting and maintenance of that membership and the generation of the required level of devotion that the groups allegedly employ techniques that most provoke their critics.

BRAINWASHING

Perhaps the most commonly-used accusations against movements are that their recruitment amounts to "mental kidnapping" and their conversions to "brainwashing" or "mental coercion." Proponents of this argument begin by acknowledging that many of those who join the movements show no symptoms of clinical illness or unusual emotional instability. They are seemingly normal, often intelligent, people. In encounters with standard persuasive techniques of appeals to reason or arguments from faith, such people would tend to be critical and resist ideas that were strikingly out of keeping with their own interests or sentiments. To critics of movements, the doctrines, practices, and real objectives of groups are starkly out of keeping with members' interests. Hence, to attract functionally normal and intelligent people, the groups allegedly employ recruitment and indoctrination techniques that are deceptive and mind-manipulative. As Toronto psychiatrist Dr. Andrew Malcolm has said: "The intellect is the enemy and the techniques of

---

Reprinted with permission from *Study of Mind Development Groups, Sects and Cults in Ontario,* June 1980.

persuasion are all designed to destabilize this most vital of all human attributes.''

As indicated earlier in this report, recruitment techniques employed by groups appear to vary widely. Yet, critics of movements contend that the differences are more apparent than real. All methods are designed to ensnare recruits' minds before they know fully what membership entails, or in some cases, the identity of the group to which they have been recruited. The result is ''mental kidnapping.''

A prominent proponent of this argument, Richard Delgado, assistant professor of law at the University of California at Berkeley, analysed the recruitment process in a 1977 article in the Southern California Law Review. He said:

> The process by which an individual becomes a member of a cult is arranged in such a way that knowledge and capacity, the classical ingredients of an informed consent, are maintained in an inverse relationship: when capacity is high, the recruit's knowledge of the cult and its practices is low; when knowledge is high, capacity is reduced.
>
> When the newcomer attends his first meeting, his capacity to make rational choices is relatively unimpaired. He may be experiencing a momentary state of depression or suggestibility; nevertheless, his rational faculties are relatively intact, and it could be expected that were he to be given full information about the cult and his future life in it should he choose to join, he would react by leaving. For this reason, the cult keeps secret its identity as a religious organization, the name of its leader or messiah, and the more onerous conditions of membership until it perceives that the victim is 'ready' to receive this information.

Delgado said the cult makes the recruit ''ready'' for disclosure of its true nature by a process most anti-cultists call brainwashing. As the process takes hold and the recruit loses capacity for independent thought and evaluation, the reality of the cult is revealed piecemeal. ''Thus,'' said Delgado, ''the recruit never has full capacity and full knowledge at any given time. One or the other is always impaired to some degree by cult design.''

LIFTON'S VIEW

While Delgado is quoted widely by anti-cultists in Canada and the United States on the legal implications of movements' practices, the brainwashing concept he and others employ is the product of work by Dr. Jay Lifton, a Yale University professor of psychiatry. Analogizing from studies of brainwashing as practised in Communist China and North Korea, Lifton and advocates of his position claim that messianic leaders have developed techniques of thought reform, which do not require bodily restraint or physical coercion of subjects. Proponents of this view say movements have learned first to minimize external influences on recruits and members and to cut them off as fully as possible from external sources of information against which to test the legitimacy of cult doctrines. This is done without resorting to outright imprisonment. Having been insulated, the individual is then immersed in the group's "sacred science." This is a system of belief, revealed by the leader, and constitutes the movement's vision of ultimate truth and the avenues of attainment. Accompanying this vision is a special language with its systems of terms, images, and forms of expression, unique to the movement. It is in this language that reality and the individual's relation to it are expressed.

As well, the group stimulates and manipulates the recruit's capacity for guilt. "Inner doubts about even the most bizarre cult doctrine and practice," said Lifton, "are then attributed to one's own evil, the influence of the devil, as represented by the society outside, or in some cases specifically by one's own parents. Control over individual guilt is perpetuated by a variety of small and large group meetings, stressing criticism, self-criticism, continuous confession — and, at times, public humiliation of those who appear to deviate." At the same time, it is impressed upon the recruit that the movement has a special, perhaps divine, mission that he has been chosen to serve.

Elaborating on this theme, Dr. Malcolm said it is during these sessions that the group employs negative and positive sanctions to wean the recruit away from doubt. If the recruit has resisted and questioned, he will be intensely criticized by devotees and will face the threat of alienation from a group, which initially showered him with love, fed his fragile ego, and promised him security. "Ostracism is hard to take," said Dr. Malcolm, "and most people would rather conform than be utterly and contemptuously rejected. And, we must not forget the prospective convert has probably invested a fair amount of time, money and energy into his own rehabilitation." On the other hand, as the recruit expresses his acceptance of the movement's credo or recants his satanic past, he is effusively lauded and lovingly forgiven. The more emotion-rending his confessional ordeal, the more immensely gratifying the approval that climaxes it.

Additionally, Lifton said the group and its leader are portrayed to the recruit as the "dispenser of existence." With the group lies salvation; without the group there is suffering, perhaps death. "Only those who have seen the light and follow the true path to virtue are entitled to exist," Lifton said.

WHO SHALL DEFINE REALITY FOR US?

RICHARD L. RUBENSTEIN

I recently received an invitation from a national magazine to do an article on the subject of the spread of torture throughout the world. My research was greatly aided by information which Amnesty International and other religious and secular organizations have assembled on the subject. When people learned of my interest in torture, they often asked me why I was devoting so much of my time to a phenomenon that had changed so little in the course of human history. In actuality, the practice of torture has changed greatly and it has been thoroughly modernized. There is currently more widespread, systematic resort to torture by governments than ever before in history. According to Amnesty International, over 60 countries currently practice systematic torture as a method of political domination. It is practiced by governments of both the right and the left and it has become thoroughly bureaucratized. Torture is no longer relegated to officially-appointed sadists. Instead, the work has been delegated to structured hierarchies of cool, impersonal professionals who are more interested in fulfilling their assigned tasks, even when the task is torture, than they are in considering the human consequences of their work. Unfortunately, once established, bureaucracies tend to possess a self-perpetuating momentum which makes them exceedingly difficult to dismantle.

Historically, torture has been used for several principal purposes. These include: punishment of dissidents, terrorization of potential dissidents, securing recalcitrant confessions, and the involuntary extraction of information that cannot be otherwise obtained. This latter purpose is often cited by governments when they wish to justify their resort to torture. One justification involves the hypothetical example of the dilemma faced by a government which has been threatened by terrorists prepared to detonate a nuclear bomb in the metropolitan center unless their demands are met within twenty-four hours. Under such circumstances, it is asked rhetorically whether a government is justified in resorting to torture to extract information from captured terrorists in order to save the city.

Richard L. Rubenstein is Distinguished Professor at Florida State University

In reality, governments today are less likely to resort to torture, to secure confessions or to punish than they are to "re-educate" dissidents. The classic literary portrayal of the use of torture to re-educate is, of course, George Orwell's novel, *1984,* in which Winston, the novel's protagonist, is tortured until he comes to love his torturer and proclaims that slavery is freedom and two and two equal five. In the novel, the protagonist had been a *cognitive dissident* who had rejected the official definition of reality. The function of torture is to "re-educate" Winston so that he can safely return to the official "world". Such torture has as its fundamental purpose reality definition. As we shall see, reality definition is today one of the principle motives for state-sponsored torture.

One of the more problematic aspects of modern life is that the task of reality definition tends to fall to ever fewer centralized institutions and that, even in non-totalitarian regimes, the state is likely to seek a monopoly on determining how reality is to be defined. For example, my grandfather tended to define reality largely on the basis of his common sense, his face-to-face encounters with peers, and some elements of his religious tradition. That is no longer the way reality is either experienced or defined by most people today. In the United States, a limited number of television networks, publishing firms and mass magazines tend to control the way much of reality is experienced by millions of Americans. An extremely important element in contemporary reality definition is the implosive effect of television. Consider the program "Roots" which was viewed by eighty million people, who had almost identical mental contents during the time they watched the program. While much can be said in praise of "Roots", it is not difficult to recognize the potential dangers involved in the capacity of a centralized institution such as a national television network to create a synthetic image of reality in a society which is structurally in crisis, as is ours.

Most Americans still believe that it is the function of government to serve as the institution of last resort for assisting them in meeting their minimal economic aspirations. In actuality, it may be that the state's fundamental task in the foreseeable future will be to keep the majority of its citizens relatively docile as they are increasingly faced with a declining standard of living, albeit one disguised by inflated dollars. President Carter's energy program has entailed a significant reduction in the living standard of the average American. This decline is hardly likely to be intolerable, but it is part of a world-wide reduction of the average person's living standard. In many countries large sectors of the population have already experienced exceedingly difficult reductions. As a result, some governments may already feel compelled to resort to force and terror to create a synthetic "reality" as a means of pacifying their populations in the face of declining per-capita resources. Where economic constraints have become intractable, a synthetic "reality" definition can become a most important instrument of political domination.

In the future, it is quite likely that even western societies will be confronted with ever greater scarcities of crucial resources. If this happens, the state may be compelled to seek means of keeping its citizens more or less docile. One means of accomplishing this would be to accord legitimacy to certain pacifying and reassuring interpretations of "reality" while limiting or excluding the expression of others. The question of whether there is any symmetry between the way "reality" is interpreted and the way it is experienced would cease to be a problem of truth and become one of political convenience.

Whether the state would succeed in such a project would depend upon whether individuals are able to sustain their own common-sense understanding of their world. Among individuals a given view of reality is sustained by means of *conversation with significant others*, as Alfred Schutz and others have observed. My wife and I have on occasion talked about this phenomenon. She says that the two of us help to correct each other's perceptions when they begin to get distorted. By contrast, were each of us placed in isolation, sooner or later our perceptions might become very strange indeed. Conversation with significant others is thus one of the most important ways in which some kind of viable definition of reality is maintained.

When a government seeks to compel a cognitive dissident to accept the official definition of reality, it will begin the process by forcibly removing the dissident from contact with those significant others who might sustain his distinctive views. This can be done through such obvious strategies as incarceration and, under extreme circumstances, solitary confinement. Moreover, when the incarcerating agency has been rationalized and bureaucratized, as are most secret police establishments, it is possible to prevent any knowledge of what is transpiring from reaching the outside world. The dissident will have no right of attorney or of communication, and will find all access to his significant others cut off.

A further step in this process would be to strip the dissident of any sense of personal dignity. According to sociologist Erving Goffman, personality is essentially a mask which we put on in order to play the drama of life in society. It is, for example, possible to tell a great deal about me by the way I dress. I tend to wear three-button, single-breasted suits and striped ties. This style of dressing is a personal statement. It is the part of the mask or persona I wear as a college professor. One of the first steps in the torture process is to deprive the victim of his/her persona. This can be accomplished by refraining from addressing the victim by his/her proper name and by stripping the victim of his/her clothing. Often, it also involves placing the victim where he/she cannot clean him/herself or eliminate waste products. The assault on the victim's sense of dignity can be total.

Recently, I was shocked to learn that many of the techniques used by torturers involved in "re-educating" their victims have also been used by so-called "deprogrammers" who, like torturers, seek to "re-educate" their charges against their wills. One of the ways the Nazis assaulted their victims was to forbid them to eliminate their waste without permission. I have been told that a similar control is often exercised in deprogramming sessions. By preventing a person from going to the toilet, the message is conveyed, "No part of you is private or inviolate. Your well-being depends entirely on how well you please us." Even when no physical assault is visited upon the victim, there will be great psychological pressure to conform.

Another way in which the victim's sense of dignity can be assaulted by both torturers and deprogrammers is by forcing him/her to betray friends or peers. When an individual has been compelled to betray friends or peer group members, it becomes emotionally difficult or impossible to return to their fellowship when and if released. All over the world, torture is so structured that the victim will be forced to betray old friends, associates and relatives. In order to assuage the inevitable guilt brought on by the betrayal, some victims will depict those whom they betray in terms that justify the betrayal. In some cases they may even come to identify with their torturers and develop a zealous sense of mission in their hostility to old associates.

The most extreme strategy in reality definition is to eliminate the cognitive dissident altogether. A vicious but less extreme strategy is to certify the dissident as "insane" or "emotionally unstable." This has been done in the Soviet Union. It also has been done in American courts where deprogramming is involved. The strategy has been documented by the brothers, Zhores and Roy A. Medvedev, in their book, *A Question of Madness*. Zhores Medvedev is a distinguished Soviet scientist who tried desperately not to give Soviet authorities reason for offense, but was nevertheless regarded as an unmanageable dissident. He was not punished in prison but was subjected to a series of psychiatric interviews and then placed in a mental institution. He was fortunate in that he was released after a short time. Most dissidents are not so lucky. There is an institution near Moscow, the Serbsky Institute of Forensic Psychiatry, whose fundamental purpose is to convey to the dissident the message, "Your way of seeing things is madness. We don't take the issues you raise seriously." The institute conveys the further message: "We can certify with all the authority of scientific psychiatry that you are an outcast from normal society. No one will have to deal with the issues you raise." The obvious terror implicit in this strategy is enormous. Nor, as we have seen, is the Soviet Union the only place where that sort of thing takes place.

Let us now turn to the question of deprogramming. In coming to understand the phenomenon, it is helpful to keep in mind the observation made by Peter Berger in *The Sacred Canopy* that religious conversion is a form of migration from one world, or global definition of reality, to another. If tomorrow I were to become convinced that Jesus Christ is Lord, my belief would not only affect the religious institution to which I belong but also the way I come to experience my world, including the way I experience my body. It would certainly affect my web of personal associations. Some old friends would have nothing to do with me; I would almost certainly gain new friends. Religious conversion is, as Berger suggests, migration from one global view of reality to another.

Unfortunately, in the United States we have traditions concerning religion that sometimes work at cross-purposes with each other. We have a tradition of religious liberty which often conflicts with another tradition, that identified by Robert Bellah as American civil religion. There is in the United States a popular consensus concerning what constitutes a permissible American religious option. As long as a group fits in, the traditions of civil religion and religious liberty are not in conflict. When, however, a person migrates to a religious world outside the consensus, his/her decision is likely to be regarded as threatening to many within the religious mainstream.

The sociologist Kai Erikson points out in his book *Wayward Pilgrims* that a society generates deviants in order to define its cognitive and behavioral boundaries. It needs such deviants as a means of defining the limits of "sanity" and appropriate behavior. However, when a society's problems change, old cultural boundaries may no longer be viable, and people on the boundaries may serve the function of testing new behavioral and cultural options. One expression of this may be the growth of new religious movements as part of the search for new, alternative ways of coping with the altered world. If that is the case, the rise of the newer religions may be pressing very close to the American nerve.

Let me suggest why this may indeed be the case. For 400 years the American experience has involved the related phenomena of *hope* and *mobility*. Both hope and mobility are deeply rooted in the experience of the Biblical religions. Biblical religion was initially the religion of wandering nomads. Such religion was especially viable in America because, until recently, there was always some place else to go and start over again. In a sense, Adam Smith's optimism concerning the intrinsic rationality of a free-market economy was based upon the underlying conviction that somehow or other the market could always be expanded, that problems could always be solved by mobility and expansion. Now, what the new religions may be expressing is the breakdown of American middle-class optimism because mobility and expansion are now perceived as having reached their limits. Perhaps, too, that is why the newer faiths seem to flourish in California. In any event, American optimism is obviously no longer working, at least for those who join the newer movements.

Moreover, by virtue of the fact that Americans have gone so far westward, it was inevitable that they would come to the East. For many Americans, the encounter with the East has had spiritual as well as economic and political consequences. It is perhaps no accident that the leader of the Unification Church is a man who comes out of the East. The encounter with the East is destined to be threatening because there are such vast social, cultural, and cognitive differences between the way reality, hope and expectation have been experienced in the East and the West. The growth of the new religions thus suggests that the traditional American ways of viewing reality are no longer entirely plausible for significant sectors of the American population and that young people are among those most likely to intuit the diminished plausibility. However, if you think that crises of this sort have not happened before in North America, I suggest that you review the history of the Great Awakening. One of the points often made by scholars about the Great Awakening is that most of the conversions involved adolescents and young adults, as is the case today.

In an historical era in which inherited assumptions about life seem to possess diminished plausibility, it is my conviction that the least adaptive religious response would be for society to throw over its established institutions. I certainly do not suggest that Catholics, Methodists, Baptists or Jews abandon their traditions. I do, however, believe that we would do well to investigate the ways in which the old views are no longer plausible and seek to modify the most dysfunctional aspects of our religious and cultural institutions. We need not ·follow the young people in their conversions, but we certainly ought to take seriously what they are saying to us by their new commitments. Unfortunately, this does not seem to be what is happening. Instead, there is a tendency to react violently against those who have experienced the problematic character of the old institutions. It is an old story. The king often prefers to decapitate the messenger bearing bad news than to give heed to the message.

It is also my conviction that one of the least helpful ways of responding to young people who turn to the newer religions is to attempt forcibly to "deprogram" them, especially as that process is outlined in the manual entitled, *DEPROGRAMMING: The Constructive Destruction of Belief — A Manual of Technique*. This manual has sections of "Food Termination," "Sleep Withdrawal," "Shame Induced Through Nudity," "Physical Correction," which is, of course, a sterilized way of referring to physical abuse, and "Verbal Stress," a sterilized way of referring to verbal abuse. Note the professionalization of the language: the fact that people are to be assaulted is disguised by neutral language. This strategy frees the deprogrammer from a sense of moral responsibility to his charges. Similar strategies have frequently been employed by bureaucracies engaged in torture when they have attempted to minimize their own or the public's awareness of the human consequences of the violence they were perpetrating.

When an assault is referred to by a mild, neutral word, it tends to cease to be what it really is: an act of violence on the victim's psyche, if not on his/her body. This is obvious in the deprogramming manual, which reads:

> This is the stage where the subject finds the Technician to be sexually attrative...a remarkably unstable and unpredictable period in the Deprog and one of the most fascinating for the Technician. Nothing in the subject's character or past behavior can be taken as a definite indication...[*et cetera*]. Further, it may prove desirable in order to sustain the relationship built up between the Technician and subject, to deliberately encourage or discourage an advance on the part of the subject. No parent or close relative could, or indeed should, be expected to deal with a situation of this nature. It takes the experience and expertise of a Technician....

I regret to report that there seems to be little difference between deprogrammers who use the procedures outlined in the manual and torturers who seek to "re-educate" their victim. Torturers tend to regard themselves as "doctors" and "professionals" instead of what they really are, men involved daily in violent assault on their fellow human beings. They tend to portray their role and function in professional terms. This is their way of denying their own violence. Apparently, deprogrammers tend to represent their work in similar professional language.

The manual continues: "There have been stories of subjects being hetero- or homo-sexually raped by Technicians.... Far from rape, what the subject has experienced is almost certainly the application of aggressive sex by the Technician (the beneficial aspects of which are dealt with above)." I see very little difference between this kind of behavior and what I found in my research on torture. As we have noted, the real aim of torture is more often than not to alter the victim's psyche rather than to punish or secure a confession. It is very strange that, although there has been much indignation in the United States concerning the fact that we send military assistance to countries such as Argentina, Brazil and Chile which are said to practice torture and violate human rights, there does not seem to be much indignation over the fact that some American courts permit the kind of violation of human rights involved in deprogramming.

It would appear that psychiatry plays a significant role in the legal sanctioning of deprogramming. The psychiatrist frequently acts as the gatekeeper of official definitions of reality. Unfortunately, in matters of religious faith, psychiatric evaluation is often inadequate. For example, if somebody says to me, as did an Arab in Jerusalem several years ago, "Abraham and Moses used to talk to me, but they no longer do," I could call that man an hallucinatory schizophrenic. Or, I could simply say that, given the world out of which he came, he was attempting to communicate to me that he had once lived in a world in which religious inspiration was direct and immediate but that today that world is past. Instead of regarding him as abnormal, I would then be attempting to translate his vision of reality and his symbols into symbols that I could understand. The question of madness is often a question of cultural incongruence and/or cognitive dissent. There are limits to the extent to which we can permit psychiatrists to evaluate the way reality is apprehended. As a long-time university chaplain, I often felt that some of my students were badly in need of psychiatric help, but I knew that such help could only be effective if the student entered therapy voluntarily. Moreover, the best results were likely to occur when the student paid for the therapy him/herself. To compel a person to submit to a consciousness-changing process is under most circumstances to assault and abuse that person. If indeed there is pathology, an enforced process of consciousness-changing is likely to result in the exchange of one form of pathology for another. I fully recognize that psychiatrists are indispensable in our culture. Nevertheless, we must be on our guard lest psychiatry be misused, as it apparently has been in both the United States and the Soviet Union.

Part of the problem of the misuse of psychiatry has to do with what is to be considered normal, especially in religion. What and whom one considers normal are often questions of one's experience and social location. The average psychiatrist is a middle-class professional, and it is not at all certain that such professionals are always competent to sit in judgement of other people's religious experience, especially when those involved experience no obvious conflict in their religious lives and are not public disturbances.

Involuntary deprogramming is in actuality a form of religious persecution. Every society responds to dissidents in its own way. In medieval society dissidents were sometimes burned at the stake. In a bureaucratic society official violence can take its own distinctive forms. A bureaucratic society will engender bureaucratized violence, including compulsory attempts to "re-educate" dissidents. It is apparently legal in some places forcibly to alter peoples' psyches, their sense of who they are and their life commitments. The process of alteration begins with psychiatric certification validated by courts of law. One wonders whether, had there been established psychiatrists at the time of the birth of Judaism, Christianity or Islam, such professionals would have certified the first adherents of each faith as "normal." I have little doubt concerning the kind of psychiatric certification the founders of the great religions would have received. Very clearly, unless there is sound reason for believing that a new religious movement constitutes a definite threat to public order, psychiatric evaluation and therapy ought to be left in the realm of free choice. The worst way to respond is to tolerate the kidnapping of adherents of the new faiths and their forcible subjection to deliberately contrived programs of psychic alteration.

If we really believe in a free society, we shall have to permit cultural, cognitive and religious minorities the right to express themselves without public interference. Forcible deprogramming is incompatible with the ideals of a free society.

MENTAL HEALTH AS
A SOCIAL WEAPON

STEPHEN CHOROVER

I want to focus on the social implications of the involuntary treatment of members of new religions, sometimes called "deprogramming." I am not concerned here with what deprogrammers actually do, but with the implications of such "deprogramming treatment" as a concept, whatever the specific methods used. I will do this by showing that this use of "mental health" is not something new. It has appeared in various disguises before our time.

I ask you to take an imaginary excursion with me for a few minutes. Assume you are a member of a staff of a large psychiatric hospital located at the outskirts of a major city. The institution is a major teaching hospital which has long reputation for giving very fine care to the patients who are entrusted to it for treatment. It is staffed by specialists in neurology, psychology, psychiatry, and perhaps even neurosurgery. In the company of other people like yourself, we are conducting a visiting dignitary on a tour of inspection through the hospital.

The visitor, who has come from the nation's capital, is both a leading medical authority in his field and a prominent mental health administrator. He is an expert on the diagnosis and classification and treatment of a large variety of nervous and mental disorders. He has written numerous influential articles in highly technical prestigious scientific and medical journals. He is an expert on alcoholism, on stress, on epilepsy, on head injury, and on brain inflamation. He is also an important administrator, a professor of psychiatry at a leading medical school, and the director of a renowned clinic. Very recently, he has become actively involved in organizing and launching a major nation-wide program involving the review, by panels of experts, of the mental health records of all of the patients in all of the nation's state mental hospitals.

As a result of the screening process that accompanied this review of records, a large number of patients were selected for inclusion in a special treatment group. More specifically, in a meeting held in the

Stephen Chorover is Professor of Brain Science at the Massachusetts Institute of Technology

nation's capital a few months before, the directors of the program decided that special treatment centers would be set up in selected institutions throughout the country. One of these new treatment centers has been created at our institution and this man has come from the nation's capital to inspect it.

The tour of inspection is almost finished. We have just finished showing the distinguished visitor through the new treatment facility and now retire into an adjacent room, from which we are to observe the first mental patients in the country receiving the new treatment.

We watch through a window as a small group of patients is led into the room. They stand around quietly as we watch them. The orderlies who have brought them in leave the room, closing the door behind them. At a signal from one of our colleagues, another orderly turns a control device that does not seem to be having any effect. The patients continue to stand around behaving quietly as they did before. But then, quite suddenly, it becomes apparent that the treatment is having an effect. In quick succession, each patient begins to gasp, grow agitated, stagger, cry out, totter, and then fall down. The treatment is over and the instrument is turned off. The manipulation has been effective. All the patients are dead.

What I have described is, in effect, mass murder. But it is mass murder conducted in a very special way. What I have described is an actual incident that took place in 1940 at the State Mental Hospital in Zunnenstein, just outside Dresden. Dr. Max DeKrinnes, a leading psychiatrist in Germany at the time, paid a visit to observe what was the first stage in a treatment program that had been planned, initiated and developed by psychiatrists who met in Berlin in July of 1939. The plan was to carry out the wholesale murder of mental patients in Germany. The project was begun early in 1940 and I won't say anything more about it except to observe that this was the first stage in a program that later resulted in the mass murder of millions of people. Most of these people we know to have been Jews, Gypsies, Slavs, and anti-Nazis of various kinds. But what very few people know is that the first group of people systematically killed in Germany were the nation's mental patients. They were murdered by the mental health profession in a program that was systematically organized and carried out in what was called "the interest of public health."

Here we are faced with a circumstance in which doctors, ostensibly charged with the care of patients, became the agents of the state. These doctors deemed it in the interest of medical practice and mental health to kill their patients rather than to attempt their cure. I won't discuss the fact that this was a violation of the Hippocratic Oath and the traditions of medicine. Rather, I want to suggest that this incident shows how the idea of mental health can be used as a social weapon.

Deprogramming does not involve, at least under present circumstances, the murder of people identified as mental patients. But deprogramming does introduce questions about who is a mental patient, and it does raise questions about what happens to people when they are defined as mental patients.

Let me give a second example of the reason why such questions are worth asking. My first example was drawn from another country in a time which is within living memory of people. My second example is not within living memory, but it has been historically documented. Let me introduce this example by saying that when we talk about deprogramming, we are talking about "patients" that involve a group of people who have not many things in common except, perhaps, the fact that they tend to be young and that they have often run away from home to join some group. As yet no word has been coined to define the mental condition from which these individuals are allegedly suffering. But that they are suffering from a mental condition is assured by the fact that they have become the object of the concern of psychiatrists, psychologists and others who utilize various behavioral manipulation techniques for so-called deprogramming.

Let me offer a name for their disease, the mental disorder. Everybody knows what "mania" means. But, how many people know what "drapeto" means? "Drapeto" is an ancient Greek word for "runaway." I wish I could say that I had invented this word. If you open a medical dictionary, however, you will discover that such a condition exists: the dictionary defines "drapeto" as "the insane desire to wan-- der away from home."

The term "drapeto" was coined, and the disease-state to which it refers was discovered (or invented) in 1850. In that year, the Louisiana State Medical Society appointed a commission of its members, headed by the distinguished physician Samuel Cartwright, to look into and to report back on the physical and psychical peculiarities of the Negro race. In 1850, one of the peculiarities of the Negro race, which in the South lived in slavery, was that this race included individuals who tended to run away.

Now, one can look at such behavior in a variety of ways. One could say, "If I were a slave, I would probably try to run away, too." One might say that the runaway slave is making a political statement about the conditions of his or her life. Finding the conditions of slavery intolerable, and finding no conceivable way to change them, the slave seeks some form of escape. The only available form of escape for the slave was to run away, perhaps to join the underground railway, hoping thereby to find a place where the conditions of his or her life would be different. That, at least, is my own interpreation of why a large number of Negro individuals who lived in the South about 1850 actively sought to run away.

But one has to recognize that, on the other hand, there were people who owned slaves, whose entire society was based on the institution of slavery. Being like you and me, these people who owned slaves did not conceive of themselves as bad people because they kept other human beings as commodities for the purpose of producing commodities. They said, "Our system, in which we rule over black people, is a system which accords with God's will." They constructed a very long and elaborate theological argument meant to show how the slavery system was God's will. But, in addition to such a theological argument, these people also constructed a biological argument (which reinforced the theological one) which also aimed to justify slavery as a "natural arrangement" that only crazy people would oppose. What was this biological argument?

Well, as everyone knew, or was supposed to know, the essential difference between black people and white people was that the white people were much more highly developed biologically. If left to their own devices, black people would inevitably fall into "sloth and torpidity" (that was the exact phrase) because they were unable to cope with civilized life. Their biology and their mental capacity were not, the argument ran, sufficiently advanced to deal with the complexities of civilization.

Since this argument supposedly showed that black people were biologically and mentally inferior to white, it followed that the social structure of domination and subordination that made white people the masters and black people the slaves, was merely a natural and inevitable reflection of the biological and psychological differences between the two races. It also followed that, from this point of view, the slave who ran away was running away from a social system which was not only natural and just, but also biologically necessary to the slave's own well-being. Since anyone who does something against his or her own well-being can easily be conceived as crazy, a slave who ran away could be conceived to suffer from "drapeto" — a mental illness.

Try to place yourself in the position of a well-regarded Louisiana physician in 1850. You would, of course, be a privileged member of a social order in which slavery was an important institution. Given your social position, it would not be at all difficult for you to imagine the mental disorder of the run-away slave.

What this example shows is how certain forms of behavior cause a person, who engages in an act that is not in conformity with the established order, to be defined as not usually healthy.

II

There is a long tradition in our culture that links medicine to science. When medicine says that such-and-such is the case, it is often presumed without further examination, that what is being asserted has the character of an objective fact. Our culture tends to receive medical opinion in the same confident spirit in which it accepts the evidence of experimental science. But I have just given you an example of how one can, without any noticeable distortion along the way, move from a description of behavior to the conclusion that this behavior is sick, or crazy. Once we arrive at such a conclusion, we have gotten to a very peculiar place outside our political and social process.

We talk about the process of law. We talk about the fact that one's behavior is presumed to be defensible, that one is presumed innocent until proven guilty. We agree that one should at least be given an opportunity to explain, justify, and defend one's actions in the adversarial process of the court of law in which there is an opportunity for the exchange of points of view. But, no such opportunity exists once a person's behavior has been presumed sick or crazy. Once the individual has been defined as mentally ill, the one thing that person needs to present a serious defense has been taken away —the validity of their thought and behavior.

The word "invalid" which we apply to sick people, gives a very interesting insight into the language of diagnosis and therapy. When applied to behavior, the notion of "mental illness" invalidates behavior. It vitiates the presumption that someone is responsible for his or her behavior or is able to defend it. You and I may or may not be capable of defending our behavior adequately or effectively, (that is, we may be found guilty) but we are at least given the opportunity to do so. But the presumption that someone is crazy removes from that person exactly this right to defense which all of us enjoy as citizens. For example, in a recent New York state mental health bill (the Lasher amendment), it is said that if a member of a religious group does not understand the need for treatment to terminate his or her membership, this is an evidence of mental incompetence.

The newspapers are full of incidents which we variously associate with contemporary totalitarian regimes. The Soviet Union is, I suppose, the most notorious case in point. We hear that in the Soviet Union it is common practice to take individuals who engage in politically dissident behavior and confine them not to prisons, but to mental hospitals. Such individuals used to be shot or exiled to Siberia. What today is being done is to ship them off to institutions for the mentally ill. There they are examined by psychiatrists and, most frequently, are found to be mentally ill. There are many examples: the biologist Medvedov is one, Bukovsky is another one. There are many more whom we don't know anything about. The only difference between them and the people I have mentioned is that they are not famous, hence they do not have a large international community to agitate against the atrocity of labeling them as crazy and putting them away.

Why are these Soviet dissidents being labeled as crazy and why are they being put away? I have two things to say. First, I have no difficulty in believing that there really are psychiatrists in the Soviet Union who are so convinced their society is the best of all possible societies that they genuinely believe anybody who would seek to change it must be mentally ill. The idea that the political dissident is a kind of crazy man comes quite easily, I think, to certain people within Soviet society.

Second, the notion of invalidation is a tremendously powerful tool which can be used against dissidents because, if a dissident is successfully labeled as crazy, it follows that it does not make any sense to pay attention to what the dissident is saying. From a political point of view, invalidating the political behavior of a dissident by "proving" it has its source in mental illness is much more effective than killing the dissident. If you kill him, you make a martyr out of him. If you call him crazy, you make suspect anything the dissident says or, for that matter, anyone else who follows in his or her footsteps.

It may be a bit hard, I suppose, for us to see any similarities between a famous political dissident in the Soviet Union and the young man or woman down the street who has run away and joined the Hare Krishna movement, the Unification Church, or some other group none of us has ever heard of. But our desire to label that young man or woman as mentally incompetent and force a treatment upon them, or lock them up, resembles what is happening in the Soviet Union to political dissidents.

We enter into discussions of what should be done or not done with members of new religious groups, but we tend to overlook the process that led us to think they are incompetent or ill. This process consists of presuming that because they dress funny and say funny things, they are suspect. Here "funny" of course, means that we do not understand what they are saying because they are different (and one of the reasons that we do not understand what they are saying is that we do not listen very carefully). Because they do not behave the way we expect young people to behave, just as the run-away slave does not behave the way the slave master expects slaves to behave, we imagine that there must be something wrong with them.

All of us know that when arguing with somebody, the easiest way to end it is just to say, "You're crazy!" What does that mean? It means, I do not have to listen to anything you are saying because you are not making any sense. But, I have my own idea what it might be, besides craziness, that leads people to join new religious groups and behave in a manner that deviates from what is expected of them. Their behavior might be a way of saying that they believe certain things are wrong with the society that we all live in. I think our society gives far too little attention to the values that are collective, shared. A lot of the people who join these groups are looking for family and they are finding it in ways that comment on the system in which they live. We do a disservice not only to them but to ourselves, if we think they are joining these groups because there must be something psychologically wrong with them. What they are doing, I think, *is* symptomatic. But anybody who knows about real diseases knows that symptoms do not always appear where the problem is.

I believe that the resort to "brainwashing-deprogramming" explanations dodges serious thinking about the dynamics of social problems. The concept of "mental health" is being used here as a way of keeping us from understanding what is going on.

We always have to remember that the steps toward the extermination of mental patients, those deemed to be mentally not the equals of the rest of us, began as a by-product of the concept of mental health that happened to prevail in German society. But there is a part to this story that I have not yet told. One of the strongest arguments that was used in Germany for killing mental patients is understandable in the context of a German society riddled wtih very severe economic problems. That argument was that, in the last analysis, it was cheaper to kill the patients than to do anything else. I think it would be mistaken to assume that that social process was fundamentally different from the social process surrounding "deprogramming" today. This, I think, is food for thought.

STATE OF NEW YORK
IN ASSEMBLY

11122—A
March 25, 1980

Introduced by M. of A. Lasher, Connelly, Larkin, Sanders, Wertz — Multi-Sponsored by — M. of A. Cohen, Greco, Harenberg, Kisor, Lipschutz, Smoler, Wilson, Yevoli — read once and referred to the Committee on Mental Health — reference changed to the Committee on Child Care — reported from said committee with amendments, ordered · reprinted as amended and placed on the order of second reading

AN ACT to amend the mental hygiene law, in relation to temporary conservator

The People of the State of New York, represented in Senate and Assembly, do enact as follows:

Section 1. The mental hygiene law is amended by adding a new article seventy-seven-A to read as follows:

ARTICLE 77-A
TEMPORARY CONSERVATORS

¶77.50 Persons for whom a temporary conservator may be appointed.

The supreme court and the county courts outside the city of New York, shall have the power to appoint one or more temporary conservators of the person and the property of any person over fifteen years of age, upon showing that such person for whom the temporary conservator is to be appointed has become closely and regularly associated with a group which practices the use of deception in the recruitment of members and which engages in systematic food or sleep deprivation or isolation from family or unusually long work schedules and that such person for whom the temporary conservator is to be appointed has undergone a sudden and radical change in behavior, lifestyle, habits and attitudes, and has become unable to care for his welfare and that his judgment has become inpaired to the extent that he is unable to understand the need for such care.

¶77.51 Petition; contents; nomination of temporary conservator.

a. A special proceeding for the appointment of a temporary conservator may be commenced by (1) a parent of the proposed temporary conservatee, (2) a spouse of the proposed temporary conscrvatee, (3) an adult child of the proposed conservatee, (4) a grandparent of the proposed temporary conservatee, or (5) an individual responsible by law for the support of the proposed temporary conservatee.

b. The petition shall be verified and affirmed under penalty of perjury and shall state facts showing (1) that the petitioner is a person enumerated in subdivision a of this section; (2) the petitioner's reasons for concern of the personal and financial welfare of the proposed temporary conservatee; (3) the necessity for the appointment of a temporary conservator; (4) the name and location of the proposed temporary conservatee; (5) a statement of the sudden and radical change in behavior, lifestyle, habits and attitudes that the proposed temporary conservatee has undergone, the extent to which the proposed temporary conservatee has become unable to care for his own welfare and that his judgment has become impaired to the extent that he is unable to understand the need for such care; and that the group with which the proposed temporary conservatee has become closely and regularly associated, practices the use of deception in the recruitment of members and engages in systematic food or sleep deprivation or isolation from family or unusually long work schedules.

¶77.52 Preliminary order of temporary conservatorship.

A. The court, upon a finding that reasonable cause exists to believe that the proposed temporary conservatee is a person for whom a temporary conservator may be appointed in accordance with the provisions of section 77.50 of this article, shall grant a preliminary order appointing a temporary conservator of the person and property of the proposed temporary conservatee.

b. The preliminary order appointing a temporary conservator shall provide the following:

(1) direct that the temporary conservator or other person specifically described in the petitioner's petition take the proposed temporary conservatee into his custody and further direct that any police officer of a municipality of the state in which the proposed temporary conservatee is located, aid the temporary conservator or the other person so directed by the court, to take the proposed temporary conservatee into custody and to further set forth that the police officer shall have the right to use whatever reasonable force is necessary in order to execute the terms of this order; and

(2) direct that the temporary conservator, upon securing the physical custody of the person of the proposed temporary conservatee shall deliver the proposed temporary conservatee to the court which issued the preliminary order of temporary conservatorship, as soon as reasonably possible, but in no event should it be later than the first day that the court has a regular session, after the custody of the proposed temporary conservatee is secured and should be that same day if at all practicable; and further

(3) provide for the assignment of counsel to represent the proposed temporary conservatee at the return of the preliminary order, and at such further proceedings as the court shall direct and direct that a copy of the preliminary order be served upon the office of the assigned counsel within twenty-four hours of the granting of the preliminary order, and directing the assigned counsel to appear at the return of the preliminary order; and further

(4) direct the temporary conservator to immediately, upon the securing of the custody of the proposed temporary conservatee, notify the assigned counsel that the custody has been secured and inform the assigned counsel of the date and time that the person of the proposed temporary conservatee will be presented to the court; and further

(5) direct that the temporary conservator provide such food, clothing, shelter and medical attention for the proposed temporary conservatee as is necessary; and

(6) provide that the preliminary order appointing a temporary conservatorship be for a specific duration and set forth in the order the length of that duration.

¶77.53 Return of preliminary order appointing a temporary conservator.

a. Upon the return of a preliminary order appointing a temporary conservator and the proposed temporary conservatee's appearance thereto, the court must immediately inform the proposed temporary conservatee, or cause him to be informed in its presence, of the contents of the petition and the relief sought by the petitioner and that proposed temporary conservatee has a right to preliminary hearing to determine whether there is reasonable cause to continue the preliminary order appointing a temporary conservator until there can be a full hearing to determine whether an order of temporary conservatorship should be granted. The court or the petitioner must furnish to the proposed temporary conservatee a copy of the petition and preliminary order of temporary conservatorship at this court appearance.

b. The proposed temporary conservatee has a right to an immediate preliminary hearing upon the petition, on the issue of whether there is sufficient evidence to warrant the court to continue the preliminary order of temporary conservatorship until a full hearing can be had on the petition, but the proposed temporary conservatee may waive such right.

c. The proposed temporary conservatee has a right to the aid of counsel at this court appearance and at every subsequent stage of this special proceeding, and even though the proposed temporary conservatee is represented at this court appearance by assigned counsel, pursuant to the preliminary order of temporary conservatorship, the proposed temporary conservatee has the following rights:

(1) to an adjournment not exceeding forty-eight hours for the purpose obtaining counsel of his own choice.

(2) to an adjournment not exceeding forty-eight hours for the purpose of communicating with the proposed temporary conservatee's assigned counsel; and

(3) to communicate free of charge, by telephone or letter, for the purpose of obtaining counsel and informing a relative or friend that there is a pending petition seeking the relief that a temporary conservator be appointed for him.

d. The court must inform the proposed temporary conservatee of all the rights specified in subdivisions a, b and c of this section. The court must accord the proposed temporary conservatee the opportunity to excercise such rights and must take such affirmative action as is necessary to effectuate them.

e. If the proposed temporary conservatee desires to proceed without the aid of counsel, the court must permit him to do so if it is satisfied that he made such decision with knowledge of the significance thereof. A proposed temporary conservatee who proceeds at the court appearance without counsel does not waive his right to counsel, and the court must inform him that he continues to have such right as well as all the rights specified in subdivision c of this section which are necessary to effectuate it, and that he may exercise such rights at any stage of the proceeding.

f. Upon the proposed temporary conservatee exercising his right to an adjournment, for whatever purpose, heretofore set forth, the court shall extend the preliminary order of temporary conservatorship until such further scheduled court proceeding and custody of the person of the proposed temporary conservatee shall remain in the temporary conservator, if it is so set forth in the preliminary order of temporary conservatorship, until such further scheduled court proceeding.

g. The court may further amend the preliminary order appointing a temporary conservator, in its discretion, to provide for the psychological and/or psychiatric treatment of the proposed temporary conservatee.

¶77.54 Preliminary hearing; procedure.

A preliminary hearing upon a petition for temporary conservatorship must be conducted as follows:

a. the proposed temporary conservatee may as a matter of right be present at such hearing;

b. all parties are entitled to be represented by counsel;

c. each witness, whether called by the petitioner or the proposed temporary conservatee, must, unless he would be authorized to give unsworn testimony at a trial, testify under oath. Any witness, including the petitioner and the proposed temporary conservatee, testifying on their own behalfs, may be cross-examined;

d. the petitioner must call and examine witnesses and offer evidence in support of the petition.

e. the proposed temporary conservatee may, as a matter of right, testify in his own behalf;

f. upon the request of the proposed temporary conservatee, the court may, as a matter of discretion, permit him to call and examine other witnesses or to produce other evidence in his behalf;

g. upon such a hearing, only non-hearsay evidence is admissible to demonstrate reasonable cause to believe that the proposed temporary conservatee has become closely and regularly associated with a group which practices the use of deception in the recruitment of members and which engages in systematic food or sleep deprivation, or isolation from family or unusually long work schedules; and that the proposed temporary conservatee has undergone a sudden and radical change in behavior, lifestyle, habits and attitudes; and has become unable to care for his welfare and that his judgment has become impaired to the extent that he is unable to understand the need for such care.

h. the court may, upon application of the proposed temporary conservatee, exclude the public from the hearing and direct that no disclosure be made of the proceeding; and

i. such hearing should be completed at one session. In the interests of justice, however, it may be adjourned by the court but, in the absence of a showing of good cause therefor, no such adjournment may be for more than one day.

¶77.55 Disposition after preliminary hearing upon petition.

At the conclusion of the preliminary hearing, the court must dispose of the petition seeking a temporary conservatorship as follows:

a. If there is reasonable cause to believe that the proposed temporary conservatee has become closely and regularly associated with a group which practices the use of deception in the recruitment of members and which engages in systematic food or sleep deprivation, or isolation from family, or unusually long work schedules; and that the proposed temporary conservatee has undergone a sudden and radical change in behavior, lifestyle, habits and attitudes; and has become unable to care for his welfare and that his judgment has become impaired to the extent that he is unable to understand the need for such care, the court must order that a full hearing be commenced upon the petition within two weeks time and that the preliminary order of temporary conservatorship be extended until such full hearing and that custody of the person of the conservatee remain in the temporary conservator, if it is so set forth in the preliminary order of temporary conservatorship, until the commencement of such hearing, or further court order.

b. If there is not reasonable cause to believe that the proposed temporary conservatee has become closely and regularly associated with a group which practices the use of deception in the recruitment of members and which engages in systematic food or sleep deprivation, or isolation from family, or unusually long work schedules; and that the proposed temporary conservatee has undergone a sudden and radical change in behavior, lifestyle, habits and attitudes; and has become unable to care for his welfare and that his judgment has become impaired to the extent that he is unable to understand the need for such care, the court must vacate the preliminary order of temporary conservatorship and release the custody of the person of the conservatee from the temporary conservator and in its discretion order that a full hearing be commenced upon the petition, or dismiss the petition.

¶77.56 Hearing; trial; judgment.

a. The proposed temporary conservatee must be present at the hearing. Any party to the proceeding may, at least five days prior to the scheduled date of the hearing demand a jury trial of such issues of fact as to the need for the appointment of a temporary conservator and the court shall order a trial by jury thereof. Failure to make such timely demand shall be deemed a waiver of the right to trial by jury.

b. No person shall have a temporary conservator appointed for him unless based upon evidence which is legally sufficient and which establishes by clear and convincing evidence the need for a temporary conservator, as set forth in section 77.50 of this article.

c. Upon the conclusion of the hearing, the court shall direct that a judgment be entered determining the rights of the parties to the proceeding.

d. A court order or judgment appointing a temporary conservator shall not extend more than forty-five days and the duration of the temporary conservatorship shall be set forth in the body of such court order or judgment.

¶77.57 Security to be given by a temporary conservator.

Before the temporary conservator enters upon the execution of his duties, the court shall require or may dispense with the giving of an undertaking as provided in section 78.09 of this chapter, and in accordance with the procedure therein prescribed, treating the proposed temporary conservatee as if he were an incompetent, the temporary conservator as if he were a committee, and the temporary conservatorship as if it were a commission.

¶77.58 Designation of clerk to receive process.

A temporary conservator shall execute, acknowledge, and file with the clerk of the court an instrument designating the clerk and his successor in office as a person on whom service of any process may be made in like manner and with like effect as if it were served personally upon the temporary conservator, whenever the temporary conservator cannot with due diligence be served within the state.

¶77.59 Powers and duties of temporary conservator.

The court order appointing a temporary conservator shall set forth (1) the duration of the temporary conservatorship; (2) the right of physical custody of temporary conservatee in the temporary conservator; (3) the duty of the temporary conservator to provide physical and mental treatment for the temporary conservatee; (4) the extent of the income and assets of the temporary conservatee which are to be placed under the temporary conservatorship; and (5) the court approved plan for the preservation, maintenance and care of the temporary conservatee's income, assets and personal well-being, including the provision of necessary personal and social protective services to the temporary conservatee. Subject to such limitations and directions, a temporary conservator shall have control, charge, and management of the estate, real and personal, of the temporary conservatee, and shall have all of the powers and duties granted to or imposed upon a committee of the property of an incompetent appointed pursuant to article seventy-eight of this chapter, subject to the jurisdiction of the court and in accordance with the procedure therein specified, and shall have such additional powers as the court by order may specify. However, the court may add, withdraw, restrict, or limit any of the aforesaid powers during the term of the temporary conservatorship.

¶77.60 Maintenance of the temporary conservatee and persons dependent upon temporary conservatee.

To the extent of the net estate available therefor, a temporary conservator shall provide for the maintenance, support, and personal well-being of the temporary conservatee and then for the maintenance and support of persons legally dependent upon the temporary conservatee. With the approval of the court, a temporary conservator may also provide for the maintenance and support of other persons who had been receiving maintenance and support payments from the temporary conservatee prior to the appointment of the temporary conservator.

¶77.61 No temporary conservator's fee.

The temporary conservator shall serve without fee.

¶77.62 Final Accounting.

A temporary conservator for the person and property of a temporary conservatee shall not have to file an accounting of all his proceedings unless within ten days after the expiration of the order of the court appointing the temporary conservator, the temporary conservatee serves upon the temporary conservator a demand for an accounting. In such a case, the temporary conservator shall serve notice of the filing of an account under his section upon the temporary conservatee and the court may appoint a guardian ad litem for the temporary conservatee, for the protection of his rights and interest with regard to such account. The court may appoint a referee to take and state such account and report to the court on the matters therein. Upon the motion for a confirmation of a report of the referee, or if the accounting is had before the court, upon the court's determination, the account shall be judicially determined and filed. The compensation of the referee and of the guardian ad litem shall be fixed by the court and shall be payable out of the estate of the temporary conservatee.

¶77.63 Decree on filing instruments approving accounts.

a. A temporary conservator or the personal representative of the temporary conservator may present to the court a petition showing the names and post-office addresses of the temporary conservatee, that all taxes have been paid or that no taxes are due and that the petitioner has fully accounted and has made full disclosure in writing of all his proceedings affecting the property of the temporary conservatee to all persons interested and praying for a decree releasing and discharging the petitioner.
b. The petitioner shall also file with the petition acknowledged instruments executed by all persons interested or in the case of an infant, incompetent, or conservatee whose claim has been paid, by the guardian, committee, or conservator of his property or person receiving payment, approving the account of the petitioner and releasing and discharging the petitioner.
c. The court may thereupon make a decree releasing and discharging the petitioner and the sureties on his bond, if any, from any further liability to the persons interested.

¶77.64 Resignation or suspension of powers of temporary conservator.

The court appointing a temporary conservator may allow him to resign or may suspend the powers of a temporary conservator.

¶77.65 Vacancy in office.

A vacancy created by the death, removal, discharge, resignation or suspension of a temporary conservator may be filled by the court.

¶77.66 Extension of order of temporary conservatorship.

a. The temporary conservator may petition the court for an order extending the appointment of the temporary conservator for an additional forty-five days. Notice of such petition must be served upon the temporary conservatee and he shall have the same rights as provided in sections 77.53 and 77.56 of this article.
b. No more than one extension shall be granted.
c. If no petition for extension is filed and within ten days after the expiration of the order, and no demand for an accounting is made, the temporary conservator shall be discharged from his duties without further proceeding and the sureties on his bond if any shall be released from any further liability to the persons interested.

¶77.67 Compensation for assigned counsel.

a. If the court is satisfied that the proposed temporary conservatee is indigent and financially unable to obtain his own counsel, the assigned counsel shall be compensated pursuant to section thirty-five of the judiciary law.
b. If the proposed temporary conservatee has sufficient funds, the counsel assigned to represent him shall act in the capacity of a guardian ad litem and the court shall fix the compensation of the assigned counsel and it shall be payable out of the estate of the proposed temporary conservatee.

¶77.68 Effect of appointment; civil rights; evidence.

a. A temporary conservatee shall not be deprived of any civil right solely by reason of the appointment of a temporary conservator, nor shall such appointment modify or vary any civil right of a temporary conservatee, including but not limited to civil service ranking and appointment or rights relating to the granting, forfeiture, or denial of a license, permit, privilege, or benefit pursuant to any law.
b. Appointment of a temporary conservator shall not be evidence of the competency or incompetency of the temporary conservatee.
c. To the extent permitted by the court order appointing a temporary conservator, any contracts, conveyances, or dispositions made by the temporary conservatee shall be voidable at the option of the temporary conservator, provided, however, that nothing herein shall be deemed to limit the power of the temporary conservatee to dispose of property by will, if he possesses the requisite testamentary capacity.
d. The title to all property of the temporary conservatee shall be in the temporary conservatee and not in the temporary conservator. To the extent permitted by the court order appointing a temporary

conservator, the property shall be subject to the possession of the temporary conservator and to the control of the court for the purposes of administration, sale or other disposition.

¶77.69 Venue.

A petition for the appointment of a temporary conservator shall be made to:

a. A special term of the supreme court, held in the judicial district in which the proposed temporary conservatee is located; or

b. Any justice of the supreme court; or

c. A county judge being or residing within the county in which the proposed temporary conservatee is located; where there is no judge within the county capable of issuing a preliminary order appointing a temporary conservator, or if all within the county capable of doing so have refused, the petition may be made to a county judge being or residing within an adjoining county.

¶2. This act shall take effect on the first day of September next succeeding the date on which it shall have become a law.

MEMORANDUM IN SUPPORT

INTRODUCED BY: Assemblyman Howard L. Lasher   A. 11122

Senator Joseph R. Pisani   S. 9730

AN ACT to amend the Mental Hygiene Law, in relation to temporary conservator

PURPOSE:

To protect individuals from the undue influence of organizations which practice systematic and sophisticated techniques aimed at radically altering their members' behavior, lifestyle and attitudes.

SUMMARY:

The Mental Hygiene Law would be amended by adding a new Article 77-A which would authorize the courts to appoint a temporary conservator for individuals over 15 years old who have undergone sudden radical changes in behavior coinciding with the individual's close association with certain groups.

A petition to commence proceedings for a temporary conservatorship may be initiated by a parent, spouse, adult child, a grandparent or an individual responsible by law for the support of the proposed conservatee.

The court, upon finding that reasonable cause exists, may appoint a preliminary temporary conservator. The preliminary order shall set forth the time, date and place for a preliminary hearing which shall be held no later than 72 hours after the granting of the order.

A preliminary hearing will be held on the issue of whether there is sufficient evidence to warrant the court to continue the preliminary temporary conservatorship. If sufficient evidence exists, the court may extend the temporary conservatorship until a full hearing may be held for a maximum period of two weeks.

A full hearing will be held in order to determine if there is sufficient evidence to continue the temporary conservatorship for a maximum time period of forty-five days. The conservatee is entitled to assigned counsel or the counsel of their choice at all proceedings.

The court order shall set forth the duty of the temporary conservator to provide physical and mental treatment for the temporary conservatee.

JUSTIFICATION:

Some organizations are posing serious problems for our society by recruiting members under fraudulent pretenses. Research has shown that young people between the ages of fifteen and thirty, who may be at a crossroads in their lives and unsure of their direction, are particularly susceptible to the deceptive recruitment techniques of certain organizations. Potential members are deceived as to the true identity of the organization they are associating themselves with, often until well after initial contact. By that time the recruits have been subjected to systematic and sophisticated attempts to alter their perception of reality to the extent that they may not be able to make a rational decision in regard to joining the group.

A conservatorship statute is necessary to ensure that young people are afforded a temporary opportunity to reassess their options before committing themselves to groups which demand the renunciation of family, friends, former lifestyle and values.

FISCAL IMPLICATIONS: None to state.

EFFECTIVE DATE: First day of September following enactment.

THE GENERAL ASSEMBLY OF PENNSYLVANIA
HOUSE RESOLUTION
No. 20   Session of 1979

INTRODUCED BY Messrs. Goebel, Lashinger and Pott, March 6, 1979

REFERRED TO Committee on Rules, March 6, 1979

In the House of Representatives, March 6, 1979

WHEREAS, It is alleged that The Spirit Association for the Unification of World Christianity, also known as the Unification Church, and the following religious societies; Scientology, Children of God, International Society Krishna Consciousness, Divine Light Mission, Church of Bible Understanding, Council for Social Development, Neo-American Church and The Way International, may utilize improper mind control techniques in their recruitment and subsequent retention of members; and

WHEREAS, It is important to ascertain whether or not the Unification Church or the other entities mentioned above recruit and/or retain their membership by way of techniques which undermine voluntary consent, involve the use of duress, interfere with free will or otherwise involve improper mind control practices; and

WHEREAS, It is necessary to determine whether the parents of individuals who have become members of the Unification Church, and who are commonly referred to as "Moonies", or the other entities employ similar recruitment and/or membership retention practices have adequate remedy under existing law to ascertain whether or not such initial or continued membership is voluntary and not the result of improper mind control techniques or other forms of duress; and

WHEREAS, It is alleged that the Unification Church and the other entities have engaged in improper and misleading fund-raising practices and that such deceptive fund-raising is facilitated by their alleged status as religious organizations; and

WHEREAS, It is necessary to determine whether the fund-raising practices of the Unification Church and the other entities are improper and misleading and, if so, whether existing law adequately regulates or prohibits such conduct; therefore, be it

RESOLVED, That the Speaker of the House of Representatives appoint a select committee consisting of seven members, four from the majority party and three from the minority party, to study, investigate and report to the House on the Recruitment and membership retention techniques and fund-raising practices of the Unification Church and the other entities alluded to in the foregoing and the possible need for remedial legislation; and be it further

RESOLVED, That such select committee shall not conduct its study or investigation so as to in any manner interfere with the free exercise of religion and religious beliefs by members of the Unification Church (commonly referred to as "Moonies") or by the other entities; and be it further

RESOLVED, That the committee may hold hearings, take testimony, and make its investigations at such places as it deems necessary. It may issue subpoenas under the hand and seal of its chairman commanding any person to appear before it and to answer questions touching matters properly being inquired into by the committee and to produce such books, papers, records and documents as the committee deems necessary. Such subpoenas may be served upon any person and shall have the force and effect of subpeonas issued out of the courts of this Commonwealth. Any person who willfully neglects or refuses to testify before the committee or to produce any books, papers, records or documents, shall be subject to the penalties provided by the laws of the Commonwealth in such case. Each member of the committee shall have power to administer oaths and affirmations to witnesses appearing before the committee; and be it further

RESOLVED, That within thirty calendar days after the committee has made its report, the chairman of the committee shall cause a record of all expenses incurred by the committee, or the members thereof, which are payable at Commonwealth expense, to be filed with the Speaker of the House and the Speaker shall cause the same to be entered into the journal thereof. No expenses incurred by the committee or any member thereof shall be reimbursable by the Chief Clerk unless such expense shall first have been included as an expense item in the record heretofore required; and be it further

RESOLVED, That the committee shall report its findings, together with its recommendations for appropriate legislation or otherwise, to the General Assembly as soon as its study is completed.

BILL 12

Private Member's Bill

4TH SESSION, 31ST LEGISLATURE, ONTARIO
29 ELIZABETH II, 1980

An Act to monitor and regulate
the activities of Cults and Mind Development Groups

MR. SWEENEY

EXPLANATORY NOTE

The purpose of the Bill is to provide a mechanism for identifying cults and mind development groups that may cause a danger to the mental health of adherents. The Bill establishes "The Commission for the Investigation of Cults and Mind Development Groups" to investigate and report on the activities of such groups. The Bill also establishes certain reporting requirements for cults and groups that are designated by the Lieutenant Governor in Council. Where a person has suffered physical or mental illness as a result of adherence to a cult or mind development group, the Bill requires that the cult or group shall reimburse the Ontario Health Insurance Plan for any amounts paid by the Plan as a result of the illness.

TORONTO
PRINTED BY J. C. THATCHER, QUEEN'S PRINTER FOR ONTARIO

BILL 12   1980

An Act to monitor and regulate the activities of Cults and Mind Development Groups

HER MAJESTY, by and with the advice and consent of the Legislative Assembly of the Province of Ontario, enacts as follows:

1. In this Act,   Interpretation

(a) "Commission" means The Commission for the Investigation of Cults and Mind Development Groups established by this Act;

(b) "Minister" means the Minister of Health.

2.—(1) The Lieutenant Governor in Council may appoint three or more persons as a commission known as "The Commission for the Investigation of Cults and Mind Development Groups".   Appointment of Commission

(2) The Commission appointed under subsection 1 shall include one representative of the Ontario Medical Association.   Idem

(3) The Lieutenant Governor in Council may appoint one of the members of the Commission to be chairman.   Chairman

(4) A majority of the members of the Commission constitutes a quorum and a majority vote of the members present at any meeting of the Commission determines any question.   Quorum

3.—(1) The objects of the Commission are to investigate and report upon any cult or mind development group, adherence to which is alleged to constitute a danger to the mental health of any person, and to recommend to the Lieutenant Governor in Council whether the cult or group should be designated for the purposes of this Act.   Objects

(2) For the purposes of an investigation under this Act, the Commission has the powers of a commission under Part II of *The*   Powers 1971, c. 49

Public Inquiries Act, 1971. which Part applies to such investigation as if it were an inquiry under that Act.

Designation   4. The Lieutenant Governor in Council may designate any cult or mind development group as a cult or group that shall comply with the reporting requirements of section 5.

Report   5.—(1) Every cult and mind development group designated under section 4 shall file with the Minister, within fourteen days of the date of the designation, a report describing,

    (a) the practices and techniques used by the cult or group with respect to the soliciting of adherents, the counselling of members, and the nature and content of seminars conducted by the group;

    (b) the qualification of counsellors; and

    (c) the manner of financing the cult or group, including a statement indicating the sources and application of funds used by the cult or group.

Additional report   (2) The Minister may at any time by notice require any designated cult or group to file within the time specified in the notice a return upon any subject connected with its affairs and, in the opinion of the Minister, relevant to the public interest.

Inquiry by Commission   6.—(1) Where a person who is or has been an adherent of a cult or group receives treatment for illness, whether physical or mental, and a payment is made in respect of such treatment from the Ontario Health Insurance Plan, the Commission shall make an inquiry to determine whether the illness was a direct result of that person's adherence to the cult or group.

Assessment for health insurance costs   (2) Where the Commission determines that a person's illness is a direct result of adherence to a designated cult or group, the Commission shall assess the cult or group for the full amount of the payment made from the Ontario Health Insurance Plan and such amount shall be a debt due to the Crown and is recoverable by proceedings in a court of competent jurisdiction.

Regulations   7. The Minister may, subject to the approval of the Lieutenant Governor in Council, make regulations,

    (a) prescribing qualification requirements for counsellors providing services on behalf of a designated cult or group;

    (b) prohibiting a designated cult or group from permitting persons under a specified age from participating in the activities of the cult or group, and specifying a minimum age for that purpose;

(c) prohibiting a cult or group from accepting a full commitment to the cult or group by a person who has not been permitted a period of time to consider the consequences of such commitment away from the influences of the cult or group and specifying periods of time for that purpose.

8. This Act comes into force on the day it receives Royal Assent. Commencement

9. The short title of this Act is *The Cult Regulation Act, 1980.* Short title

PART II

SPECIAL INTEREST GROUPS

JEWS AGAINST "MESSIANIC" JEWS

DAVID RAUSCH

The brief excerpt in a Jewish newspaper caught my eye. It noted that the Jewish Defense League and a local rabbi were opposing a "Jews for Jesus" group evangelizing in another city. Since I was doing research on the Messianic Jewish movement, several questions came to mind. Was this Moshe Rosen's evangelistic enterprise, Jews for Jesus? Was one of the Christian missions to the Jews involved? Who was the rabbi cooperating with the JDL? What form was the opposition taking?

Upon further investigation, I was surprised to learn that the group involved was the Messianic congregation, Melech Yisrael ("King of Israel"). This seemed unusual to me because I had found that Messianic synagogues are not overtly evangelistic and rarely incur the wrath of the Jewish community. They are generally polite individuals, who try to avoid irritating the Jewish people. I had visited several of their congregations across the United States and had found them primarily concerned with providing a place for Jewish persons who accept the Messiah but who do not want to give up their Jewish heritage. They believe that Jewish people who accept the Messiah should not have to stop being a Jew. Some Christians consider this stand to lack evangelical fervor, and call them "Judaizers." In Minneapolis, where I was located, the Anti-Defamation League did not bother with them, and rabbis were not overly concerned as they had been with Jews for Jesus. What could they have possibly done to stir up the rabbi and the JDL?

Surprisingly, the problem had been precipitated by a brief holiday greeting carried in their local *Jewish News* on December 13, 1979. The greeting read: "Chanukah blessings to Am Yisrael and the Jewish Community." It included the congregation's name in Hebrew and in English, their Star of David insignia and their postal box number.

A local member of the Hasidic Lubavitch movement, Rabbi J. Emmanuel Schochet, castigated this greeting in a letter to the editor January 3, 1980. Schochet stated:

David Rausch is Professor of History at Ashland College

> I protest the callousness of the JN staff in allowing the publication of an ad by an insidious missionary cult of "Jews" for Jeshu and "Hebrew"-Christian cults who go by the name of "Congregation Melech Israel."
>
> "Congregation Melech Israel" is a local missionary group preying especially on youth. They are listed in the telephone book without an address and are led by a Dutch Gentile minister by the name of Hans Vandervouf, who lives and works on Overbrook Place, in the Bathurst Manor. He calls himself "rabbi" and leads his followers in weekly "Shabbat" services on Friday nights, as well as on Sundays, at the Muir Park Hotel, 2900 Yonge St. — using talit, tefillen and Torah scroll.
>
> The "implications" of the friendly Chanukah greeting with the post office box address in the ad are self evident.

The letter was captioned " 'Shul' lures Jews into cult."

Upon further investigation I found that Rabbi Schochet had previously crusaded against "cults." He tried to "deprogram" Bob Dylan in Los Angeles and frequently travels to speak on cults and their dangers. At his recent meeting at a Chicago synagogue he distributed material from which I quote: "STOP THE SOUL SNATCHERS — We can expose and *eliminate* the cults from our society — Listen to the man most *feared* by all cults and missionaries." According to the *Globe and Mail* ("Charismatics Upset Jewish Activists," Jan. 12, 1980), Schochet led twelve young Jews from an activist organization in picketing Hans Vanderwerff's home. Signs such as "Missionaries are spiritual Nazis!" "Jews Don't Switch" and "Leave Jews to Judaism" were carried in front of press photographers. One of the demonstrators was Meir Halevi, the leader of the local chapter of the Jewish Defense League, who described Hans Vanderwerff as a "cancer" and noted that they "want to deal with a cancer in the way we feel he should be dealt with." Rabbi Schochet added that Melech Yisrael attracted people who "know nothing about Judaism,"— people who believed that they could be both Jews and Christians.

The theological issue is whether or not one can be Jewish and Christian at the same time. Schochet told the *Willowdale Mirror* ("Rabbi in Rage Over Phonies," Jan. 9, 1980): "They call themselves Jews when they're not. They give their 'congregation' a Hebrew name (Melech Israel, meaning King of Israel), and use traditional Jewish symbols and religious items — to teach them about Jesus." Schochet claimed that Vanderwerff had called himself a "rabbi" during meetings and that his followers preyed on children and senior citizens.

Vanderwerff replied in *The North York Mirror* ("Group Leader Denies Preying on Jews," Jan. 16, 1980) that he was upset that Schochet charged him with calling himself a "rabbi." "I've never called myself a rabbi because I'm not one. I'm Dutch, I'm gentile, and I've never been ordained." Responding to Schochet's claim that his congregations were "soul-snatchers" Vanderwerff explained: "We've never gone out of our way to bring people here. We don't even mail out literature — if people want to find out about us, we ask them to come in person." Vanderwerff found it incredible that a single "Happy Chanukah" in the *Jewish News* could cause so much trouble.

That same week Rabbi Schochet was organizing his young people. Thirty of them assembled outside the Muir Park Hotel on Friday evening to picket congregation Melech Yisrael's weekly meeting. They were joined by Meir Halevi and his Jewish Defense League and called themselves "Jews for Judaism." Schochet again angrily claimed that Melech Yisrael was composed of "soul snatchers" and was "one of the missionary cults preying on Jewish youngsters." Speaking to the *Jewish News* at this demonstration, Schochet did concede that Congregation Yelech Yisrael "does not use isolated, controlled environments, but it operates primarily on the emotional level rather than the rational." He described it as "very low key," as working on emotional tie-ins and as generating "an emotional dependence" before it brings in the religious element (Group Stages Protest Against Jews for Jesus," Jan. 24, 1980). Police broke up Schochet's demonstration at 10 p.m.

An editorial in the *North York Mirror*, "Jews and Jesus," questioned whether Rabbi Schochet was approaching the issue rationally. It stated:

> It's almost impossible to pick right and wrong when dealing with different religions. Each side claims a monopoly on truth, using values that often defy human logic.
>
> Such is the case in the dispute between Rabbi Immanual Schochet and the messianic Melech Yisrael congregation. The truth, says Schochet, is that Jews and Jesus can't mix — and he can't understand how anyone would think otherwise of their own free will.
>
> Well, some people have. And though some Melech Yisrael congregants pray with the zeal of a southern Baptist, it's clear nobody's been brainwashed. They just believe in a different truth.
>
> Schochet has done nothing to challenge messianic Judaism as an authentic religious belief. And that means Schochet's protests are little less than persecution — the same kind of persecution traditional Jews have experienced through the centuries.

Indeed, Hans Vanderwerff has been persecuted though Rabbi Schochet has never met with him personally to discuss their differences. There has been an effort to terrorize and liquidate the congregation. Two incidents occurred *before* the Schochet incident, which suggests that the four year old congregation has been under surveillance for quite some time. During the summer of 1978, the Vanderwerff family was harassed at home. A car with a number of JDL members came in the middle of the night and rang their doorbell. When Vanderwerff opened the door, they fled. He found their mailbox marked with a swastika. A message: "Nazi Vanderwerff — GET OUT!!" was signed "JDL." Police traced the car to a JDL member who lived nearby. Vanderwerff believes that Marvin Weinstein (real name of Meir Halevi, the leader of the JDL) was with the driver that night.

Like Rabbi Schochet, Meir Halevi has a history of crusading activity.

He was a convert to Christianity and was baptized by a Christian outreach organization in Toronto. Those who remember him recall his tendency, even as a "Christian," to be fanatic, marked by a lack of love and concern. In his radical fashion, he would try to expel an individual from the group who did not believe exactly as he did. If a person had a different interpretation of the Bible, Meir (Marvin) wanted to "boot him out" of the Christian Bible study. He later turned from his Christian beliefs, went to study in a yeshiva in New Jersey and came back to lead the JDL. His bitterness — evident to those who interview him — is now leveled at Hans Vanderwerff and Congregation Melech Yisrael. Halevi calls his own group "Bnai Akiba" (sons of Akiba), in memory of a rabbi in Palestine in the second century A.D. who declared the warrior, Bar Kochba, the Messiah.

The second incident was in June, 1979, when a conference of Messianic Jews was to meet in Pennsylvania. A male voice phoned Vanderwerff to ask if he was going to the conference the next day. Vanderwerff thought he might want a ride and said, "Yes." The caller said, "I just wanted to tell you that you will never get there because I planted a bomb in your car." The caller hung up. The police bomb squad had to be called out. There was no bomb.

Since this bomb threat, there had been no other such activity until the Chanukah greeting and the harassment led by Rabbi Schochet. With that incident, however, the floodgates were opened. Bomb threats and vile language now abound in telephone messages. "Drop dead;" "You'll burn in Hell;" "I will break your neck and smash your face if you don't leave our Jewish people alone" are among the gentlest. This puts a burden on the Vanderwerff family and Mrs. Vanderwerff agonizes for her husband. They are not used to such outbursts. Their daughter has even been accused of "enticing" Jewish young men with sexual favors to get them to become Christians. Vanderwerff has stated, "It is *never* pleasant as a human being to be defamed, especially by Jews whom I love and who had to form an Anti-Defamation League because *they* have been defamed so throughout history." What hurts him most is the fact that none of these individuals have sat down with him and asked, "Hans, who are you? What are your intentions?" He feels that they have a right to their beliefs, but that they should not be entitled to infringe on his rights by such malicious conduct and false accusations to the media.

My opportunity to view the situation for myself came in March, 1980, two months after Rabbi Schochet's initial letter to the *Jewish News*. Congregation Melech Yisrael was sponsoring a Messianic singing group from Philadelphia, Kol Sincha, to present a Hasidic song festival. There was to be *no* evangelism and so it was *not* advertised as a missionary outreach. Nevertheless, Rabbi Schochet and his young people threatened a protest. There were threats received by Congregation Melech Yisrael and it appeared that violence could break out.

Friday evening services were held in a large rented room of the Muir Park Hotel, located only a few minutes from the city's principle business and shopping districts. Seats were arranged surrounding a corner of the room in which there was a table holding Shabbat candles, an ark containing a Torah scroll and a podium. Several guitarists and violin players sat off to the side of the podium. Over fifty percent of the congregation was from a Jewish background and over three-fourths of the men wore yalmulkes. The leaders assembled at the front wore prayer shawls. I found no evidence that the group "preyed" on children, for there were only two teenagers present in the congregation of over one hundred. Many were couples over the age of twenty-five and a good number of middle-aged congregants were also present.

Fifty year old Hans Vanderwerff, dressed in a dark suit with a red yarmulke and blue and white prayer shawl, began the service with the singing of "Shabat Shalom." His exuberance was contagious and as the singing of Hebrew songs progressed the congregation clapped, a few tambourines rang and voices resounded. Yet the service was tinged with anxiety about the rumored violence that was to occur at the song festival the next evening. A few Jewish couples had already been pressured to forsake the congregation. Visitors from as far away as New York, Philadelphia and Michigan had traveled in for the concert.

Mrs. Vanderwerff came forward, covered her head and lit the Sabbath candles, saying the traditional Jewish blessing over them. The Torah scroll was removed from the ark and carried in the traditional manner around for the congregation to touch while they sang the traditional blessing. Blessings were chanted in Hebrew and the text read in English by those called to the "Bema" by their Hebrew names. In addition, there was a New Testament reading. Like those of many Jewish messianic congregations, the service was a combination of elements familiar to the Jewish community with Christian elements. Songs such as *Hine Ma Tov* and "Sabbath Prayer" (from "Fiddler on the Roof) were interspersed with those such as "We're Marching to Zion." Prayers were sung and read in Hebrew and English. Fervent spontaneous prayer occurred as well.

Some Jewish members said they worshipped there because they did not feel comfortable in the cultural and social trappings of a Christian church. They noted that they identified with the first century Jewish Christians who allowed Gentiles to worship *with them.* The Gentiles were fervent in their singing of the "Shema" in Hebrew, believing that Jews had a right to worship in their own milieu even *after* accepting Jesus as their Messiah.

One of the most touching parts of the service was the prayer for Rabbi Schochet. Vanderwerff acknowledged the congregation's anxiety about the potential violence at the concert the following evening and called forward those undergoing direct pressures related to the performance. Tears poured down the faces of young and old alike as they made their way to the front while the congregation sang softly, "Thou Art Worthy." "It would be foolish to deny that we are human," Hans Vanderwerff told them, hugging each one separately and speaking words of encouragement.

Vanderwerff prayed that God would give them strength. Then in a concise, pastoral manner he began his message. "I love the Bible . . . ."

He spoke about what it means to "defame." "To defame is to harm or destroy the good name or reputation of someone." He pointed out that Yeshua said, "Turn the other cheek," and that the "Word of God" has an antidote for defamation. He turned to II Samuel 16, which tells of the curse of Shimei upon David the King. "Get out, get out, you man of bloodshed, and worthless fellow!" Shimei had cried and cursed at him. "This man had a chip on his shoulder," Vanderwerff explained, "and he started doing things that you may well expect tomorrow . . . he threw rocks at David and to add to his content he threw dust, an act of contempt." He noted that the rocks were not only thrown at David but at the people around him.

Vanderwerff pointed out that those surrounding David wanted to react with violence, but that David's answer was a "godly answer." "It is my prayer that you will be so zapped with the Holy Spirit that the spirit that was in David will also be in you," he exclaimed and then added, "David said, 'Let him alone, let him curse, it may be that the Lord will repay me good for his curse.' That is a step in faith . . . that is the word of faith," Hans Vanderwerff concluded. He reminded them that because of the strength of the Lord they "need not fear anything or anyone." As I listened to him, I was fascinated because this service was such a contrast to the approach of Moshe Rosen's "Jews for Jesus" which thrives on and even encourages confrontation.

Saturday evening Hans Vanderwerff appeared visibly nervous. Before leaving their apartment for the concert, he and his wife gathered their followers and joining hands prayed for their congregation, for the concert and for Rabbi Schochet. Someone there had obtained a leaflet entitled "THE SOUL-SNATCHERS ARE AT IT . . . AGAIN!" which was distributed by Rabbi Schochet's group and which called for a protest of the concert at 7:45 p.m. It stated:

> DON'T BE A STUPID JEW! ON SATURDAY MARCH 15, THE MISSIONARIES WILL STAGE A DECEPTIVE "CHASSIDIC" CONCERT. THE PURPOSE IS TO CONVERT OUR YOUTH TO CHRISTIANITY. "Congregation Melech Yisrael" is a Christian Missionary cult preying on Jewish youngsters in Toronto and vicinity under false pretences. Their "trade-name" seeks to convey the image of a Jewish congregation. Their leader is a Dutch GENTILE minister, Hans Vandervouf, who pretends to be Jewish, utilizes Jewish religious objects, and has himself called "rabbi."

The protest was signed: "York Jewish Student Federation; B'nai Akiva; Jewish Defense League; North American Jewish Students' Network." The Jewish Defense League's star with a fist over it and the words "Never Again" was displayed at the bottom. It is interesting to note that Rabbi Schochet and his group consistently misspell Hans Vanderwerff's last name I feel that this is indicative of their information on him and on the messianic Jewish congregation as a whole.

About two hundred Jewish demonstrators attended the concert at Northview Heights Secondary School. Most were young people carrying signs such as "Take A *Stand* — Missionary Cults Must Be Banned" and "Jews and Jesus Do *Not* Mix." When I tried to speak to them, they noticed the camera around my neck and someone yelled, "There is the press!" Many signs turned in my direction and two men unfurled a large banner, "Don't Mix Jews & Jesus," so I could photograph it. A smartly dressed young woman proudly held her yellow sign aloft: "Vandervouf Is A *PHONEY* — Melech Israel Is Full Of BALONEY." Some middle aged Jews looked on and chanted slogans such as "Jews Don't Switch." A number of bullhorns blared chants, breaking the silence of a dark, cool night.

My question, "Where is the leader of the JDL?" brought me face to face with Meir Halevi (Marvin Weinstein). When I asked him why he was protesting, he informed me that Congregation Melech Israel was a cult that preyed on Jewish young people, pretending to be Jewish so it could get them to convert to Christianity. "You mean they actually go after teenagers?" I questioned. "Have they succeeded in converting these children?" "Yes, that is true," he nodded, "Yes, they have." He reemphasized his position that a Jew could not be a Christian — a Jew could not believe in Jesus.

"If a Jew can be an atheist and a Jew, why can't he believe in Jesus and stay a Jew, as these Messianic Jews claim to do. Shouldn't they have freedom of worship?" I asked. "Not when they steal Jewish children," he replied and informed me that Hans Vanderwerff claimed to be "Jewish" *and* a "rabbi." "Are you sure?" I asked. "Yes," he affirmed.

Another young man informed me that he was "personally" responsible for "alerting" the Jewish community to the danger of the cult, Melech Israel. "How do you know it *is* a cult?" I questioned. "Oh, it fulfills the ten criteria used to determine what a cult is!" he replied. "What are those criteria?" I asked. His face dropped and he stammered, "I...I...can not remember them all." "Can you name just one?" "Not right now," he answered, "but I can tell you that they certainly fulfill *all* of them!" He told me that "terrible things" happened in the messianic congregation meetings. "Have you ever been to one of their meetings?" I asked. "Yes . . . but it was too sickening . . . I couldn't stand it." Further questioning revealed that this young man in his twenties had *never* set foot in Melech Israel's service.

With the help of the police the concert goers and protesters filed into the auditorium and the concert began without incident. Hans Vanderwerff prefaced his introduction of the program with an explanation of the messianic belief of the Melech Israel congregation.

As Joseph Finkelstein, a member of the Kol Simcha, introduced the group, explaining that Kol Simcha was from the Philadelphia congregation Beth Yeshua, a sister congregation of Melech Israel, whistles began in protest from the back of the audience. He continued, "we are a messianic Jewish congregation, and we are Jews who believe that Yeshua, Jesus, is the promised Jewish Messiah . . . ." Over twenty Jewish protesters arose at the back of the room shouting "Jews don't switch! . . . Jews don't switch!" Finkelstein paid no attention to the

shouting protesters as the police escorted them out. He continued his
introduction. By the time he was finished, the police had moved the
noisy group outside. The police thought that this was the last of the
demonstrators, but it was in fact a ploy. Quite a few had kept silence so
that they could disrupt and mock the rest of the concert. The police,
now in the foyer, had no idea what was happening inside. Contrary to
what Rabbi Schochet was to write in the *Star* on April 12 (i.e., "some
students infiltrated the concert on their own, to chant from within, but
were soon ejected. Instructions of the police were followed meticu-
lously.") the demonstrators did not listen to the police, but tried to
disrupt the concert by staging a fight, coughing, mocking, booing, and
whistling loudly. Two Hasidic Lubavitchers from Rabbi Schochet's
group led the group in booing, chanting, and coughing. These individuals were not there to protest — they were there to harass!

I asked a protester in her twenties "Do you feel that it is ethical to
defraud this whole audience of the money they paid for this concert? Is
this the 'Jewish' thing to do? Do you care?" "No . . . I *don't* care," she
flippantly answered and then told me that the Messianic Jews were
playing at being Jews and were deceptive. "What makes you any
different than Nazi brownshirts?" I asked another protester who was
standing at the back chanting. "Those are the Nazis," he angrily
shouted, "the *spiritual* Nazis."

Before the last song, Finkelstein told the audience:

> Well, we want to thank you so much for being able to be
> here. . . . We want to thank all of you for your patience, and
> just want you to know that we know this has been a somewhat
> controversial concert. . . . [The whole audience broke out in
> laughter and clapped] and I want you to know, and we mean
> this and are not just saying words, that we love every one of
> you . . . . We certainly would not ask anyone to believe
> because we'd feel good about it. All we're asking is that you
> look into the Tenach, examine it with an open heart and see
> for yourself. . . . We have seen a fulfillment of prophecy how
> God has brought our people back to the Land. . . . We are
> asking you to examine the Scriptures to see if Yeshua is the
> Messiah. If you think we are Meschumid [a "traitor" or
> "deserter"], fine. But look into the scriptures and see. After
> the concert, we are available. If you want to chew our ears
> off. . . fine.

The final song was "Shema Yisrael Adonai Eloheynu Adonai
Echad." They were given a standing ovation by their followers. As they
blew the shofar before the final blessing, a protester in the back
screamed "Sacrilege!" After the concert protesters inside and out
conversed with the Messianic Jews. Sometimes with intense and angry
words they castigated the Jewish believers in Yeshua, while these believers explained patiently that they had a right to hold on to their
Jewish heritage.

Who wins in such a situation? Certainly not the Jewish community, most of whom deplore such tactics. Neither does the Messianic community "win" from this situation. Nor does the community as a whole win.

Rabbi Schochet's call for "both Jew and Christian and all who care for honesty and decency" to condemn and protest against these Messianic Jews should be carefully analyzed in light of history. As history has shown, words *do* become actions, people *do* get hurt, and communities *do* suffer from personal vendettas, whether religious or political.

Attacks of this sort bring with them great danger wherever they occur. It is a short step from here to the pogrom, to the legally sanctioned extermination of those whose belief differs from that of the dominant group. Concerned citizens need to resist all such attempts at abridging religious freedom.

"CULTS" vs. "SHRINKS":
Psychiatry and the Control of
Religious Movements

THOMAS ROBBINS
DICK ANTHONY

The trauma of Jonestown has recently intensified the popular hostility to "cults" which has been building since the middle seventies. This hostility bears some relationship to the "neo-conservative" reassertion of loyalties to traditional structures: the family, the churches, the state and civil religion, and to the growing mood of antipathy to the student protest and social experimentation associated with the "counterculture" of the late sixties and early seventies. The charge of "mind control" leveled against "cults" has elements of mystification. Models of "coercive persuasion" have definite heuristic value in the analysis of indoctrination in authoritarian movements, yet most applications of "brainwashing" and related concepts to contemporary religious movements have been evocative more of occult demonology than scientific analysis. Psychiatrists and clinical psychologists have been in the forefront of anti-cult polemics. Gurus and "cults" are competitors of "legitimate" therapists; however, the latter have opportunities to develop successful roles as rehabilitators of the alleged victims of unorthodox groups. The agitation against cultist "mind control" thus represents an additional modern instance of the prevalent "medicalization of deviance."

INCREASING STIGMATIZATION OF "CULTS"

The horror of Jonestown has drastically shifted the climate of public opinion regarding "cults." In this connection it is important to realize that the trauma of Jonestown has merely tremendously intensified a transformation of public attitudes towards "cults" which has already been building up for several years. In the early seventies social scientists who studied "new religions" were often concerned with their "integrative" and "adaptive" properties, e.g., rehabilitating drug users, reassimilating bohemian drop-outs into conventional expressive roles, and providing expressive compensations which rendered

Dr. Thomas Robbins is Post-Doctoral Fellow in the Sociology Department at Yale University. Dr. Dick Anthony is with the Program for the Study of New Religions at Graduate Theological Union.

devotees better able to tolerate bureaucratic routine. (Robbins, et al., 1975; Mausund Petersen, 1974). Criticisms of novel religious and therapeutic mystiques tended initially to come primarily from socially conscious left-liberal intelligentsia who discerned a latent conservatism and implicit support for the status quo lurking behind the superficial alienation of the guru movements (Schur, 1976; Marin, 1976; Nolan, 1971). Typical of such critiques was an early piece on the Divine Light Mission of guru Maharaj-ji in which McAfee (1973) argued that devotion to an exotic spiritual master provided a cover behind which young persons from affluent backgrounds could resume enjoyment of class privileges while continuing to define themselves in total opposition to American culture.

At the end of the seventies, however, we are increasingly treated to depictions of "cults" as subversive of social order. Attempting to prosecute the Hare Krishna for using "mind control" to illegally imprison converts, an assistant district attorney in Queens, New York (1977) evoked a spectre of "an army of zombies or robots, who could undermine the government and law enforcement."[1] More recently Dr. Flo Conway and Jim Siegelman (1979:217) warn the readers of *Playboy* about a coming world in which the cults have taken over and "you cannot get a job in certain professions unless you have first taken 'the training', or where you cannot run-for office unless you have accepted Jesus Christ as your personal savior." Particularly sinister in their view is the Maharishi Maheesh Yogi's World Government for the Age of Enlightenment and the Maharishi's plan to resolve international tensions by spreading his techniques of meditation. An ominous future is projected in which "large numbers of people in other countries may be laid open to mind control at the direction of self-appointed religious, social and political leaders" (Conway and Siegelman, 1979:218). Dr. John Clark, a psychiatrist concerned with "mind control," sees "cults" as consciously striving "to change the very fabric of the society, which they would place under . . . totalitarian controls at all levels" (Clark, 1979:1). Dr. Clark is concerned with the possibility that "guards at prison, military, atomic, and other critical installations, atomic submarine crews and the like," might be susceptible to mind control (Clark, 1979:9).[2]

To some degree, the increasing stigmatization of "cults" is related to the present "neo-conservative" reassertion of traditional loyalties to the state, the family and the social order. "Cults" are widely perceived as movements which denounce the established social order as totally depraved and evil, seek a total (authoritarian) transformation of society, and seduce unwary young persons away from institutionalized roles in families, schools, churches, and orthodox psychotheraphy in order to encapsulate them in "totalistic" communal structures. (Enroth, 1977; Stoner and Park, 1977). Like radical feminists and militant gays, "cults" are seen as threatening the integrity of the American Family. There is an interesting irony in the present assault on "cults." Many of today's exotic spiritual groups manifest distinctly conservative social attitudes in areas such as the role of women, homosexuality and drug use; and some movements such as The Unification Church are distinctly right-wing. Nevertheless, the stigmatization of "cults" is clearly linked to a general reaction against modes of radical non-conformity and dissent which were flamboyantly assertive in the late sixties and early seventies. Militant gays, feminists and "cults" are suffering retaliation for their iconoclastic stridency in the past decade; each is moreover a convenient scapegoat for the problem of contemporary American familism (Robbins and Anthony, 1978).

The decline of The New Left has also been a factor in the anti-cult hysteria. When radical students were occupying campus buildings, Hare Krishna may have seemed relatively innocuous.[3] The disappearance of student radicals and hippies creates a vacancy for the role of "The people our parents warned us against" which "dangerous youth" then filled. The hostility of "cults" is thus linked to hostility to groups such as feminists and radicals, to which many of the "cults" are themselves antagonistic and with which they appear on the surface to have very little in common. Nevertheless, with the passing of the New Left, austere authoritarian sects such as The Unification Church or Communal Jesus groups represent an increasingly rare source of overtly articulated "value-oriented" dissidence in America. This may not apply, of course, to the numerous conformist and "narcissistic" therapy-guru mystiques which promise worldly success or more meaningful relationships to achievers. The latter "world-accepting" groups may have somewhat better prospects in the emerging late capitalist society (Wallis, 1978). Nevertheless, the more austere utopian ("world-rejecting") communal sects articulate an implicit indictment of consumerist culture and, moreover, suggest a disturbing prophecy of the crumbling of moral order. They are natural scapegoats for the party of order, which must see in every "cult" a replica of the People's Temple. As an activist anti-cult rabbi put it at the Dole hearings, "The path of cults leads to Jonestown."[4]

THE ISSUE OF "BRAINWASHING"

There is perhaps one striking respect in which "cults" differ from other contemporary scapegoats. The relatively "totalistic" milieu of a few communal groups as well as the explicit emphasis on "consciousness" and techniques to "alter" consciousness in many novel religious and therapeutic movements provide a surface plausibility to allegations that such groups "brainwash" converts through methods of "mind control." However, government intervention or investigation in this area raises the issue of the "therapeutic state" and how extensive should be the government's concern for citizens' mental health? (Robbins, 1979, Robbins, Anthony and McCarthy, 1979). Government surveillance of "mind control" could entail government scrutiny of "consciousness."

Allegations of "brainwashing" by deviant sects derive in part from assumptions to the effect that sane persons could not possibly accept certain unconventional life-styles or ideologies voluntarily.[5] Such assumptions ignore the fact that for centuries people have joined authoritarian and totalistic movements and willingly surrendered intellectual flexibility and freedom in exchange for a sense of meaning and purpose in their lives. In *Pagan and Christian in an Age of Anxiety*, E.R. Dodds argues that Christianity attracted persons in the later Roman Empire partly because "it lifted the burden of freedom from the shoulders of the individual: one choice, one irrevocable choice, and the road to salvation was clear. . . . In an age of anxiety any 'totalist' creed exerts a powerful attraction." (Dodds, 1963: 133-134). Or as David Moberg has commented in his recent Jonestown articles in *In These Times*, it is at "times when cultures are disrupted and people feel that they are powerless to act effectively to put their world in order in deliberate rational fashion, they frequently turn to leaders who claim supernatural visions. . . . With the decline of corporate liberal consensus of the decades after World War II and the frustration of the new forces for change in the U.S. during the late 60s, it was not surprising that cults of various types began to develop and appeal to those desperate for meaning and effective power. . . ." (Moberg, 1978:14).

Authoritarian sects which demand heavy sacrifices from participants tend to produce embittered authoritarian apostates, hence the legions of "deprogrammers" who are largely recruited from former Moonies and other ex-sectarians and who now lecture forcibly confined devotees on the evils of cultism and agitate for decisive government action. These activists bear some resemblence to the anti-communist ex-communists of the fifties, who were often in the vanguard of McCarthyism and whose Stalinist proclivities did not always altogether disappear when they left the party but were redirected into efforts to strike back against "the God that failed."[6] They are the "friendly witnesses" who appear at legislative hearings and on T.V. programs to expose what David Susskind has labelled the "terrifying reality" of cultism.

The problem of evaluating the "witness of apostates" is one of several serious issues which arise in the application of models of "coercive persuasion" and "thought reform" to today's unorthodox religious and therapeutic movements (Robbins and Anthony, 1979a). Studies which endeavor to apply "brainwashing" notions to "cults" in a particularly stigmatizing and pejorative manner generally rely exclusively or primarily upon accounts provided by "deprogrammed" ex-devotees (e.g., Enroth, 1977; Patrick, 1977; Conway and Seigelman, 1979; Singer, 1979a). While these accounts contain valuable material, caution must be urged in the interpretation of accounts which have previously been negotiated in persuasive relationships with therapists and deprogrammers. The retrospective accounts of ex-devotees can also be said to be "situated" in the sense that they necessarily reflect the shifting attitudes, needs and interests of the respondent in his or her present situation. As Peter Berger has noted, individuals continually reconstruct their past experiences to bring them into line with their present orientations; thus, "we have as many lives as we have points of view" (Berger, 1963:57). A convert to a religious sect may, without intending to deceive, exaggerate the depths of depravity and disorientation to which he or she had sunk prior to being "saved." Similarly, a disillusioned ex-sectarian may exaggerate the degree to which he or she was "brainwashed," regimented or involved in spectacularly bizarre and depraved scenes prior to being "saved" by deprogramming. Such reinterpretations may be reinforced by various significant others such as parents, therapists or deprogrammers; moreover, "brainwashing" conceptualizations of past sectarian experiences may be highly functional and psychologically rewarding (Bedford, 1977). Dean Kelley has recently commented,"After a person has doubly defected—once from parental values and then from the religious group—strong pressures for self-justification and the expiation of guilt are set in motion. These often take the form of insisting, 'I was fooled, I was victimized'." (Kelley, 1977:31).7 "Mind control" interpretations of past foibles may facilitate reintegration of the ex-sectarian with relatives and former friends, who can now attribute past conflicts with the ex-convert to ego-alien mind controlling forces. In effect the ex-convert is seen as having been "possessed" by external demonic spirits; once these have been "exorcised" there transpires a restoration of the "real" personality of the ex-devotee, which is characterized by a natural affinity for the styles and orientations of parents, therapists and non-sectarian peers.8

The above considerations are hardly adequate to totally "explain away" the negative accounts of apostates from authoritarian sects; indeed, much of what is said by ex-devotees concerning deception, manipulation, and regimentation in relatively totalistic "cults" such as The Unification Church is probably true. It is disconcerting, however, that few of the authors of pejorative analyses of "mind control" in "cults" have indicated any awareness of the serious methodological problems entailed in the utilization of the accounts of overtly counterindoctrinated ("deprogrammed") apostates as a dominant data source for the study of highly controversial social movements. 9

Beyond the question of evaluating apostate accounts, several other issues have been raised by the present authors regarding the application of "coercive persuasion" and "thought reform" models to commitment processes within contemporary religious movements (Robbins and Anthony, 1978; 1979a; 1979b; 1979c; 1979d; Robbins, 1979a; 1979b; Robbins, Anthony and McCarthy, 1979):

1. Discussions of alleged cultist "mind control" generally involve the purveyance of over-generalized stereotypes. We will not here discuss the multiple current definitions of "cult" (Robbins and Anthony, 1979c); however, at present there appears to be a pervasive "cult" stereotype in which the perceived features of The Unification Church of Rev. Sun Myung Moon and/or The People's Temple community of Jonestown are projected onto diverse groups. Most "new religions" are substantially less authoritarian and regimented that Hare Krishna or the Unification Church.10Moreover, those movements which do tend to encapsulate converts in totalistic communal structures rarely exhibit the extreme duplicity and fraud in recruitment patterns which appar-

ently characterize some "Moonie" groups.[11] Whenever an "atrocity" is linked to a discernible tiny cognitive minority, the offending group is immediately labeled a "cult" and made to bear the stigma of Jim Jones or Charles Manson. The imprecise generalizations which are made about "cults" by the proponents of "cracking down" against the alleged abuses of such groups are disturbing because they suggest the likelihood that any program of state intervention or coercive control would cast a wide net in which diverse and heterogeneous fish would be trapped. The operative criteria for whom to crack down which would eventually emerge would probably rely upon some notion of respectability or conventionality (Robbins, 1979a).

2. Use of terms such as "thought reform" or "brainwashing" to typify conversion and acculturation processes within religious groups tends to implicitly equate such formally voluntary associations with government operated institutions such as POW camps or re-education programs in which psychological and peer group pressures operate within a context of manifest physical constraint. The degree of isolation of "milieu control" in groups such as Hare Krishna or The Unification Church falls significantly short of the degree to which these factors are developed within "classical brainwashing" contexts (Scheflin and Opton, 1978:52-63). Moreover, it is a questionable procedure to collapse the distinction between physical coercion in which dispositions and proclivities are forcefully overcome and manipulative-seductive "mental coercion" in which proclivities and dispositions are exploited. Parenthetically, it should be noted that there are substantial reasons for suspecting that too much was made of the alleged Maoist "brainwashing" of Korean War POWs; this was not an effective persuasive tactic (Scheflin and Opton, 1979:89; Segal, 1957).

3. Legitimations for deprogramming and involuntary therapy generally affirm that sectarian devotees have lost the capacity to rationally evaluate their commitment and exercise free choice, i.e., they have lost free will (e.g. Delgado, 1979). It is too readily assumed that because individuals have been subjected to manipulative techniques of persuasion they must therefore henceforth be viewed as mental incompetents bereft of personal autonomy and rationality. In our view "free will" is not a routinely measurable empirical concept, it is rather a philosophical premise which underlies "a system of law informed by the imagery that man is in control of his destiny" (Glock, 1972:14). Two inferences follow from this clarification of the essentially metaphysical status of "free will": (1) Bracketing cases of extreme visible disorganization, psychiatric designations as to who does and who does not have "free will" are not strictly scientific and are even somewhat evocative of occult demonology (Shupe et al., 1977); and (2) A system which traditionally presumes personal autonomy and rationality cannot lightly withhold this presumption with regard to members of "cults" (Robbins, 1979a).

4. Various sociologists and other social scientists have linked the present spiritual ferment and upsurge of unconventional movements to structural dislocations in American society (Robbins and Anthony,

1972; Coleman, 1970; Marx and Ellison, 1975) or to a sociocultural context of normative flux and value dissensus (Bellah, 1976; Clock, 1976;
Wuthnow, 1976; Anthony and Robbins, 1975; Anthony et al., 1977). It
is arguable that these sociocultural analyses are not really incompatible
with psychologistic "brainwashing" formulations; the prevailing normative ambiguity and cultural confusion simply renders individuals
less resistant to cultist mind control (Singer, 1979b). There is some
merit to this argument; however, the emphasis on techniques of persuasion which allegedly produces a conditioned mental incompetence
has the implication that no uncoerced person in his or her right mind
could possibly accept a given deviant ideology or life-style. Harvey Cox
has analyzed the "myth of the evil eye" whereby "it is thought that no
sane person could possibly belong to a movement 'like this' and therefore the participant must be there involuntarily" (Cox, 1978:127). In
contrast, analyses of deviant movements as responses to normative
breakdown or cultural disorganization imply that a situation is
emerging in which individuals can voluntarily opt for seemingly bizarre patterns because either the "normal" constraints on religo-ideo-
logical deviance have eroded or needs for meaning and affiliation have
emerged which cannot be adequately met by traditional institutions.
Perhaps "protean man", as Robert Lifton (1968) has termed a prevalent modern identity type, must continually experiment with exotic
and sometimes authoritarian and fanatical role-identities; or perhaps
only surrender to an overwhelmingly totalitarian demiurge can produce
for some persons the sense of autonomy and decisive, authentic
decision-making which is systematically undermined by an impersonal
bureaucratic milieu.12

Studies and formulations which, in the opinion of the present writers,
have been unduly heavy-handed and pejorative in characterizing sectarian commitment processes as "mind control", have generally in-
dulged in some of the mystifications discussed above: overgeneralized
stereotyping; crude equations of religious groups with "classical"
coercive persuasion contexts involving tangible physical constraint;
reification of philosophical and metaphysical constructs; and a-priori
assumptions that certain ideologies and movements, being pernicious
and illegitimate, must therefore be "coercive" with regard to creation
and maintenance of commitment.13 More careful studies which have
explored the possible application of "coercive persuasion" and
"thought reform" models to contemporary religious movements have
concluded that while such models have a definite if limited heuristic
value in the analysis of indoctrination and conversion patterns in some
authoritarian sects, they are also sources of serious distortions and can
obscure salient aspects of even relatively "totalistic" movements
(Galanter et al., 1979; Kim, 1976; Barker, 1977; 1978; Scheflin and
Opton, 1978; Richardson et al., 1972).14

Finally, in the opinion of the present writers, "mind control"
explanations for sectarian conversions are contravened by indications
that: (1) relatively authoritarian groups such as The Unification Church
have a substantial voluntary turnover (Judah, 1977; Welles, 1976;
Lefland, 1974; Soloman, 1979); (2) conversion to a given movement is

not a simple "discrete event" but is more often an aspect of a broader "conversion career" involving a series of "conversions" and experimentations with unconventional life-styles which commenced prior to any given sectarian affiliation (Richardson, 1978; Richardson et al., 1977; Downton, 1979a); (3) persons attracted to oriental mystical ideologies tend to come from different backgrounds than converts to quasi-fundamentalist ("Jesus") groups (Wuthnow, 1978; 1976a; Anthony and Robbins, 1977); and (4) involvement in youth culture religious movements have various "adaptive," "problem-solving" and "integrative" consequences for devotees (Robbins et al., 1975; Robbins and Anthony, 1972; Anthony et al., 1977; Zaretsky and Leone, 1974; Snelling and Whitely, 1974). The evidence on these points is hardly conclusive; however, existing data seems to indicate definite elements of *choice* involved in conversion to "new religions."[15]As the authors have stated elsewhere, the findings of available sociological research is "not consistent with a model of 'psychological kidnapping' in which an otherwise dutiful and conformist young citizen is [suddenly]hypnotically overwhelmed and imprisoned in a deviant lifestyle which would otherwise be anathema" (Robbins and Anthony, 1978:82).

"CULTS," "SHRINKS," AND THE MEDICAL MODEL

Much of the literature discussing the alleged "mind control" techniques of cultist indoctrination is authored by psychiatrists and psychologists (e.g., Gelper, 1975; Singer, 1979; Clark, 1977; 1979; Miller, 1979). This is to be expected since the authors are putative experts in the human mind and might be expected to be concerned with the consequences of heavyhanded cultist indoctrination. The possibility might be considered, however, that in crusading against "cults" the mental health community is responding to two conditions: (1) "cults" and "shrinks" are competitors, i.e., many persons attempt to improve themselves or resolve their difficulties with the assistance of scientology or gurus instead of employing "legitimate" therapists;[16](2) Religious "deprogramming" and auxiliary services for the "rehabilitation" of cultists and ex-cultists expand vocational opportunities for psychiatrists and psychologists as well as for social workers, lawyers, detectives, clergy and ex-devotees. The institutional interests of psychiatry and clinical psychology thus confronts unorthodox gurus and movements in two areas; gurus and unorthodox therapies must not receive the support and subsidies from private and public health programs which psychiatrists hope to obtain (Marshall, 1978); moreover, the "abuses" of unorthodox groups may produce clients for the services of orthodox practitioners, thereby further pointing up the salience of such service and the need for public support.

As one journalist has recently pointed out, scientologists, human potential awareness experts and Indian mystics have "done the psychiatrists image no good. The public begins to wonder whether mental therapy has anything in common with medicine" (Marshall,

1978:18-19). The *medical model* is thus vitally significant to the interaction of psychiatry-psychology with "cults." It is precisely the
medical model which legitimates the "scientific" status of psychiatry,
thereby (1) differentiating psychiatry from gurus and unorthodox therapists, and (2) establishing the specialized competence of psychiatrists
to evaluate the authenticity of ideological commitments developed in a
context of close-knit group solidarity and to identify psychopathology
underlying what might be otherwise accepted as a legitimate if unconventional spiritual involvement.

The use of "mind control" concepts to stigmatize deviant spiritual
movement thus "involves an application of the medical model to
religion. Certain religious beliefs are consigned to the realm of
involuntary pathological symptoms" (Robbins and Anthony, 1978:80).
"The brainwashee's thought processes are viewed as involuntary
symptoms, i.e., he can no more control his thoughts than someone with
measles can control his skin rash. He must therefore be restrained and
controlled for his own good so that he may be 'cured' " (Robbins, et al.,
1979). 17 As one M.D. has already argued, "Destructive Cultism" is an
actual disease syndrome which can be diagnosed as standard physical
illness (Shapiro, 1977).18

The prevalent conceptualization of converts to "cults" as victims of
"mind control" thus represents a topical instance of *the medicalization
of deviance*, a modern process of expansion of the social control
functions of medicine, which has been extensively commented upon by
sociologists (Conrad,(1975; 1978;1979; Conrad and Schneider, 1980;
Friedson, 1970; Zola, 1972; Kittrie, 1971; Robbins, 1979c).
Medicalization entails the assimilation of more and more areas of social
interaction to the medical model of deviance. Despite growing criticism
from "anti-psychiatrists" and sociologists associated with "labeling
theory," the medical has been continually extended to new areas of
social life including alcoholism (Schneider, 1978); hyperactive children (Conrad, 1975); child abuse (Pfohl, 1977); "compulsive gambling"
(Skilnick, 1979); and even habituation to caffein or tobacco (Goleman,
1978). Medicalization has been linked to the rise of the "Therapeutic
State" (Kittrie, 1971) which has generated a clientele "by developing
categories of deviance which reflected an assumption of illness.
Psychopath, alcoholic, and drug addict are categories applied to those
whose sexual, drinking and drug behavior is thought to be beyond control" (Stivers, 1975:384). What is presently emerging is a special
category identifying those whose religious behavior is viewed as having
gone beyond their control.19

A fundamental element of the medical model *qua* ideology is the assumption that it is less reprehensible to impose a possibly unnecessary
course of treatment than to risk leaving a pathological condition un-
treated (Sagarin, 1975:190-192; Scheff, 1966:109-10). The risk entailed
in rejecting the hypothesis of illness is seen as greater than the risk
involved in accepting the hypothesis. "It seems fairly clear that the
rule in medicine may be stated as: 'When in doubt, continue to suspect
illness' . . . most physicians learn early in their training that it is far

more culpable to dismiss a sick [person] than to retain a well one"
(Scheff, 1966:1009-10). An explicit and straightforward application of
this ideology to religious deprogramming and "mind control" in cults
has been made by a legal scholar (Delgado, 1977:72-73) who argues:

> In Type II error, an incompetent individual is presumed to be
> competent and his refusal of treatment is respected. As a
> result no measures are taken to bring about his release (from
> the cult and its conditioning), and the individual's stay with
> the cult will continue, perhaps indefinitely. The longer he
> remains with the group, the more entrenched the cult's
> control over his psyche will become and the lower the prob-
> ability will be that he will be able to leave on his own accord.
> Since the risks of continued membership by an unconsenting
> (mind controlled) individual appear to exceed those of
> treatment, and the time period during which those risks will
> operate is far longer, it appears reasonable to accept small
> numbers of Type I error if this is necessary in order to mini-
> mize consigning large numbers of unconsenting individuals to
> lives that they have not freely chosen . . . . The
> risk-aversiveness that we ordinarily afford to decisions to
> impose treatment on possibly competent objecting adults is
> *overborn by consideration of the greater risk of withholding*
> *treatment.* [20] (Our emphasis)

MEDICALIZATION, CULTS AND SECULARIZATION

The medicalization of deviance is related to the process
of *secularization* or declining influence of religion in modern culture
(Clarke, 1979). As Susan Sontag argues in *Illness as Metaphor* (1978),
we no longer have a religious and philosophical vocabulary to conceptu-
alize evil, so we use a medical vocabulary: evil becomes "pathology."
The decline of theistic beliefs in American culture is a contributory
factor underlying a broader moral ambiguity in the cultural milieu
which can be viewed as secularization of *civil religion* (Robbins et al.,
1976; Anthony and Robbins, 1977; 78). The role of the medical model
"is likely to be enhanced in a society in moral flux in which authorities
are hesitant to acknowledge a punitive intent and thus increasingly rely
on social scientists to provide therapeutic legitimations for social
control" (Robbins and Anthony, 1978:80). Psychiatric medical-model
ideology operates as a religious surrogate.[21]

The issue of secularization, however, is more directly involved in the
question of "cults." Attacks on "cults" are essentially attacks on
religious groups which share some of the following traits: authoritarian,
communal, emotionally fervent, experiential-mystical, overtly theistic
or supernaturalistic, and not concerned with social reform. Religions
sharing several of these attributes are deviant in twentieth century
America and are thus assumed to be regressive and pathological
(Anthony and Robbins, 1979). The attack on these types of religiosity
represent in part a thrust in the direction of enhancing and formalizing
secularization by defining authoritarian, life-consuming, and
emotional-experiential religiosity as illegitimate. The "Secular" and

"privatized" pattern of sedate Sunday-Saturday 'limited liability' religiosity is made explicitly normative. Any religious leader who wants to elicit a more intense or comprehensive commitment may be encouraging psychopathology and had better check with HEW!

NOTES

[1]Quoted in Robbins (1977a:241).

[2]Elsewhere (Robbins and Anthony, 1979b). The authors have compared the present agitation against "cults" with eighteenth century "counter-subversion" campaigns against Freemasons, Mormons and Catholics. The latter groups were viewed as repudiating basic Americanism and posing a threat to civil order.

[3]In the early seventies a sociologist writing on social movements and their relationships to social change in America (Howard, 1974:206-207) could write, "Krishna consciousness offers for its membership the possibility of safe deviance." The Krishna movement was seen as providing "a relatively safe vehicle for the expression of deep estrangement from mainstream culture."

[4]Rabbi Maurice Davis quoted in *The Washington Post,* Feb. 6, 1979.

[5]See Cox (1978) for a discussion of this premise of "brainwashing" analyses. See also Robbins and Anthony (1979d).

[6]On ex-communists witnesses before congressional committees in the late forties and early fifties, see Caute (1978:122-139).

[7]Dr. Margaret Singer, who has worked with ex-converts and who supports both "mind control" formulations and some forms of deprogramming, has noted the difficulties faced by ex-converts in trying to explain how they could have been attracted to such bizarre and authoritarian groups (Singer, 1979a; 1979b). One can infer from Dr. Singer's account that deterministic-mechanistic "brainwashing" explanations should be psychologically rewarding and comforting to ex-devotees.

[8]See Shupe *et al.* (1977) for an incisive discussion of the phenomenological convergence between "brainwashing" conceptualizations of cultist conversion processes and late medieval notions of "spirit possession." See also Shupe and Bromley (1980).

[9]Data gathered by Solomon (1980) indicate that ex-Moonists who have been deprogrammed are more likely than other ex-Moonies to have intense negative views of The Unification Church and to believe that they had been victimized by "brainwashing." Beckford (1977) reports that English ex-Moonists, who are less likely to have been deprogrammed, are less likely to see themselves as having been "brainwashed."

[10]See Pilarzyak (1978) for a comparison of Hare Krishna and The Divine

Light Mission of Guru Maharaj-ji which stresses the diminished communal insulation and authoritarian totalism of the latter. See also Messer (1976) on the DLM. In a definitive sociological monograph on Scientology, Wallis (1976) acknowledges that scientology has "some totalitarian features" (1976:180) but also points out that "most scientologists remain in full-time employment outside the movement, utilizing scientology facilities only occasionally and limiting their involvement to a level compatible with their occupational and domestic responsibilities" (1976:189). On the "integrative" properties of the Meher Baba movement, in which devotees are urged to seek full-time work in "the world" and often also become involved with professional psychotherapists, see Robbins and Anthony (1972) and Anthony *et al.* (1977). See Robbins *et al.* (1975) for a distinction between "adaptive" and "marginal" movements, and Wallis (1978) for a somewhat similar distinction between "world-accepting" and "world-rejecting" groups.

[11]Delgado (1979) presents a model of cultist "thought reform" in which the "cult" initially deceives the potential convert by concealing its deviant nature and stringent membership requirements, and subsequently destroys his capacity to exercise free-will through totalistic regimentation, conditioning and fatigue. Bracketing the issue of "free will" (see below), our analysis above suggests that such a model is inapplicable to most groups, which are either (1) not communal and totalistic, or (2) not deceptive in a gross sense in their recruitment processes (e.g. can one join Hare Krishna without knowing at the outset that one has encountered a deviant "cult"?). However, see Banner (1976) on the manipulative techniques of one west coast Moonist commune.

[12]See the account of Rassmussen (1976) who researched a Moonist workshop as a participant observer. Rasmussen comments, "The desire to abandon reason for emotion had to be present before the person came to the workshop . . . and the new identity that emerged from the workshop experience was an assertion of self that came from submission . . . it was a willful submission." (1976:15).

[13]See Robbins and Anthony (1979a) for a more extensive critique of these studies and formulations.

[14]See also Galanter and Buckley (1979) and Ungerleider and Wellisch (1979) on the personality patterns of converts.

[15]See particularly Richardson (1979); Downton (1979b); Rassmussen (1976); and Robbins and Anthony (1979B).

[16]Discussing psychiatry's "image problem," Marshall (1978) notes that "psychiatrists who want to receive an insured income must get the public to believe that all forms of mental therapy are hogwash, except for those forms practiced by psychiatrists, psychologists or their assistants" (1978:19). "Psychiatry has proclaimed itself a science, and now it wants to reap the institutional rewards that other forms of medicine have won in the U.S. If there is to be a national health insurance plan, for example, the APA wants it to be 'non-discriminatory' — by which it means that psychiatric care should get the lavish subsidy that is given to physical health care. Yet the APA would impose an important limitation: mental therapy is *not* to be subsidized unless it is given under the direct supervision of a psychiatrist or a psychologist. No gurus or social workers are to be allowed in on their own" (Marshall, 1978:19).

[17]See Shupe *et al.* (1977) for documentation that supporters of deprogramming actually see "cult" converts in this light. See West (1975); Clark (1976); and Merritt (1975) for pertinent anti-cult formulations.

[18]Dr. Shapiro and other "authorities" are quoted in "Teens in Religious Cults Develop Dangerous Disease," *National Enquirer,* October 10, 1977. Dr. Shapiro's son, Edward, is a devotee of Hare Krishna; he has been abducted and deprogrammed more than once. He was involved, as an alleged victim of "mind control" in the important case of *People v. Murphy.* See Robbins (1977a; LeMoult, 1978).

[19]On HEW and NIMH involvement with anti-cult psychiatrists, psychologists and deprogrammers, see Rich (1978).

[20]Delgado uses the term "Type I" and "Type II" in an opposite manner from their usage by Scheff (1966) and Sagarin (1975). Nevertheless, it is clear that he views the "error" of forcing treatment on a competent devotee to be more tolerable than the error of withholding imposed therapy from a person underging induced personality alteration. For Delgado, an "unconsenting" devotee may appear to have verbally consented to his involvement but his affirmation has been elicited in a context of totalistic "thought reform" in which his or her capacity to rationally evaluate his participation is diminished. Such an "unconsenting" participant is "released" through deprogramming or imposed therapy.

[21]Thomas Szasz notes: Modern psychiatric ideology is an adaptation — to a scientific age — of the traditional ideology of Christian Theology. Instead of life being a vale of tears, it is a vale of diseases. And, as in his journey from the cradle to the grave man was formerly guided by the priest, so now he is guided by the physician. In short, whereas in the Age of Faith the ideology was Christian, the technology clerical, and the expert priestly; in the Age of Madness the ideology is medical, the technology clinical, and the expert psychiatric (Szasz, 1970:5). See also Clarke (1979) who argues that in the process of modernization, secularization or the diminution of the social control powers of religion is linked to a corresponding increase in the social control authority of medicine; "normality and abnormality are increasingly defined as medical conditions" (1971:1).

REFERENCES

Anthony, Dick, Thomas Robbins, Madlyn Doucas and Thomas Curtis, 1977, "Patients and Pilgrims: Changing Attitudes Toward Psychotherapy of Converts to Eastern Mysticism," *American Behavioral Scientist,* 20,6:861-886.

Anthony, Dick and Thomas Robbins, "Youth Culture Religious Movements and the Confusion of Moral Meanings," paper presented to the Society for the Scientific Study of Religion, 1975.

Barker, Eileen, "Conversion into the Rev. Moon's Unification Church in Britain," paper presented to the British Sociological Association's Sociology of Religion Group at the London School of Economics, 1977.

Barker, Eileen, "Living the Divine Principle: Inside the Reverend Moon's Unification Church." *Archives de Sciences Sociales des Religions,* (1978).

Beckford, James, "Through the Looking-Glass and out the Other Side: Withdrawal from Rev. Moon's Unification Church," paper presented to the Fourteenth International Conference for the Sociology of Religion, 1977.

Bellah, Robert, "The New Religious Consciousness and the Crisis of Modernity." In *The New Religious Consciousness,* pp. 333-352. Edited by Charles Glock and Robert Bellah, Berkeley: California, 1976.

Berger, Peter, *Invitation to Sociology.* New York: Anchor, 1963.

Caute, David, *The Great Fear: The Anti-Communist Purge under Truman and Eisenhower.* New York: Simon and Schuster, 1978.

Clark, John, "Sudden Personality Change and the Maintenance of Critical Governmental Institutions," paper presented to the International Society of Political Psychology, 1979.

Clark, John, "Investigating the Effects of Some Religious Cults on the Health and Welfare of Their Converts," testimony to the Special Investigating Committee of the Vermont Senate, 1976. Arlington, Texas: National Ad Hoc Committee Engaged in Freeing Minds.

Clarke, Juanna, "Medicalization and Sacrilization," paper presented to the Association for the Sociology of Religion, 1979.

Coleman, James, "Social Inventions." *Social Forces,* (1970) 49:163-173.

Conrad, Peter, "The Medicalization of Deviants in American Cultures." *Social Problems,* (1975) 21, 1:12-21.

Conway, Flo and Jim Siegelman, *Snapping:America's Epidemic of Sudden Personality Change.* New York: Lippincott, 1978.

Conway, Flow and Jim Siegelman, "Snapping: Welcome to the Eighties." *Playboy,* (March,1979) 59:217-219.

Cox Harvey, "Deep Structures in the Study of New Religions." In *Understanding New Religions,* pp. 122-130. Edited by L. Needleman and G. Bauer, New York: Seabury, 1978.

Delgado, Richard, "Investigating Cults," *New York Times,* Op-Ed Page, Jan. 27, 1979

Dodds, E.R., *Pagan and Christian in an Age of Anxiety.* New York: Norton, 1973.

Downton, James, *Sacred Journeys: Conversion of Young Americans to the Divine Light Mission.* New York: Columbia, 1979a.

Downton, James, "The Conservative Nature of Change: An Evolutionary Theory of Conversion," paper presented to the International Society of Political Psychology, 1979b.·

Enroth, Ronald, *Youth, Brainwashing, and Extremist Cults,* Grand Rapids, Mich: Zondervan, 1977.

Galanter, Marc, Richard Rabkin, Judith Rabkin, and Alexander Deutsch, "The 'Moonies' a Psychological Study of Conversion and Membership in a Contemporary Religious Sect." *American Journal of Psychiatry* (1979) 136, 2:165-169.

Gelper, Marvin, "The Cult Indoctrinee: A New Clinical Syndrome," paper presented to the Tampa-St. Petersburg Psychiatric Society, 1976.

Glock, Charles, "Consciousness Among Contemporary Youth: An Interpretation." In *The New Religious Consciousness,* pp. 353-366. Edited by C. Glock and R. Bellah, Berkeley: California, 1976.

Goleman, Daniel, "Who is Mentally Ill?" *Psychology Today,* (1978) 11, 8:34-41.

Kelley, Dean, "Deprogramming and Religious Liberty." *Civil Liberties Review* (1977) 4, 2:23-33.

Kim, Byong-Suh, "Indoctrination in the Unification Church," paper presented to the Society for the Scientific Study of Religion, 1976.

Kitterie, Nicholas, *The Right To Be Different.* Baltimore: Johns Hopkins, 1971.

Lifton, Robert, "Protean Man." *Partisan Review,* 1968.

Lofland, John, "Doomsday Cult Re-Visited," paper presented to the American Sociological Association, Boston, 1979.

McAfee, Kathy, "Blissing Out: Divine Light or Divine Hype." *University Review* (May, 1973).

Marshall, Eliot, "It's All in the Mind." *New Republic,* (Aug. 5, 1978) 17-19.

Marin, Peter, "The New Narcissism." *Harpers* (1975)251:45-56.

Mauss, Armand and Donald Petersen, "Les 'Jesus Freaks' et Retour à la Respectabilitie, ou la Prediction des Fils Prodiques." *Social Compass* (1974) 21, 3:283-301.

Marx, John and David Ellison, "Sensitivity Training and Communes: Contemporary Quests for Community." *Pacific Sociological Review* (1975) 18, 4:442-460.

Merritt, Jean, "Open Letter." Lincoln, Mass.: Return to Personal Choice, 1975.

Miller, Jesse, "The Unification of Hypnotic Techniques by Religious and Therapy Cults," paper presented to the International Society of Political Psychology, 1979.

Nolan, James, "Jesus Now: Hogwash and Holy Water." *Ramparts* (1971) 10:20-26.

Patrick, Ted (with Tom Dulack), *Let Our Children Go*. New York: Dutton, 1977.

Pfohl, Stephen, "The 'Discovery' of Child Abuse," *Social Problems,* (Feb. 1977) 24:310-323.

Rich, Jerome, "Secret HEW Huddle on Religious Cults is Cut Short when Cultists Show Up." *Washington Post* (June 28, 1979) :A3.

Richardson, James, T., R.B. Simmonds and M.W. Harder, "Thought Reform and the Jesus Movement." *Youth and Society* (1972) 4:185-200.

Richardson, James T., *Conversion Careers: In and Out of New Religious Groups*. Beverly Hills: Sage, 1978.

Richardson, James T., "Types of Conversion and Conversion Careers in New Religious Movements," paper presented to the American Association for the Advancement of Science.1977.

Robbins, Thomas, " 'Cults' and the Therapeutic State." *Social Policy* (1979) 10, 1:42-46.

Robbins, Thomas, " 'Deprogramming' the 'Brainwashed': Even a Moonie Has Civil Rights." *Society* (1978) 4:77-83.

Robbins, Thomas and Dick Anthony, " 'Cults,' 'Brainwashing' and Counter- as an Explanation for Conversion to Authoritarian Sects," paper presented to the International Society of Political Psychology, 1979a.

Robbins, Thomas, and Dick Anthony, " 'Cults,' 'Brainwashing' and Counter-Subversion." *The Annals,* 1979b.

Robbins, Thomas and Dick Anthony, "The Sociology of Contemporary Religious Movements." *Annual Review of Sociology* (1979c) 5.

Robbins, Thomas, and Dick Anthony, "Brainwashing and the Persecution of Cults." *Journal of Religion and Health* (1980).

Sagarin, Edward, *Deviants and Deviance*. New York: Praeger, 1975.

Shapiro, Eli, "Destructive Cultism." *American Family Physician* (1977) 15, 2:80-83.

Scheff, Thomas, *Being Mentally Ill: A Sociological Theory*. Chicago: Aldine, 1966.

Shupe, Anson, J.C. Ventimiglia and Sam Stigall, "Deprogramming: The New Exorcism." *American Behavioral Scientist* (1977) 20, 6:941-956.

Schur, Edwin, *The Awareness Trap*. New York: McGraw-Hill, 1976.

Segal, Julius, "Correlates of Collaborative and Resistance Behavior of U.S. Army POW's in Korea," *Social Issues* (1957) 13, 3.

Singer, Margaret, T., "Coming Out of the Cults." *Psychology Today* (1979a) 12, 8:72-82.

Singer, Margaret T., "Cults as an Exercise in Political Psychology," paper presented to the International Society of Political Psychology, 1979b.

Skolnick, Jerome, "The Social Risks of Casino Gambling." *Psychology Today* (1979) 13, 2:52-58, 63-64.

Snelling, Clarence H., and Oliver Whitely, "Problem-Solving Behavior in Religious and Para-Religious Groups." In *Changing Perspectives in the Scientific Study of Religion*. Edited by A. Eister, New York: Wiley, 1974.

Solomon, Trudy, "Integrating the Moonie Experience: A Survey of Ex-Members of the Unification Church," (1980). In *In Gods We Trust: New Patterns of Religious Pluralism*. Edited by T. Robbins and D. Anthony, transaction forthcoming.

Stivers, Richard, "Social Control in the Technological Society." In *The Collective Definition of Deviance*. Edited by R. Stivers and F.D. Davis, New York: The Free Press, 1975.

Stoner, Carroll and Jo Anne Parke, *All God's Children: The Cult Experience —Salvation or Slavery?*, Philadelphia: Chilton, 1977.

Szasz, Thomas, *Ideology and Insanity*, New York: Doubleday, 1969.

Ungerleider, Thomas, and David K. Wellisch, "Coercive Persuasion (Brainwashing), Religious Cults and Deprogramming." *American Journal of Psychiatry* (1979) 136, 3:279-282.

Wallis, Roy, *Rebirth of the Gods: Reflection on the New Religions of the West*. Published lecture delivered at Queens University of Belfast, 1978.

Welles, Chris, "The Eclipse of Sun Myung Moon," *New York Magazine* (1976). Reprinted in *Science, Sin and Scholarship: The Politics of Reverend Moon and the Unification Church*. Edited by I. Horowitz, Boston: MIT, 1978.

West, W., "In Defense of Deprogramming," (Pamphlet) Arlington, TX: International Foundation for Individual Freedom, 1975.

Wuthnow, Robert, *The Consciousness Reformation*. Berkeley: California, 1976.

Zaretsky, Irving and Mark Leone, *Religious Movements in Contemporary America*. Princeton, 1974.

PROFESSIONAL vs. TRADITIONAL:
Methods of Influencing Behavior

RICHARD WEISMAN

The rumours of a decade ago echoed in such works as Philip Rieff's *Triumph of the Therapeutic* or Paul Halmos' *Personal Service Society* have proven not to be exaggerated. The language of psychotherapy and its derivatives has so permeated the popular consciousness in North America that it has become virtually impossible to conceive of a problem affecting one's biography for which someone has not proposed and administered a therapeutic remedy.

Psychotherapy has begun to fulfill its promise as an overarching frame of reference to which persons may refer their experience whether in denunciation or justification of their moral conduct. Increasingly, it is in terms of such criteria as emotional well-being or psychological growth that individuals decide on the merits and worth of their personal relationships and their work. The triumph of the therapeutic is no longer a messianic conceit—psychotherapy has replaced religion and law as the ultimate frame of reference for the crucial experiences encountered by ever larger segments of the North American population.

It would be misleading to conceive of this new psychotherapeutic ethos as a purely spontaneous outpouring. For all its ingenuous claim to disinterested humanitarianism, the new consciousness is not without its subtle orchestration. Underlying the personal service society is a service economy, and underlying the new psychotherapeutic ethos is what Hans Enzensburger has aptly called a "consciousness industry." This is why the recent increase in governmental involvement in the organization and control of mental health services cannot be appreciated apart from the political and economic relationships which exist between the occupational groupings that provide these services.

The commissions, inquiries, and political lobbying to control new religious groups represent as much the self-interestedness of the professionals who seek to expand their market as the public who seek their services. The current debate concerns the right to shape human

Richard Weisman is Professor of Sociology at York University

behavior and administer therapies — religious or psychological. Conflicting ideas over which kind of behavior shaping best serves the public are rooted in the struggle of contending occupational groupings who command unequal political and economic resources and who are engaged in competition both for the right to define what constitutes right consciousness and for control of the market of those who seek help.

For present purposes, it is crucial to distinguish between at least two of these contending groups: professional psychologists and leaders of religious or psychological self-help groups. The professional psychologists have already obtained their mandate to perform therapy through the authority of the state. Included within this category are those helping-healing human service associations ranging from psychiatry, clinical psychology and psychiatric social work, to counseling, with its many institutional affiliations, corrections, and vocational guidance. Characteristically, the members of these occupations receive training at an institute, college, or university accredited by the state, are organized into local, provincial and national associations which are recognized by the state, and are granted jurisdiction to perform their task through legal sanctions ranging in restrictiveness from registration to certification to licensing.

The second group of occupations, including religious leaders, form a class more by default than by design. It consists of those members who perform therapy without specific authority from the state. They include voluntary self-help organizations, private therapy groups which offer their own training programs independently of state-assisted institutions, and popular movements which incorporate psychotherapy more or less eclectically within religious, political, or communitarian value systems. It may be suggested parenthetically that the media representation of these groups as cults, fringe groups, sects and so forth (with all the pejorative connotations of these terms) merely reflects an unacknowledged bias in favour of state-authorized service.

What both groups of servicers have in common is a need for consumers of their services. Where they differ is in the strategies they employ to attract these consumers. For several of the occupations within the first group, there has been a discernible trend over the past decade to control the market through a process of professionalization[1] In this process, a group lays claim to a particular cognitive skill and, on this basis, seeks to persuade an elite — in this case, influential members of the government — that it should exercise autonomous and exclusive control over how the skill is to be defined, how it is to be evaluated, and who is to be allowed to practice it.

Within the second group, including all religious organizations, one of the more conspicuous methods for attracting and maintaining client support has been through a process of proselytization in which recruits are encouraged to become adherents who pledge their resources to the survival or, in some cases, the propagation of the group. The aggressiveness with which this course of action is pursued may, of course, vary greatly from case to case.

The process of professionalization may be understood schematically as a collective strategy for controlling a particular market of skills. The attempt to gain legal sanction for autonomous practice by means of registration, certification, and especially licensing, is analogous to building boundaries on claimed territory.

These boundaries are drawn when a professional association is able to convince those in political power that it alone is competent to define and evaluate a particular skill. If this claim to exclusive competence is granted legal sanction, the profession will have gained a virtual monopoly over the distribution of its resources. From this privileged legal position, the profession increases its capacity to regulate supply and demand according to its own priorities. By eliminating external competition through licensure and by restricting membership and therefore the supply of services, it is able to make its resources scarce. By eliminating or at least discouraging internal competition through sanctions against advertising and kickbacks, it orients members towards identifying their individual interest with the collective interest of the profession. In short, professionalization may be viewed as a collective strategy for transforming skills into scarce resources and, in turn, for transforming those scarce resources into another scarce resource, for example, money.

In contrast to those occupations such as clinical psychotherapy and psychiatric social work which are in a position to seek domination of psychological services through the mediation of the state, de-professionalized helpers, such as religious leaders, must promote their services in full view of the public. The strategy of professionalization entails the control of a market through the indirect creation of a captive population who must either accept the services of the profession or do without altogether. The strategy of proselytization, on the other hand, bears the character of groups who must compete on a relatively open market, and who must therefore occasionally appear in the somewhat undignified posture of helpers who need clients.

The professional option as a strategy for domination of health or psychological services remains open only to those occupations that can presume to claim exclusive competence regarding a vital technical skill. Moreover, in contemporary North America, such a claim is likely to be respected by political leaders only if it is accompanied by evidence of a systematic body of knowledge and then only if this knowledge has been approved within accredited training institutes or universities. That self-help and non-university trained groups, such as new religious movements, often appear crude and venal in their efforts to attract clients stems in large measure from their relative lack of access to the political resources with which to pursue the professional option. In New York State, for example, the legislature has recently passed a bill (later vetoed) which would require all proselytes of religions to undergo "deprogramming" administered by professional psychiatrists. In addition to the questions of "religious freedom" or "mental health," this New York initiative should also be viewed as the attempt to create a larger "market share" for professional psychiatrists and to reduce the clientele for non-university trained prophets.

NOTE

[1]For my analysis of professionalization, I have drawn upon Eliot Friedson, *Profession of Medicine* (1970), Jeffrey Berlant, *Profession and Monopoly* (1975), and M.S. Larson, *The Rise of Professionalism* (1977).

MEDIA ETHICS:
The Elimination of Perspective

M. DARROL BRYANT

What are the obligations of public affairs broadcasting? What are the ethical principles that should guide both the process of research and presentation? Can public affairs broadcasting avoid being anything other than the occasion for airing the views and prejudices of the team of producers, researchers, writers and hosts of the show? Can public affairs broadcasting offer the audience nothing more than a pleasing flattery of the views and prejudices already held by the audience?

These questions, large yet particular, were raised anew recently in relation to the CBC *fifth estate*'s program on the Unification Church. Under the guise of raising public awareness of important and controversial public issues, the *fifth estate* proceeded to present a prejudicial portrait of the Unfication movement. The show seemed designed to create public hysteria rather than public understanding and debate. When only one way of viewing the Unification Church is presented, there is no longer any controversy. The consequence is that a prejudiced view becomes, in the context of the show, fact. Last year the *fifth estate* offered a similarly outrageous sensationalized portrait of the Apostles of Infinite Love. I am therefore inclined to question whether they are seeking to increase public understanding and discussion or to promote fear and hostility to the so-called new religions.

In many respects the *fifth estate* presented what has by now become the standard media portrait of the Unification Church: young men and women brought into the church by devious means ("brainwashed") and then put to work to build an economic and political empire for their leader, Sun Myung Moon. The larger editorial framework for the show was provided by the assertion that the new religions offer "simple solutions to the complex issues of modern society." Having then established the "simplemindedness" of the new religions, the show proceeded.

M. Darrol Bryant is Professor of Religious Studies at the University of Waterloo

Now what makes this particularly objectionable is that I know that the researchers for the program had access to more informed opinion about the Unification Church. Early in September I was approached by the researcher for the program. She presented herself as one engaged in general research in relation to the new religions. In our initial conversations, she indicated a desire to speak to me and others within the academic community who might be able to shed some light on these contemporary movements. She further indicated the she desired to do something "other than the normal stuff" which she felt was not very balanced. The upshot of these initial conversations was that she came to Waterloo where Professor Rodney Sawatsky and myself spent an afternoon talking with her. In these conversations we stressed the importance of seeing contemporary religious movements as religious movements! We stressed the importance of seeing these movements in relation to the larger perspectives of the history of religion. We suggested that conversion rather than "brainwashing" might be the appropriate category for understanding what happens to people who join this and other new religious communities. We suggested that these movements be seen as responses to deep structural crises within contemporary societies.

I also provided her with scholarly publications on the Unification Church, documentation on the issue of "deprogramming" and several suggestions concerning people both within the Church and within the academic community with whom she might profitably be in touch. We further agreed with her concern that the program focus on Canada rather than simply importing the already established media material from the U.S.A.

Subsequently, I did learn that she approached several of the people I suggested she contact. I have also learned — much to my dismay — that in some instances she suggested that I was involved in and supportive of the *fifth estate* project in a way that I was not.

Against this background, the reader can perhaps understand my dismay at the program that finally appeared on November 14th. The body of material that had been provided, as well as the contacts and conversations with more neutral observers of this movement, were simply ignored. Instead we were presented with a program drawing almost wholly on American material, a positive portrait of deprogrammers as concerned young people seeking to save others from the cults, and no commentary whatsoever from people trained in the study of religion.

An especially noteworthy feature of the show was an undercover visit by the intrepid Eric Malling to Camp K, the supposed center of California Moonie Brainwashing operations. We were informed that it was only with great difficulty that the *fifth estate* was able to secure permission to film the activities of the Camp. However, Eric, never put off the trail, then posed as a Canadian visiting the Bay Area who innocently fell in with the Moonies and, incidently, the cameras that were filming Moonie activity in San Francisco and Camp K. This double-con was carried through with a commentary about how deceptive the members of the Unification Church are. In the midst of this commentary we are treated to film clips of Eric talking, singing and playing games at Camp K. However, this visual material did not mean what it appeared to mean. Rather, our host and commentator, Eric Malling, assured us that something most peculiar was going on. (Indeed it was. But it was by the *fifth estate*, not by members of the Unification Church.) But the film clip itself showed that what was going on was simply what one might expect at any religiously based camp seeking to encourage people to join their group, to gain converts.

The whole style of presentation of this episode would appear to be a stock feature of the new media myth of the "new reporter." The *new* reporter is the one who risks all, even the washing of his brain, in pursuit of the "real" story. I thought that this schtick went out with grade B westerns, but it appears to have resurfaced in the new reporter. (I say this as one, who in the pursuit of my research, went through Camp K and found it to be a high intensity experience, but certainly not pernicious.)

In the program Eric Malling interviewed one young Canadian who had joined the Unification Church and subsequently left. The young man was obviously unsure what he thought about the Moonies. But the questions of our intrepid interviewer clearly led him towards a negative statement of his experience with the Unification Church. It was Eric who suggested that the young man must be "afraid" for his "safety" and that he had been "brainwashed." The interviewer's questions, then, were designed to elicit responses that would confirm his, the interviewer's, prejudices.

Those who have studied the Unification Church are aware that people in the movement come and go with great regularity. The overwhelming percentage of those who leave leave voluntarily — they are not "deprogrammed" (an appalling Orwellian doublespeak term used to cover activities which courts in the U.S.A.have determined to be criminal.) However, in a perspective that insists that people who join the movement are "brainwashed," such information must be ignored. If it were stated, it would suggest the obvious contradiction: how could "brainwashed" people leave on their own accord if they were truly "brainwashed"?

ITEM: They showed one set of tearful parents concerned about a son who had joined the Moonies in California. Since these were the only parents interviewed, the viewer is left with the impression that *all* parents feel this way. However, there are parents, perhaps the majority, who support their sons and daughters who have joined the movement. I have spoken to many such parents.

ITEM: In the commentary on the footage from Camp K, it was suggested that only young and confused kids join this movement. But I noticed in the footage from Camp K a man who has a Ph.D. in engineering, taught at Cornell and joined the movement in his mid-thirties. The commentary did not mention him. Indeed, the evidence suggests that the average age of people joining the Unification Church is 23-24 years of age, usually with some college education.

ITEM: In the program one psychologist was interviewed. The viewer is thereby left with the impression that all psychologists view this group negatively. However, many psychologists who have studied the new religions differ with this psychologist on the question of the psychological health of people in this, and other, new religious groups.

ITEM: Not one person trained in the study of religion was interviewed on the program. Why not?

My point here is not a defense of the Unification Church but simply to suggest some of the contrary evidence that makes this whole movement more complex than the program portrays. Moreover, these items simply point up the bias of the *fifth estate's* presentation.

After the program was aired, I contacted the executive producer of the *fifth estate* to raise some questions concerning what had been aired. In that conversation, the producer denied that there was anything unfair or prejudicial or even one-sided about the program. He likened my objections to the presentation of the deprogrammers to objecting to a whole profession on the basis of some bad members within the profession. I tried to suggest that there was hardly anything "professional" about the "deprogrammers," that they were rather engaged in activities to deny civil liberties to persons of legal age. When I raised the issue of the responsibility of the *fifth estate* to take seriously its own research, he again claimed that they had and that the script was based on that research. Throughout our lengthy conversation he assured me, again and again, that they had presented the material in a fair and balanced way. I began to wonder if perhaps we were talking about different shows.

I also received a note from the original researcher from the *fifth estate*. She said that "she had not been able to agree with my point of view on the Unification Church." But, she continued, she hoped "I had found the program interesting." At issue here is not *my*, or any other particular, point of view, but simply the obligation of public affairs broadcasting to do its job. As I understand it, that job is to assist in raising the level of public understanding. When a program is aired that simply decided to ignore information and perspectives that might contribute to a fair-minded presentation of controversial topics, then one is allowed to wonder if the media is misusing its considerable power and influence.

Here it should be noted that in the program itself it was stated that they had interviewed in the Summer people caught by the Moonies. What then of the seeming open-mindedness presented by the researcher? Was there willful duplicity here? Had the content of the show already been determined? Was the researcher simply looking for additional confirmation or further ammunition for attack?

Regardless of the answers to these questions, it is clear that we did not get a program on the controversial Unification Church. By the time the show was presented, the controversy had been resolved within the staff of the *fifth estate*. In the perspective of the program there is no controversy: the group is simply dangerous and bad. Anyone viewing the program would be left with the impression that there is no other perspective than the one presented. Indeed how could there be another perspective on such a reprehensible group? Here is where the lie is exposed. Rather than providing the viewer with information and a range of opinion that would allow the viewer to make his own determination, the *fifth estate* decided the question in advance. Having already determined that the Unification Church is essentially evil and pernicious, they then simply selected and framed their material in ways that would confirm their original bias. One has a right to expect more from the CBC.

These issues are not confined to only media presentations on the new religions. Recently, the Anglican Church of Canada asked for a hearing before the Canadian Radio and Television Commission in relation to a Canadian television presentation on the Anglican Church, "A House Divided." Their brief makes it clear that they too believe that we must be vigilant and insist that television broadcasting live up to its own stated responsibilities.

It Would Have Been Nice
To Hear From You . . . .
On *fifth estate*'s "Moonstruck"

BART TESTA

I missed the broadcast of CBC's film "Moonstruck" when it was aired on the network's Sunday news "magazine" *fifth estate.**
However, that same evening I visited a friend of mine, a newspaper editor, and she described the film to me as "another CBC non-documentary." Neither a film critic nor especially sympathetic to "new religions," my friend was annoyed not so much at the film's glaring bias against the Unification Church (the Moonies) but at the film's apparent violations of the conventional "objectivity" associated, at least morally, with documentary filmmaking. Hence her expression "non-documentary."

Darrol Bryant's piece in this volume gives his account of why "Moonstruck" is so biased against the Moonies by describing from his personal experience how certain inputs — ideas, anecdotes, research, etc. — were excluded from the film. Bryant's criticism is based on what may be termed "elimination of perspective." Bryant knows about such elimination because a perspective different from the one the film takes was elicited from him by the producers of "Moonstruck" and ignored by the film itself.

My concern in this short essay differs from those of my editor friend and Bryant but does relate to both the conventions of documentary and the suppression (not only by elimination) of perspectives to which their criticisms of the film directed my attention. "Moonstruck" strives to create a discourse which presents itself as authoritatively "subjective," that is "authentic," but the film fails, not only in comparison to some ideal "other" film about the Moonies which could have been made, but *within the film itself* as it now stands.

Bart Testa is Instructor in Cinema Studies at the University of Toronto

* "Moonstruck" was screened for me by the CBC public affairs library. I would like to thank the library staff for their consideration in allowing me to study the film at length and in private on their office video tape machine.

In his essay, "Theory and Film: Principles of Realism and Pleasure," Colin MacCabe posits: "There is no discourse that produces a certain reality" but rather "a set of contradictory discourses transformed by specific practices. Within a film there may be different 'views' of reality which are articulated together in different ways.'[1] In the case of traditional documentary films, the two most basic discourses are those of the image and the soundtrack. MacCabe observes: "Most documentaries... bind the images together by verbal interpretation of the voice-over commentary."[2] In such films, the voice-over text becomes the dominant discourse to which the images submit for interpretations, thus becoming "illustrations" of the off-screen commentary to which they are seen to "correspond."

However, to some degree, in the last fifteen years, documentary films, and especially those made for television, have developed alternate strategies for the soundtrack. Among the crucial influences on this development has been *cinema verite* and its displacement of the voice-over in favor of a soundtrack composed of direct-sound interview material and "eye-witness" on-camera commentary. By situating the verbal text within the image rather than as a disembodied, voiced authority over it, the *cinema verite* style creates a relative equality between sound and image which allows the viewer to be aware of the verbal discourse as one view of reality rather than compelling him to accept the soundtrack as a plenary explanation of the image.

The effect of such an equalization of image and sound has been to bring greater authenticity to documentary films, though at a cost to their "authority." The viewer loses something in global explanation, full interpretation and "efficiency." However, in exchange, the viewer gains a much greater density, complexity and multiplicity of textual experience. Both kinds of documentary style incarnate their own kinds of pleasure. Today, it is conventional to combine both modes, using the older method to provide exposition and the newer to leave room for debate within the film by giving voice (literally) to "views" of reality.

In light of such developments in documentary filmmaking, "Moonstruck" is retrogressive. It uses the newer techniques of interview and "eye-witness" but the film's dominant strategy is to give the voice-over complete authority, to make it the sole discourse of the film. However, the problem with "Moonstruck" is not that the film is conservative in style but that it perversely seizes integrity from its materials to give the voice-over its authority. In this film not only are the images relegated to the role of "illustrating" the soundtrack, sound materials rooted in the image — "direct sound" — are also used to "footnote" the voice-over. MacCabe's "contradiction" is systematically suppressed within the film.

The extent to which this strategy extends in "Moonstruck" can be suggested by briefly describing the diverse materials the film assembles. These fall into five categories.

1. The in-studio preface. It sets up the Moonies as a "mystery" we cannot readily understand by using phrases like

"...cults and the iron hold they have over so many young people." Spoken by an announcer in the conventional position of authority, behind a desk in "our studios," such phrases prepare the viewer for a "discourse of answers," not a documentary of multiple views.

2. Stock footage. Six different sources of footage not shot by the makers of "Moonstruck" have been inserted into the film. Most of this material consists of news clips (e.g., "historical material") and as is usual for stock footage usage, the role of this material is to be "objective" because its inherent rhetoric is that of "historical record."
   However, as we shall see, this role is abused at several points in the film.

3. Expository material. These shots (and they are usually single shots) are used to "cover" events for which the film-makers have no footage, such as John Quinlan's deprogramming, which is related by the voice-over as the viewer sees a traveling shot from a car (Quinlan, we are told, traveled by car to see the deprogrammers.)

4. Interview material. The subject faces the camera and answers off-screen questions put by Eric Malling, the film's on-screen reporter. There are six such interviews in this conventional mode, but their use changes on the soundtrack as when the deprogrammers' voices take over the role of the voice-over during the "Moonie mass marriage" sequence taken from stock footage.

5. Eye-witness material. The longest single sequence in "Moonstruck" is reporter Eric Malling's sojourn among the Moonies of San Francisco. Such visits are by now a journalistic cliche in stories about the Moonies. The reporter goes to the Moonies' center incognito, is transported to one of their rural training centers, stays a few days and later writes up his (usually horrific) impressions. 3

Of course, this cliche presents some difficulties for filmmakers since the camera has to make the vist along with the reporter. These difficulties were overcome by the makers of "Moonstruck" when they obtained permission from the Moonies to film their activities. Malling still visited incognito, as the camera's main subject of interest. However, while the reporter's spoken account, a dubbed-in voice-over, and the camera's "views" of reality are two different texts, they are conflated so that Malling's voice-over and the camera appear to be *one* textual source. That is, his voice-over commentary is used to seem synchronous with the images.

This effect is achieved by suppressing the direct-sound recorded on location and inserting Malling's voice in its place. And, when direct sound is heard, it is immediately qualified, ironized or explained away by Malling's voice-over.

Two examples: First, Moonie recruiter Richard Lewis, who has agreed to be tape-recorded with a microphone hidden on his body, approaches Malling and identifies himself as a representative of the Unification Church. The voice-over immediately takes over the sound-track to explain that such admissions are not usually made and that Lewis is "obviously" playing for the camera and microphone. Second, when Malling is at the Moonies' urban center for dinner, the viewer sees people moving around a table serving themselves food, buffet--style. Malling's voice-over, however, complains, "They heaped my plate," then goes on to recite dialogue he supposedly had with the Moonies over dinner. The images don't show anything related in the voice-over text.

With the exception of 5, this inventory of materials in "Moonstruck" is conventional for contemporary documentaries. And one would expect that they would provide ample opportunity for a multiplicity of perspectives. But such is not the case. Malling's impressions are the dominant perspective of the film and the rest of the material is used to supplement it so that his discourse is presented as the "authentic" one, not presuming to "objectivity" but to subjective sincerity copasetic with the objective facts the other materials bring to bear on the film.

The overall strategy of voice-over dominance, whether the voice is Malling's or someone else's, which works in "Moonstruck" is based on this principle: images and sounds appear at the beckoning of the voice-over. The voice-over tells us Rev. Moon arrived in the U.S. in 1971. Stock footage immediately shows the viewer Moon getting off a jet plane. The voice-over says, "He had enough followers, enough John Quinlans, to stage this rally." Stock footage shows the Moonies rallying around the Washington Monument. At the level of direct-sound the voice-over commands the same powers. The rally footage soundtrack (direct-sound) includes Moon's translator saying, "God summoned Rev. Moon to lead young people back to God." The voice-over picks up "young people" and continues, "Once young people get into the Moonies, few have the strength to walk out themselves." The meaning of "young people" is excised from one discourse and reappears immediately inside another, linking them aurally. Similarly, when Malling addresses the camera in his car after leaving the Moonie ranch, he says in conclusion, "...anything in their lives." There is a straight cut to a close-up of psychiatrist Margaret Singer who utters one word, "Any," before the voice-over cuts in to give her capsule biography. In this way, one word links Malling to Dr. Singer whose remarks accordingly become a "footnote" by an authority to his impressions. In both cases, the switch in discourse leads from reflections of "God" and "commitment" into a discourse on "brainwashing," the film's dominant theme-account of why people join the Moonies. That is, the former sound materials become illustrations of the "brainwashing" explanation.

Instances of such tactical match-ups, in which the structure of interpretation seizes words and images in order to bleed their content to nourish the authority of the explanation — "brainwashing" — could be enumerated throughout "Moonstruck" because this is the film's basic strategy. But let's limit ourselves to two further obvious examples of such shifts, this time into *connotative* directions.

After Dr. Singer gives her theories of brainwashing in the Moonies,[4] the film resumes an interrupted interview with two deprogrammers — itself an interesting seizure of talk from one "expert" interviewer to another — who suggest the viewer compare Moon and Jesus, as they do during their deprogrammings. Immediately, there is a straight cut to Moon (stock footage apparently shot in Korea at a Moonie "mass marriage"). As we shall see, the deprogrammers are about to take over the voice-over role. They are already able to beckon images. But before this happens, the announcer's voice-over returns to give details of Moon's theology of the "perfect family" and some information about the custom of mass marriage. Then, the deprogrammers' voices return and take over the voice-over role to assert that Moon is against individualism and that his intentions are imperial. The camera cuts to Moon dressed as a king, apparently for this marriage ceremony. This shot is followed by one composed in a rigidly geometrical manner, an allusion really to the Nazi propaganda film, *Triumph of the Will.* [5] That it is a compositional allusion to this famous Nazi movie is probably not obvious to the average viewer but its political connotations as a composition, read through a generation of newsreel watching in which *Triumph of the Will*'s compositions are a cliche, makes the shot an effective icon of "Nazi-type" organization. This connotation is greatly amplified by succeeding shots of the Moonies chanting "Manseis!" (Victory) which draw out the *triumph of the will* allusion to reinforce the Moonies-are-Nazi-like connotations. This whole sequence is provoked by the deprogrammers' assertion on the soundtrack, in the same way as the voice-over does throughout the film.

Now, "Moonstruck" never makes, much less substantiates, any charge that the Moonies are Nazi-like or imperious. All the film charges directly is that the Unification Church behaves (in Congressman Donald Frazer's words) at times like a "multi-national corporation." However, in interpreting images and mixing the soundtrack in certain ways, "Moonstruck" implies the vague but connotatively abundant charges of "Nazi-like" and "brainwashing" as if these were the sole possibilities for interpreting images seen.

Our second example of this tactic in the film is even more obvious. During the "Moonies in Canada" sequence the voice-over tells about Moonie activities in Canada, accompanied by matching images of Moonies marching up Toronto's Yonge Street, their sheep farm in rural Ontario, etc. Then, the voice-over, continuing right along, talks about the church's "funny" dealings with Canadian Customs and a shot appears of a truck driving down a back road at dusk. The intended meaning to be grasped from this match of sound and image, coming as it does at the end of a string of like and obviously, objectively, matched couplings, is: "Moonie truck running the border." But, of course, the shot is fictional, staged. Even if Moonie trucks do run the border (and the film never *says* so explicitly) *this* truck isn't one of them.

This shot, moreover, is no more fictional than the sequences used to establish and repeat the "Nazi-like" connotation, though this is more obvious in the case of the truck. The truck doesn't have a denotative relation to the soundtrack one can believe, while Rev. Moon's image from stock footage obviously does denote "here is Rev. Moon." In the latter case, it is the connotation which is fictional.

These few examples instance the extreme degree of deformation which the dominance of the voice-over enjoys in "Moonstruck" in over-determining the viewer's reading of the materials assembled by the film as a unilinear, closed discourse. The examples have been chosen that might likely pass by the average viewer unnoticed.

But there are other places where only the viewer predisposed to believe vaguely put allegations about the Moonies would feel comfortable with "Moonstruck." The indifferent viewer watching TV on a Sunday evening, like my editor friend, would likely feel annoyed because in these places "Moonstruck" is simply botched. The most obvious instance of this is Eric Malling's clownish "performance" as an incognito reporter.

For one thing, his voice-over during the "Moonie sojourn" sequence is too gleefully sarcastic, not only about his deception of the Moonies but about everything. Malling seems a buffoon, whereas the whole tone of the lead-in and the very moving interviews with John Quinlan's parents, cause the viewer to expect a more dignified tone when the film travels to the scene of John's conversion to the Moonies. Malling is supposed to be following in John's footsteps, undergoing the "brainwashing" John underwent.

Malling relishes his role as buffoon and plays the voice-over as comedy. The images are, however, normal, banal, sober, silent. When the direct-sound intrudes, for snatches of conversation, songs and bits of a lecture, the viewer feels pleasure, at least at escaping Malling's unfunny sarcasm. For example, one shot shows a black boy singing Stevie Wonder's "You are the Sunshine of My Life" in a rich feelingful voice. The viewer wants to hear at least a bit more, for the sake of the sounds themselves, but Malling cuts it off to complain the tune alludes to Sun Moon. Whether or not that was the case, the interpretation Malling provides isn't worth the frustration of cutting the song off.

But the frustration is more general, for the viewer would always like to hear *from the image,* which is the pleasure principle of synchronous sound ever since Al Jolson made the first talkie. The few admissions of direct sound in this sequence creates a desire in the viewer to hear more simply because the direct-sound is richer, denser, more "real" than the voice-over, a sour comedy monologue, is. The most glaring case here is the lecture. Malling says, "I didn't understand the lecture at all. But the rest loved it." The viewer hears only small bits of this lecture, a joke on the Moonies' beaming solicitude and a fragment of the lecturer saying how people feel uncomfortable using the word "God." The joke comes as a shock — who would have thought the Moonies were so self-mocking? The fragment is, of course, a banal commonplace, not hard to understand at all. The viewer at this point finds it difficult to *believe* Malling's voice-over or to enjoy his wit, because the pleasure of hearing the direct-sound is now frustrated on two levels—the cinematic one of synchronous sound and the content one, for the Moonies' own talk and singing are more interesting, complex and, in the case of the joke, funnier, than Malling's verbal account of them. It would at this point have been a pleasure to hear from the Moonies, but the film frustrates that opportunity too clumsily, too often and without adequately pleasing compensation.

I think the failure of "Moonstruck" as a documentary film, though particularly extreme, is typical of the media's failure to deal with the Moonies, not only on the moral level of "objectivity" but on the level of pleasure as well. The media stir up desire in their audience to know fully the phenomenon to which the media directs its attention. This desire may be of short duration but it is intense. In the case of the Moonies, however, this attention and desire is persistently deflected away from the "Moon phenomenon" as a concrete reality and into its interpretation by anyone but Moonies. The problem, at the level of pleasure, is that this interpretation emerges not out of a direct confrontation of camera and microphone with the Moonies, but out of a strangely perverse refusal to enact such a confrontation, a refusal that underlies the whole strategy of "Moonstruck." This refusal provokes nothing but frustration on the part of the casual, indifferent viewer who feels he (or she) is being manipulated *before* and *instead of* being informed. The Moonies—and Darrol Bryant—are not the only people who are annoyed by a film like "Moonstruck." Anyone who viewed it should be annoyed by this CBC "non-documentary" because it violates the pleasure principles of viewing a film.

NOTES

[1]*Screen,* (Autumn, 1976), 17:3, 11.

[2]*Ibid.*

[3]See my "Making Crime Seem Natural" in *A Time for Consideration,* edited by M.D. Bryant and H.W. Richardson (New York and Toronto: The Edwin Mellen Press, 1978) for a detailed description of this journalistic practice.

[4]Dr. Singer's account of "brainwashing" in the Moonies has three arguments: (1) Moonies use love, by giving it and withdrawing it, to control people; (2) their lectures induce hypnosis; (3) their constant chanting in groups and privately produce an altered state of consciousness which precludes self-reflection.

[5]The notorious *Triumph of the Will* was made by Leni Riefenstahl in 1934, on commission for Adolph Hitler who wanted it as a documentary-propaganda piece of the Nuremberg Party Rally of 1934. Footage from the film frequently appears as stock footage for newsreels, historical documentaries and even some fiction films.

PART III

JUDICIAL DECISIONS & GOVERNMENTAL STUDIES

THE QUEENS COUNTY HARE KRISHNA CASE:
Court Memorandum

This is an omnibus motion made on behalf of the three named defendants for an order, *inter alia,* dismissing the indictments herein upon the ground that the evidence before the Grand Jury was not legally sufficient to establish the commission by the defendants of the offenses charged or any lesser included offense. Said motion (pursuant to the provisions of subdivisions [1] and [2] of section 210.30 of the Criminal Procedure Law) is accompanied by a motion to inspect the Grand Jury minutes for the purpose of determining whether the evidence before the Grand Jury was legally sufficient to support the charges or any lesser charge contained in such indictments.

The court will address itself specifically to the prayer for the aforementioned relief sought in defendants' omnibus motion.

The motion to inspect the Grand Jury minutes is granted, and based upon such inspection, all of the papers submitted hereon and the thorough and protracted arguments of all counsel, the court makes the following findings and conclusions.

In view of the unusual factual background to the original presentment of this case to the Grand Jury and, above all, the unique theory of mental culpability advanced by the People as the foundation upon which they rely for the finding of criminal responsibility herein, and the potentially far-reaching ramifications of the court's legal conclusions in regard thereto, the court is constrained to review in detail the underlying facts, applicable law and the legal conclusions to be drawn therefrom.

At the outset, the court wishes to commend both defense counsel and the District Attorney's office on their obviously assiduous labors in the preparation of their memoranda of law and legal arguments based thereon.

Under indictment number 2012/76, the Grand Jury accused the defendants, Angus Murphy and Iskcon, Inc., of acting in concert to commit the crimes of (1) Attempted Grand Larceny in the First Degree, in that on or about April 12, 1976 they did attempt to steal from Eli Shapiro property, namely money by extortion by instilling fear in Eli Shapiro that physical injury would be caused to his son, Edward Shapiro, in the future, and (2) the crime of Unlawful Imprisonment in the First Degree, in that between May, 1973 and September 7, 1976 they did restrain the aforementioned Edward Shapiro under circumstances that exposed the said Edward Shapiro to a risk of serious physical injury.

Under indictment number 2114/76, the Grand Jury indicted the defendants, Harold Conley, a/k/a Trai Das, and Iskcon, Inc., for the crime of Unlawful Imprisonment in the First Degree, in that on or about and between August 3, 1976 and September 7, 1976 the said defendants while acting in concert did restrain one, Merylee Kreshour, under circumstances that exposed her to a risk of serious physical injury.

It is noted that the Grand Jury's initial investigation which commenced on September 7, 1976 was on the complaint of Merylee Kreshour alleging that she was kidnapped — not by the named defendants herein — but rather by her mother, Edith Kreshour, and one, Galen Kelly. The uncontradicted testimony adduced in respect thereto shows that Merylee Kreshour (who at the time was and to the present day remains a member of Iskcon, Inc.) was forcibly taken from a street in Queens County on August 3, 1976 by her mother and others and for a period of four days was subjected to a treatment referred to as "deprogramming". This treatment, the mother testified, was administered in order to liberate her daughter's mind and to restore her "free will". The mother testified further that her daughter was the victim of "mental kidnapping" by the defendant Iskcon, Inc. and that by physically taking her daughter into custody she was "rescuing her".

On September 8, 1976 the Grand Jury voted not to indict either Galen Kelly or Edith Kreshour, and instructed the District Attorney's office to continue its investigation into any alleged illegal activities of the said Iskcon, Inc.

Thereafter, numerous witnesses, comprised of experts in the fields of psychiatry, medicine, social work, religion and also parents and relatives of former members of the defendant corporation, as well as former members themselves, appeared and testified before the Grand Jury. As a result thereof, the Grand Jury returned the two instant indictments that are the subject of this motion.

The defendant Iskcon, Inc. is a nonprofit religious corporation, a legal entity by virtue of the issuance of a certificate of incorporation for the International Society for Krishna Consciousness pursuant to the Religious Corporations Law of the State of New York (Religious Corporations Law, Book 50). The defendant Harold Conley was the Supervisor of Women at the New York Temple for the International Society for Krishna Consciousness (Iskcon, Inc.). The defendant Angus Murphy was President of the New York Temple.

Merylee Kreshour became interested in the Hare Krishna Cult during the summer of 1974 while working as a secretary before returning to college in September. After going to meetings she decided to join the organization and moved into the Temple. Her average day started before 4 o'clock by praying, studying, meditation and chanting until about 8:30 a.m. when breakfast was served. The chanting lasted two to three hours each day, consisting of repeating the Hare Krishna Mantra

Meditation continuously. In order to keep track of the chanting, each time a chant is finished a bead is moved from a strand of 108 beads worn around the neck. After breakfast the day's activities began with Merylee leaving the Temple to distribute Krishna literature, selling magazines and soliciting contributions. Lunch was served at 3:30 p.m. and consisted of fruit, vegetables and juice. She had two meals a day and went to sleep at 7:30 p.m. The money she received from selling books and literature, as well as the donations, were turned over to the treasury of the organization and in return she was provided food, clothing and shelter.

Edward Shapiro became interested in the Cult when he was in high school and during the first year of college he became an active member. However, he did not live in a Temple because he is a diabetic, requiring daily insulin and a special diet which does not conform to the religious beliefs of the Krishna organization. He ultimately left college and started living at a Temple. On April 12, 1976 Edward returned from a pilgrimage to India. His father went to Kennedy Airport to greet him when he returned from India and it was obvious to his father as a medical doctor that his son needed immediate medical attention. He wanted Edward to have a checkup but his son said he would not talk to his father unless his father wrote out a check for $20,000 to the President of the New York Temple; otherwise, he would have nothing to do with his father.

Based on the aforestated facts, the defendants were charged, as heretofore recited, with the crime of Unlawful Imprisonment in the First Degree, in that they restrained the said Merylee Kreshour and Edward Shapiro under circumstances that exposed them to a risk of serious physical injury and, further, the defendants, Angus Murphy and Iskcon, Inc., were charged with Attempted Grand Larceny in the First Degree.

In reference to the charge of unlawful imprisonment, section 135.10 of the Penal Law provides as follows:

A person is guilty of unlawful imprisonment in the first degree when he *restrains* another person under circumstances which *expose* the latter to a risk of *serious physical injury* [emphasis added].

The two elements of this crime are *restraint* of another person thereby exposing such a person to a risk of *serious physical injury*. The term "restrain" is defined in section 135.00 of the Penal Law as restricting a person's movements intentionally and *unlawfully* in a manner as to interfere substantially with such person's liberty by moving him from one place to another, or by confining him either in the place where restriction commences or to a place to which he has been moved, *without consent*, and with knowledge that the restriction is unlawful. A person is so moved or confined "without consent" when it is accomplished by:

(a) physical force, intimidation or deception or

(b) any means whatever, including acquiescence of the victim, if he is a child less than sixteen years old or an incompetent person and the parent, guardian or other person or institution having lawful control or custody of him has not acquiesced in the movement or confinement."

It is conceded by the People that no physical force was utilized by the defendants against Merylee Kreshour or Edward Shapiro, and, further, that the said two individuals entered the Hare Krishna movement voluntarily and submitted themselves to the regimen, rules and regulations of said so-called Hare Krishna religion, and it is also conceded that the alleged victims were not in any way *physically* restrained from leaving the defendant organization. However, it is posited by the People that the nature and quality of the consent of the two alleged victims must be examined as it is asserted by the People that such consent was obtained by deception, and by the device of intimidation, control and the continued restraint was maintained over them. From this premise the People draw the conclusion that the two alleged victims were deceived or inveigled into submitting themselves "unknowingly to techniques intended to subject their will to that of the defendants * * *" and that same resulted in "* * * an evil consequence * * *". The entire crux of the argument propounded by the People is that through "mind control", "brainwashing", and/or "manipulation of mental processes" the defendants destroyed the free will of the alleged victims, obtaining over them mind control to the point of absolute domination and thereby coming within the purview of the issue of unlawful imprisonment.

It appears to the court that the People rest their case on an erroneous minor premise to arrive at a falacious conclusion. The record is devoid of one specific allegation of a misrepresentation or act of deception on the party of any defendant. Concededly, both Merylee Kreshour and Edward Shapiro entered the Hare Krishna movement voluntarily where they remain to this day as devotees of that religion. There is not an iota of evidence to even suggest that false promises were made to either of them or to indicate any act or conduct on the part of the defendants that might be construed as deceptive.

As to the premise posed by the People that the religious rituals, daily activities and teachings of the Hare Krishna religion constitute a form of intimidation to maintain restraint over the two alleged victims, the court finds not only no legal foundation or precedent for same but a concept that is fraught with danger in its potential for utilization in the suppression — if not outright destruction — of our citizens' right to pursue, join and practice the religion of their choice, free from a government created, controlled or dominated religion, as such right is inviolatedly protected under the First Amendment to the Constitution of the United States and article 1, section 3 of the N.Y. State Constitution.

It is at this juncture the court sounds the dire caveat to prosecutional agencies throughout the length and breadth of our great nation that *all* of the rights of *all* our people so dearly gained and provided for, under the Constitution of the United States and the Constitutions of all States of our Nation shall be zealously protected to the full extent of the law. The entire and basic issue before this court is whether or not the two alleged victims in this case, and the defendants, will be allowed to practice the religion of their choice — and this must be answered with a resounding affirmation. The First Amendment to the United States Constitution prohibits the establishment of religion by our federal legislators. Neither congress nor the states may establish a religion or compel individuals to favor one religion over the other. This precept was set forth by the forefathers of our country in the most explicit and unequivocal language in the articles in addition to and in amendment of the Constitution of the United States. In Amendment I it is mandated that:

"Congress shall make no law respecting an establishment of religion, or *prohibiting the free exercise thereof*" (emphasis added).

We are given further guidance by the provision of the Constitution of the State of New York that confirms, enhances and elaborates upon this cherished right. Article 1, section 3 provides:

"The free exercise and enjoyment of religious profession and worship, without discrimination or preference, shall forever be allowed in this state to all mankind; and no person shall be rendered incompetent to be a witness on account of his opinion on matters of religious belief; but the liberty of conscience hereby secured shall not be so construed as to excuse acts of licentiousness, or justify practices inconsistent with the peace or safety of this state."

Our country is a pluralistic society in religion. The First Amendment of the Constitution of the United States lays the foundation of the full play and interplay of *all* faiths. The freedom of religion is not to be abridged because it is unconventional in its beliefs and practices, or because it is approved or disapproved of by the mainstream of society or more conventional religions. Without this proliferation and freedom to follow the dictates of one's own conscience in his search for and approach to God, the freedom of religion will be a meaningless right as provided for in the Constitution.

Any attempt, be it circuitous, direct, well intentioned or not, presents a clear and present danger to this most fundamental, basic and eternally needed right of our citizens — freedom of religion.

The Hare Krishna religion is a bona fide religion with roots in India, that go back thousands of years. It behooved Merylee Kreshour and Edward Shapiro to follow the tenets of that faith and their inalienable right to do so will not be trammeled upon. The separation of church and state must be maintained. We are, and must remain, a nation of laws, not of men. The presentment and indictment by the Grand Jury herein was in direct and blatant violation of defendants' constitutional rights.

The giving up of one's worldly possessions, social contacts, and former way of life — and the court clearly recognizes and sympathizes with the resultant hurt, fear and loneliness of loved ones left behind — is not a matter under the present facts to be subject to judicial scrutiny *by way of the invocation of criminal prosecution*. Other than showing that Merylee Kreshour, Edward Shapiro and others subjected themselves to the discipline and regimentation of this particular legally licensed, religious group, whereby they are apparently seeking their individual *self-chosen* road to eternal salvation, there was not a scintilla of evidence presented to the Grand Jury to indicate the practice of fraud, deception, intimidation or restraint, physical or otherwise, on the part of these defendants. Religious proselytizing and the recruitment of and maintenance of belief through a strict regimen, meditation, chanting, self-denial and the communication of other religious teachings cannot under our laws — as presently enacted — be construed as criminal in nature and serve as a basis for a criminal indictment.

The court points out that the numerous and well-documented cases cited by the People do, in fact, show, and correctly so, that "physical restraint" need not be shown as a basis for prosecution herein, but that the unlawful restraint may be accomplished by "inveiglement" (former Penal Law, 1909) or by a "fraudulent misrepresentation" that could constitute "deception negating consent". Succinctly stated, in one case a victim was induced to leave New York for Panama on the promise of a job as a governess when in fact while enroute the victim learned the job was with a house of prostitution (*People* v. *Deleon,* 109 N.Y. 226). In another case, the complainants were induced to enter defendant's car *upon the fradulent representation* that they were needed as babysitters, when in fact the defendant wanted to engage them in indecent sexual advances (*State of North Carolina* v. *Gough,* 126 S.E. 2d 118). A third case involves the inducement of the victim to enter a wooded area upon the representation they would search for squirrels, when in fact it was defendant's purpose to assault the complainant (*State of North Carolina* v. *Murphy,* 184 S.E. 2d 845).

The further cases cited in the People's memorandum involve psychologically induced confessions, mental disease or defect, hypnosis to destroy a free will, intoxication, and coverture. However, in every case cited the criminal intent was shown, by the proof adduced therein, of the defendants seeking to compel their victims to perform some *illegal act* and that same was accomplished by *false representations.* In the case at hand, neither of these elements are present.

The final thrust of the People's argument aims at the unlawful restraint of an individual who has been declared incompetent and, therefore, by law the consent of the parent or guardian must be obtained, as set forth in subdivision (1) of section 135.00 of the Penal Law. In the case of Edward Shapiro, a Massachusetts Court issued an order appointing Mrs. Shapiro as conservator of his property. There is a serious issue as to whether under the United States Constitution full faith and credit would be given to our sister state's aforesaid order. This question is moot, however, in view of the court's finding that the order does not come within the purview of our statute — as same merely appoints a conservator of the property rather than a guardian of his person.

To sustain this indictment would open the so-called "Pandora's Box" to a plethora of unjustified investigations, accusations and prosecutions that would go on ad infinitum, to the detriment of the citizens of our state and placing in jeopardy our Federal and State Constitutions.

The concept of mind control or brainwashing is not a crime in and of itself. The fact that indoctrination and constant chanting may be used as a defense mechanism to ward off what another person is saying or doing is devastating and it is equally devastating when used as a technique for brainwashing or mind control. It may even destroy healthy brain cells. It may also cause an inability to think, to be reasonable or logical. However, this does not constitute a crime. Neither brainwashing nor mind control per se is a crime. It cannot be used as the basis for making out the elements of the crimes charged herein.

The court finds that as to both indictments, numbered 2012/76 and 2114/76, there is insufficient legal evidence to sustain the offenses charged or any lesser included offense.

Based on the foregoing, the motions to inspect the Grand Jury minutes and to dismiss the indictments on the ground of insufficient legal evidence are granted. The balance of these motions is denied as moot. The indictments are hereby dismissed.

John J. Leahy

Critique of the Goelters Report

Juegendliche in destructiven religioesen Gruppen

(Youth in Destructive Religious Groups)

HERBERT RICHARDSON

A government report appears. It wears the uniform of the social sciences, the costume of important social problems seriously considered in light of evidence carefully gathered and carefully weighed.

Are new religious groups, the *neue Jugendreligionen*, apparently so attractive to a segment of the youth population, a serious social problem? Do they represent a real danger to society and its members? Such questions have become a matter of urgent concern to some government officials. Unknown until the 1970s, at first praised for providing alternatives to the radical political groups and, in some cases, even provided with state funds to carry out drug rehabilitation programs, more recently these groups have been sharply criticized as at least potentially destructive. Many both inside and outside government consider them dangerous.

In response to the controversy, a scientific project of research has been undertaken by George Goelters, the Minister for Social Affairs, Health and Sports of the Rhineland Pfalz Government. This report, entitled *Youth in Destructive Religious Groups (Juegendliche in destructive religioesen Gruppen)*, presents the research data. But this report also presents much else: a sketch of the socio-economic landscape through which these youth-sects move; the legal resources the state possesses to combat these groups; and, throughout the report, the *impression* that these groups are destructive to their memberships. This impression, however, is nowhere substantiated in the data presented in the report. Yet, this impression has given the report its very title.

Goelters' report consists of four chapters. The first is a prefacing account of the controversy surrounding the new religious groups. The second prepares for and gives the results of the research. (The data are also provided in an appendix in computer data-sheet form.) The third

---

Herbert Richardson is Professor of Religious Studies at the University of Toronto

chapter is taken up with speculation on the social causes, mainly the problems facing contemporary youth, behind the rise of the youth-sects. The fourth chapter surveys the legal and educational resources available to counteract these new religious groups.

The first chapter of *Youth in Destructive Religious Groups* concludes its brief history of the controversy surrounding the groups with an un-critical summary of a document submitted by a private German anti-sect organization (p. 2). This document asserts that membership in youth-sects leads to psychological disorders that make it difficult for ex-members to be reintegrated into society. In addition to accepting its psychological assertion, Goelters also reads this document politically as saying that the new religious groups violate the basic values of society and even man's inherent dignity. This anti-sect document, or rather Goelters' reading of it, forms the sole basis for his use of the label "destructive" prior to presenting his own data or indicating his re-quirements for the use of such a strong and unscientific term.

The first part of the second chapter of *Youth in Destructive Religious Groups* uses tendentious psychiatric rhetoric to prepare the reader for the results of the research presented in this chapter. Having labeled the groups "destructive," Goelters now seeks to define such destructive-ness in ways that exclude the youth-sects' religiousness.

Aware that by attacking "sectarianism" he would be violating what he himself calls "the fundamental law" that protects religious free-dom, Goelters focuses on the "extra-religious" *behavior* in these groups which is "not in harmony" with the basic system of values in society. (p.4) He says that the issue does not concern doctrine. It is "the destructive effects on young persons, not their religious partiality or 'sectarian tightness' that demand the attention of the state." (p. 4) Moreover, these youth-sects do not all operate in the same way (for example, some are communal groups where one lives full-time, others require only part-time commitments); so, their effects on young people vary and must be *specified*. These new religious groups, it must also be acknowledged, are only part of a wider new religious enthusiasm among the young and "no religious group is fully free from the danger of destructive effects in individual cases." (p. 5) So, writes Goelters, what needs to be shown is how the "evil practices of influence" on the part of these youth-sects have an *obvious* and *typical* destructive effect on the young people who join them.

This is an ambitious array of requirements for proof that these youth-sects are "destructive," because what Goelters calls for is proof of extra-doctrinal, behavioral, specific, typical practices that are destruc-tive to the psychological health of those who become involved in youth-sects. This set of ambitious requirements overshadows what Goelters terms his "little survey" of "the most important destructive religious groups." I think the reader is meant to take the author at his word and expect that Chapter 2 of *Youth in Destructive Religious Groups* will meet these requirements for the use of the label "destructive." Sadly, as one reads on, the chapter does not do this at all. Goelters freely *speculates* on the destructive potential of these groups but there is little hard data to be found among what are basically doctrinal and historical accounts of some of these groups. The burden of proof, which becomes heavier as one passes through the "little survey," will have to fall squarely on the later presentation of the research.

Goelters' "little survey" is set out according to a three-part typology of youth-sects intended to describe their organizational style. It proceeds as follows:

I. Unification Church/Children of God. Goelters says these two groups have little in common except that both "demand total integration in a community and unconditional subjugation to a religious leader who perceives himself as a Messiah or prophet." (p. 7) However, rather than argue that this organizational "totalism" (the term comes from the American psychologist Dr. Robert Jay Lifton) makes the organizational behavior destructive, Goelters says that their presumably shared doctrine of absolute choice of either God (the sect) or Satan (the world) has caused ex-members to experience difficulty shaking the notion that they have opted for Satan. This indicates that the ex-members have continued to believe the attributed dualist *doctrinal* systems of these two sects even after leaving them. It does not say anything about the destructiveness of the specific behavior of the group, nor, I might add, about the destructive effects of anyone holding such a dualist view of things. This view would have been quite conventional to Luther, Calvin or the Protestant Pietist religious groups of past centuries. Such dualist doctrines, in fact, have been commonplace within traditional "sectarianism."

II. Transcendental Meditation/Scientology. The author describes both groups as promoting a "variety of courses" which they claim lead to enlightenment: TM courses teach meditation and Scientology courses teach "applied philosophy." The first criticism the author levels at these groups is that they don't deliver on what they promise for their courses. This, Goelters says, is a matter of consumer fraud, not precisely one of his requirements for "destructiveness." The second criticism the author makes is that both groups have a cadre organization of young people who give "unconditional dedication and subordination to the leader-personality" and that these requirements effect the emotional development of the cadre-members in destructive ways. This charge is similar to the one implied against Unification Church and the Children of God above and it is not substantiated. Dedication and subordination are not specific behaviors, particularly not in the case of groups where the cadre-members' involvement in the group is identical to that of the "course-taking" members except that the former are much more deeply involved in the practical day-to-day running of the organizations. It should also be added that both Transcendental Meditation and Scientology, unlike the Unification Church and the Children of God, are not doctrinally tightly defined religions, but possess belief systems which mainly involve commitments to the techniques of enlightenment. In such cases, a member's relationship to the leader-personality has far less importance than his practice of the techniques. A third criticism is presented as well: that the meditation techniques can be dangerous to young people because they can lead to a "narrowing of consciousness" that will cause members to "drop out of social relations and to develop ideas of delusion." (p. 9) The source for this last charge is Dr. D. Langen, Director of the Clinic for Psychotherapy of the University of Mainz. It is not said whether Dr. Langen was speculating about a possibility or had actually noticed and then analyzed this consequence of Transcendental Meditation or Scientology involvement.

III. Hare Krishna and Other Indian Associations. Goelters asserts, "there are charlatans among them but also serious religious leaders who are recognized in India." (p. 10) There is no suggestion here whether or not Goelters considers the founder of Hare Krishna a charlatan, although among Eastern religion scholars in North America it is generally accepted that this man, Bhaktividanta Swami Prabhupada, was a "serious religious figure." Drawing rather obviously on *Turning East*, a study of Eastern religions in the West by Harvard University theologian Harvey Cox, Goelters emphasizes the great gulf between Eastern Religions and the culture of the West. But Goelters' criticism of the Indian youth-sects takes just the opposite tack from Cox's criticism. Cox says the Eastern religions will be remodeled to fit Western expectations, becoming just another item in Western consumer society. Goelters claims there is a danger that members of these groups will lose touch with Western social reality. How this conclusion is reached is mysterious. But what is more problematic is how this conclusion fits the author's ambitious requirements for a proof of destructiveness.

Even further removed from those requirements is Goelters' summary where he tries to set out the common characteristics of "destructive religious groups." While admitting that the scholarly literature on the subject has failed to stand up under close scrutiny, the author derives three common features:

1. A savior figure who is the leader.
2. Totalitarian thought and volition. Personal thinking and criticism are shut off. "For young people who have grown up in our society, which is dominated by rational-analytical thinking, this means a serious and often a personality-changing shock." (p.11)
3. Apocalypticism. These "destructive" groups believe that the end of the world is imminent and, concomitantly, that one has to choose between absolute good and evil.

The author admits that (1.) is common to all new religions throughout history. He could also have added that doctrinal rigor, (2.), has also been common to moments of strong religious revivalism, often led by the "totalitarian" monastic movements in Catholicism and the strictly governed *cuius regio, eius religio* principle in Europe during the aftermath of the Protestant Reformation. He quite correctly points out that Apocalypticism (3.) is not a feature of Eastern religions. He might also have added that one finds no trace of Apocalypticism, nor of its concomitant Good-Bad absolutism, in Scientology or Transcendental Meditation, while the Unification Church holds a non-apocalyptic doctrine that they are founding the Kingdom of God on earth with their 'perfect families.' Therefore, these three features of "destructive" new religious groups do not apply to the groups instanced in Goelters' "little survey."

Goelters then proceeds to consider the "disintegration" (*Desintegration*) of young people from society, a question on which he expands in chapter 3. Briefly, he addresses the psychological issue here, the socio-economic and political issues in chapter 3. His psychological view is that young people who associate themselves with these youth-sects are mainly those burdened with personal problems and that these young people believe they can find meaning and security through membership in these sects. What they do not understand, says Goelters, is that the fellowship the young people receive from these groups is a double-illusion: "they perceive their environment as hostile" and fellowship is really the result of "doctrinaire pressure." (p. 12) This illusion would be dispelled, or the danger it involves would at least be diminished, Goelter suggests, if the young people knew at the outset the whole doctrine of the group to which they commit themselves rather than accepting bits of belief as they sink deeper into the false fellowship of the group.

Whether or not it is true that a full understanding of the doctrines of a group would act as a deterrent from joining, the fact is these groups do not deliberately withhold doctrine. Hare Krishna scriptures are ancient and have been the subject of long scholarship and the devotees themselves carry on a veritable bombardment explaining their beliefs. Sun Moon's *Divine Principle*, which contains the doctrines of the Unification Church, is freely available. L. Ron Hubbard's books which form the basis of Scientology, both popular paperbacks and 'technical' manuals, are very openly for sale. And so on.

However, far more important to the rest of his report is Goelters' last psychological assertion that these new religions do not draw members because of their religious beliefs and practices but that membership is the result of a compulsion young people have to shut out contemporary reality. The author greatly expands this theme in chapter 3 in terms of social and economic factors; here he works through psychological rhetoric, claiming that the youth-sects seize on this compulsion to shut out the world and use it for their "destructive" ends, whether these ends are calculated or merely the inadvertent consequences of the groups' inner psycho-social dynamics. So far, Goelters has advanced no evidence that suggests young people who join these youth-sects have such a compulsion to shut out reality nor has any argument been given that adequately shows what "destructiveness" results when this hypothetical compulsion meets the psycho-social dynamics of one or another of these groups. Rather, Goelters has given his own doctrinal presentation — a loose and, at several points, wholly inaccurate, account of the beliefs of the groups in a Messiah-leader, in the worth of meditation, in uncritical adherence to a belief system as a requirement for membership, in an absolute distinction between Good and Evil — which has been applied to support the otherwise unfounded assertion that to hold such beliefs must of itself require a preexisting compulsion. This hypothetical compulsion becomes the cause of belief while the unusually tight doctrinal strictness of the beliefs become the proof of the existence of the compulsion. This reasoning is circular and hardly scientific. As for how the *product* of such reasoning shows how these groups are "destructive," we haven't been shown anything at all that meets Goelters' ambitious requirements. We have only the rhetorical label of "destructive" and a few vague and unscientific speculations about "maybes" and "potentially destructive."

At this point in *Youth in Destructive Religious Groups*, the burden of proof rests very heavily indeed on the research data to follow. The reader looks forward to the scientific information that will substantiate the charges so loosely made of "destructiveness" and that will give real human experience to the psychological rhetoric that has dressed up the report in the somber garb of serious, governmental discourse. The reader is anxious now for the hard data that will satisfy Goelters' ambitious requirements for proving that these sects are destructive, re-membering that this label has been boldly impressed into the report's title. The reader desires scientific proof. The reader desires not specu-lation, conjecture, the musings of a culture ministry bureaucrat or ideo-logical folderol, but hard empirical data that will tell him something about this serious social problem.

And just what is it that the reader gets? He gets an opinion poll.

201 persons between 16 and 25 years of age were asked questions about youth-sects. Only 25% even knew the name of a group, excepting Hare Krishna, where the percentage jumps to 50%. Goelters attributes Hare Krishna's high profile here to their "eye-catching appeal" (that is, their costumes and public chanting). The average, when one adds the Krishna group, is 30% who can name a youth-sect. Only 4% have ever attended a youth-sect meeting, 9% more had other direct contact with youth-sect members (that is, they were approached on a school campus or in the street). The overwhelming majority (73%) heard about the groups through the media; 46% from friends and relations. A near-majority of 46% said that public information on the sects was in-sufficient. No wonder, since these survey respondents were so poorly informed about the youth-sects.

It is appalling that this opinion poll among young people would be passed off as determining a portrait of these new religious groups. Where did these young people get their "insufficient" information? From the mass media, and from friends and relations who probably got their information from the media as well. (Only 4%, we recall, have actually attended a sect meeting.) The report calls the media's information "objective." This is laughable. For, where do the media get their information, whether it is presented responsibly or sensation-ally? The media get their information from reports like this one! Circular reasoning is matched by circular flow of information, or rather, of the non-information of hearsay and gossip, which passes from one hand to another.

But let us turn to the opinions expressed by the young people surveyed briefly. In describing their reactions to contact *they have not had* with the youth-sects, 4% said they were very interested, 17% said they might consider joining one of these groups, and 44% said they would not mind taking a look though they doubted they would be seriously interested. 33% said they didn't want a thing to do with these groups. When asked why people join these groups (and of course almost none of the respondents knew sect-members personally) the same 44% who said they personally were curious about sects also said that curiosity and a desire to break out of a day-to-day routine was the main reason people joined. 59% said the complexities of modern life drove people into these groups. Others cited personal problems with families, work and school. It should be recalled that these respondents were speculating. They had, most of them, no contact with anyone in a youth-sect.

Yet, what is interesting is that the respondents saw the members of the new religions as people very much like themselves. This is clear from their responses to the question about what should be done about these groups. 61% said more attention should be paid to the problems of youth. 45% said youth should be provided with more opportunities. These answers correlate highly with the reasons given for young people deciding to become members, i.e., the complexity of modern life, lack of goals, etc. Moreover, while responses to some very leading questions about what life inside a youth-sect is like suggested that the respondents felt sect life was repressive and narrow, the majority of respondents, 71%, said that the groups would continue to grow, indicating that their own interest in these groups and their speculations as to the groups' attraction to youth overpower their speculations about the unpleasantness of sect life. This suggests that the respondents, even without knowing the groups themselves, saw them performing a function they thought should be performed in today's society even though they expressed distaste for what they guessed the life in such a group would be like.

However, let us return from these interesting correlations among the opinions and speculations of the respondents to the fact that this so-called "scientific research data" is nothing but an opinion poll. It is clear that this information in no way constitutes scientific data about the youth-sects or their supposed "destructiveness." This research data only tells us what some young people feel about these groups on the basis of what they learned from the media and from hearsay. This is hardly the "scientific report" chapter 2 of *Youth in Destructive Religious Groups* has prepared the reader for. Yet he *Youth in Destructive Religious Groups* as a whole has been devised and presented on the supposition that this opinion poll is scientific research. Worse, on the basis of this transparently false presentation, the report goes on, in chapters 3 and 4, to formulate political approaches to understand and combat the youth-sects.

It is too bad that Goelters did not arrange to make the serious scientific studies of these new religions that have been done in North America. For reasons of space, and because this paper is not intended to give an exhaustive account of the serious research into new religions, I can here only recommend two sources that would give a reader information about how to find and relate the various kinds of research in this area now being conducted in North America. The first is *Religious*

Movements in Contemporary America, a collection of seminal essays edited by Irving Zaretsky and Mark P. Leone, and published by the Princeton University Press in 1971. Updating work since the Zaretsky-Leone volume is Thomas Robbins, et al., "Theory and Research on Today's New Religions" in *Sociological Analysis* (Vol. 39, No. 2, pp. 95-122. 1978).

In order to instance the kind of empirical research that a government report should have done, I would like to turn briefly to four research projects on new religious groups conducted in North America by psychiatrist Dr. Charles Norton, fiscal analyst J.B. Sawadogo, medical doctor Dr. Toomas B. Sauks, and my own study.

THE NORTON REPORT

The Norton study consists of computer analysis of 342 problems of decision-making that range over a whole gamut of practical, spiritual, social and internal aspects of the decision-making process. Through computer analysis comparing the individual responses to a psychological test to a 450-member reference group, Norton is able to construct a behavioral and decision-making profile for each individual person. The profile consists of 105 psychological characteristics and describes behavior in three contexts: purely individual, communal, and survival.

The profile is rendered mathematically as fractional variations from the base-normal through that range of variation which includes the majority of the population (therefore, the normal range) through behavior that is idiosyncratic and but not disturbed, to traits which correspond to medically diagnosed disorders. Then, by computer analysis, a typical profile can be constructed for the membership of each individual religious sect and then, finally, for the total membership of all the sects studied.

Norton studied the nearly total membership (117) of six sects in a North American urban center. This was not a mere sample of the membership, but included almost every member of four of these groups. The groups studied were from all three of Goelters' categories in *Youth in Destructive Religious Groups*: I, Unification Church; II, Church of Scientology, 3HO, People Searching Inside; III, Hare Krishna, Ananda Marga. Norton also studied members of an older sect, the Jehovah's Witnesses.

In addition, Norton compares the sect-members' profiles to the profiles from three control groups:

1. a group of clergy (pastoral counsellors) from large Protestant and Catholic denominations.
2. a group of young adult apartment dwellers selected at random.
3. a group of non-religious adults who regularly met together for study.

The results of the Norton report are as follows:

1. The psychological profiles of the sect-members closely re-sembled the profiles of clergy (pastoral counsellors) from the traditional denominations.

2. There was *no* pattern similarity between the psychological profile of sect-members and the psychological profile of six medically diagnosed disturbed persons.

3. The behavior of all sect-members evidenced healthy differ-entiation between intra-group behavior and individual be-havior outside the group. Thus, Norton's report gives no support to the charge that group members continue group-typical behavior after they are away from their groups or after they have given up their membership.

4. Three of the seven groups studied evidenced an unusual homogeneity of membership. The other four religious groups were not homogeneous but evidenced a heterogeneity comparable to that of the apartment dwellers of the control group.

5. The incidence of psychological disorders was lower among sect-members than among the control groups. Norton found one case of serious psychological disorder among the members of the control groups (1 in 36) and one case of serious disorder among sect members (1 in 117).* A second borderline case was also found among sect-members. Both cases of psychological disorder among sect-members were found in the heterogeneous rather than the homogeneous sects.

6. The individual personality profile of sect members evidenced a somewhat higher than average individuality and also a higher than average sociability. That is, David Riesman's inner-directed, other-directed characteristics were both found among sect-members. The Norton study therefore showed that intensive group involvement is not incompatible with highly developed individuality.

7. The Norton report found that an objective sense of group membership and mutual responsibility were the basis for interaction within the religious groups. It showed that the manipulation of feelings such as love and guilt was not a significant basis for group interaction. (Interestingly, Norton found that guilt feelings were much higher in the control groups than among sect-members.) Norton also found that

---

*   The Norton results, modified since the writing of this essay by a re-evaluation of raw data using more refined tools, now report 3 cases of psychological disorder among the 36 controls, and 2 cases among 117 sect members.

there was a higher than average participation in group decision-making and that a higher than average autonomy was preserved among group-members. His results also indicated that group members evidenced a tendency to listen, to be influenced by other people, yet also a higher than average tendency to make up their own minds. (Certain popular psychologies suggest that the evidence of making one's own decision is *not* listening to or being influenced by other people. The Norton report shows this popular view to be false.)

8. The Norton report showed that sect-members tend to have above average trust in God relating to matters of survival, health, sickness and death. They also have low fear of death but they have a high love of life and show high-normal self-protectiveness, carefulness and implications-awareness.

9. Norton also tested to see whether sect-members showed tendencies toward violence in survival-type situations. He found no such tendencies. In fact, in the survival context, these religious persons tended to show high assurance towards others and they tended not to be fierce.

10. Norton's research showed a tendency for the behavior of group-members to change slightly towards group typicality over the time of their membership. But since he judged this group-typicality to be well within the range of the normal, he saw no problems in such change. Moreover, he inclined to the view that recruitment of group-similar members rather than specific group processes played the major role in accounting for this change.

Norton also conducted more subjective clinical examinations with persons in each of the sects (except for the Jehovah's Witnesses). He found a wide range of idiosyncratic elements, including attractive and unattractive features from group to group. He also found variations of paraphernalia, language, and costume. But these idiosyncracies and paraphernalia proved to have little relation to the characteristics his scientific testing disclosed. His clinical examinations of sect members did not disconfirm for him the results of the computer-based report discussed above.

THE SAUKS REPORT

In this context it is also worth reporting the results of the medical examinations of 47 sect-members selected at random from six sects (including the Church of Scientology, Hare Krishna, and Unification Church, one group each from Goelters' three-part typology). This study, conducted by Toomas Sauks, M.D. and two medical colleagues, compared the health of 47 sect-members (average 27.7 years) with the health of a control group of 26 persons (average age 25.7 years). The results of this study were that Sauks found "No abnormalities within the 'cult' subjects [which] could be attributable to 'cult' affiliation." Dr. Sauks provided the following chart to illustrate his conclusions:

	Sect Members	*Control Group*
Unqualified Fit and Well	44.7%	15.4%
Minor Abnormalities	34.0%	69.2%
Significant Abnormalities	21.3%	15.4%

Sauks noted that the major medical problems for sect-members stemmed from events in their lives antedating sect-membership. He added, "In contradistinction, the control group's liver and lung problems were related to their present lifestyle." (p. 5) The overall finding of the Sauks report is that there are no health problems arising from sect-membership.

THE SAWADOGO REPORT

A third study, which deals with the financial transactions and business practices of new religious groups, was conducted by J.B. Sawadogo, M.B.A. Sawadogo compared the financial transactions and business practices of five new religious groups and five parish churches from established North American denominations, including the Roman Catholic and the Lutheran, in a North American urban centre. Sawadogo's study is especially illuminating in light of the Goelters report's assertion (derived from its opinion poll) that the monies gathered by sects are funneled off to "the bosses" of the groups. (p. 18)

The results of the Sawadogo report are as follows:

1. The local organizations of Hare Krishna, the Church of Scientology and the Unification Church contribute .5%, 3.7% and 2.5% of their gross financial inflows respectively to higher-level non-local organizations. In comparison, the Roman Catholic, Lutheran and Reformed (United) Churches contribute 11.9%, 5.2% and 24.9% of their gross financial inflows respectively to higher-level, non-local organizations (the Reformed figure includes projects supported through the central office).

2. Another significant comparison is remuneration for local leadership. Remuneration for local leaders and staff of Hare Krishna, Church of Scientology, Unification Church

respectively is 2.5% (does not include the cost of food and bed while living at the center). 18.3% and 17.7% of disbursements. For the Roman Catholic, Lutheran and Reformed (United) Churches remuneration for local leaders and staff is, respectively, 26.7%, 30.8% and 40.1%

There is a major difference in expenditures between funds used for actual religious practice and teaching. Hare Krishna, Scientology and Unification Church expend respectively 24%, 18.3% and 25% of their gross financial inflows in this way. The Roman Catholics do not carry this as a separate item in their budgets; the Lutherans display a figure of 1.5%; and the Reformed (United) Church spends 9.3% of its gross financial inflows in religious practice and teaching.

Finally, the breakdown of income for both the new religions and the established churches shows that both kinds of groups rely primarily on special donations and income in conjunction with religious observances. Of course, this North American pattern will differ in Germany where a church tax is still collected through government agencies for selected denominations. One speculates whether the horror evidenced in the Goelters report against religious groups soliciting religious offerings is not a consequence of their not being protected by the *Kirchensteuer*. We find in North America where there is no church tax and churches and sect-groups must raise their own funds, that the profile for income for both established churches and new religions is about the same.

In addition to studying the flow of funds within the ten religious denominations studied, the Sawadogo also examined their recruitment and employment practices from a business point of view. The conclusion of his report: "The techniques and methods of recruitment and finance provided by the representatives of all the religious groups do not seem to have basic differences wtih standard business practices." (p. 7) An examination of the financial tables for five new religions and five traditional denominations shows that the average cost of financial disbursements in new religions is approximately equal to the disbursements of traditional churches in seven of ten categories. The three major discrepancies between new groups and traditional groups have been mentioned above: namely, traditional groups depend less on worship, donate more to central organizations, and provide higher remuneration for leaders and staff.

It may be useful at this point to include the results of my own research into the pattern of affiliation in new religious groups. To conduct this research, I solicited 25 autobiographies from members of one new religious group. The average age of the group studied was 26 years old. Each person was asked to present a 10,000 word chronological account of those important incidents, thoughts and reflections they thought had a bearing on their development towards group membership. The sample was composed of 23 university graduates and 2 persons still attending university.

From these autobiographies I constructed a questionnaire that focused on specific types of incidents to see whether a more explicit profile could be described. From a subjective reading of the autobiographies no single pattern emerged, but the questionnaire turned up the following three statistically significant findings:

> 1. A major factor in deciding to join the religious group was a knowledge of and agreement with the doctrine. For 92% of the respondents, a primary attraction of the new religion was that it "satisfied intellectual concerns."

> 2. 72% of the respondents had had a significant introduction to Oriental philosophies and/or religions through school courses, travel, or personal reading before making contact with their present religious group. This antecedent contact with Oriental religious ideas had made them question their prior religious commitments. For these respondents, membership in their new religious group represented a reconciliation of their knowledge of Oriental thought with their prior Jewish or Christian upbringing.

> 3. 56% of the respondents (14 of 25) had, at first, experienced the communal lifestyle of their new religious group as distasteful and had considered *not* joining the group for this reason. Contrary to what the Goelters report suggests, these persons joined their new religion *in spite of* and not *because of* its communal life.

Although not included in my original questionnaire, a later question presented by Prof. Herbert Anderson of Dubuque Seminary led to the discovery that, in a similar sample group, over 90% of the respondents had regarded themselves as the "identifiably responsible person" within their family. (The "i.r.p." is that brother or sister who typically accepts special responsibilities for performing family tasks or fulfilling parental expectations.) Prof. Anderson has suggested that voluntary affiliation with new religious groups may be correlated with an unusually high sense of social responsibility and personal ideals inculcated within the family structure.

Even this brief review of empirical research studies conducted in North America on youth-sects provides us with a picture very different from that found in Goelters' *Youth in Destructive Religious Groups*. The findings from scientific studies in North America are, in fact, totally contrary to his report from the German Rhineland. Is this a question of different cultures? I do not believe so. The difference is between scientific study and opinion-polling dressed up as a science.

The Goelters report is pseudo-science created for political purposes. His survey of the uninformed opinions of young people fails to confirm his statement that these new religious groups are "destructive." It does show, however, that his own prejudices and those of his informants were in agreement. Such prejudices probably also prevail in North America among those who get their knowledge of these new religious groups from the media rather than from scientific research.

There can be no denying that the presence of these new religious groups is a cause for concern, for there is no point in denying a social fact. But we should understand that the social fact is that these groups are present and that there is concern about them. This does not mean that these groups are "destructive." If anything, the seriousness of the concern requires of governments, when they choose to study the matter, that they proceed cautiously and conduct their research carefully, drafting their reports within the limits of truth rather than promoting the prejudice which so often accompanies popular discussion of religious novelty. Especially on an issue with which such a small percentage of the population have had direct experience, extreme caution is imperative.

For this reason I find chapter 3 of *Youth in Destructive Religious Groups* even less responsible than chapter 2. In chapter 3, Goelters picks up his earlier assertion that youth-sects reflect a more widespread new interest on the part of young people in religion. He says this development reflects the search of youth for warmth and for the experience of meaning." (p. 23) At first, Goelters says that there is no reason to criticize this wider interest in religion and he applauds the Ecumenical Brotherhood of Taize. (p. 21) But he then continues by explaining this interest in religion through the following description of contemporary youth:

1. Youth are worried about the 'meaningfulness' of work. They have problems because they may not achieve the professional station they desire.

2. Youth are not stable in difficult situations or in situations that they consider are unjust. They tend to give up easily rather than applying their creativity in cooperative ventures.

3. Youth have it too easy from parents and educators. Work, for youth, means expanded buying power and not the means of livelihood. They've never known the threat of not meeting the basic means of survival.

4. There has been a breakdown of authority and community to mediate that authority. This is why the youth think about dropping out.

5. As a result of permissiveness, youth, who need authority, have had too little experience with it. They tend to give in to it too readily when they meet it, as they do when they contact the youth-cults. This lack of authority and community is what the promotors of the youth-sects prey upon.

Before proceeding, it would be useful to note that none of these charges against youth is substantiated with data or even references to research available elsewhere. I am always wary of government officials pronouncing on youth. Officials can translate, quite magically, youth's demands for greater participation in the life of society into youth's need for more authority. When youth speak, even if petulantly at times, out of a practical experience of exclusion from social life, government officials are quick to translate their complaint into a plea for authority. That is what Goelters has done.

To conclude, we might ask why Goelters applauds general revival of religion among the young but calls the youth-cults "destructive." How does one distinguish the general revival of religion from the particular new religions if both are said to be rooted in the same sociological conditions? No answer to this question is found in *Youth in Destructive Religious Groups*. Goelters glosses over this issue. He provides no explanation for the revival of religion except that which he uses to "prove" that the youth-sects serve as an escape from social responsibility and are "destructively" authoritarian. Part of the problem here is that Goelters never allows any validity to the specific- ally *religious* appeal of religion to young people. Thus, it appears that the same social forces lead young people to become involved in tradi- tional established churches as lead others to become members of the youth-sects. The only difference between the two kinds of involvement that Goelters makes explicit is that the latter involves only a small minority. This minority, suddenly detached by Goelters from the majority of youth, is said to be pathological, simply for joining a "destructive" religious group. The majority, for reasons of their numbers alone, seem to escape this pathology by joining a mainstream church (even though Goelters adduces no sociological profile for the majority distinguishable from that given for the minority). Yet, it is this entire shared profile of youth from which Goelters selects features — for authority, desire to drop out, etc. — that he develops into an explanation of the minority's involvement in "destructive" groups.

We wish to ask then what, according to Goelters, distinguishes the Ecumenical Brotherhood of Taize, which he applauds, from the Hare Krishnas, which he labels as "destructive." We get no answer from *Youth in Destructive Religious Groups*. We get no answer because the purpose of this government report is not to give scientific answers to the questions it raises. Its purpose is to give us politically popular answers and to avoid the requirements of scientific investigation as truth.

First, the report seeks to marginalize the youth-sects from the current wave of youthful interest in religion. His argument fails to do so, but Goelters presses on anyway to attribute to the youth-sects an authoritarian social structure at odds with the basic values of society. Second, it is clear from chapter 4, where Goelters recommends that church and educational institutions provide information about "destructive" youth-sects, that the purpose of the report is to suggest counteracting tactics. By "information," Goelters means not scholarly information or the kind of information that derives from ecumenical dialogue, but anti-sect propaganda. Third, the report labels these groups "destructive" in its title and throughout the text. While this is done without substantiation, the fact that *Youth in Destructive Religious Groups* is a government report will greatly aid in the dissemination of the view of these groups as "destructive." It will give the label authority, thus reinforcing the prejudices the respondents to the opinion poll, representing a sample of the population, have towards the new religions.

Moreover, there is good reason to believe that Goelters' report promotes hysteria about the youth-sects. Pseudo-science in the hands of the state has been used to generate hysteria, and at times even violence, against minority groups. Goelters' opinion poll shows simply that his respondents had already formed judgments about youth-sects, although only 4% of these respondents had ever attended a meeting of any sect and only 25% could even give the name of one. These responses, by definition, are prejudice. What Goelters' report does is to give this prejudice the seal of approval from a government office and provide it with a pseudo-scientific justification.

In my view, the Goelters report is an irresponsible misuse of the authority of a government office and of the authority of science for political purposes. I think this report should be officially condemned since, having been released as an official document, it cannot be ignored.

Conclusion to the *Study of Mind Development Groups, Sects, and Cults in Ontario*

DANIEL G. HILL

BRAINWASHING AND HYPNOSIS

As the writer of a recent pop song lamented, perhaps inelegantly but nonetheless perceptively:
    Somethin's happening here.
    What it is ain't exactly clear.
To the person who penned those words, the cause for distress was not likely any aspect of the so-called "cult phenomenon." Still, they do sum up the dilemma the study faced as it attempted to evaluate allegations that the movements employ mind control techniques — specifically brainwashing and hypnosis — to convert and hold recruits.

Obviously, something has been happening. It is extraordinary to see recruits embracing radical new beliefs with suddenness and fervor and their self-sacrificing devotion to the groups. Perhaps especially in times such as ours, when secularism is said to reign and selflessness supposedly is rare, it seems it would require something more than friendly persuasion to explain such conversions. But can they really be the products of mind control? Brainwashing? Hypnosis? Mental Kidnapping? Psychological enslavement?

To a majority of anti-cultists, many of whom have undergone conversions themselves, there is no doubt. And the study must admit that their arguments have a compelling quality. The analogies they draw between classical mind control techniques and conversion practices of many cults, sects, mind development groups and new religions are strikingly apt in many respects.

In the final analysis, though, the study could not confirm that the groups' practices constitute actual brainwashing or hypnosis. And while the study believes the practices are designed to play heavily on the emotions and psyche, it could envisage no way of effectively legislating against their use.

Reprinted with permission from the *Study of Mind Development Groups, Sects and Cults in Ontario,* June 1980.

There is no doubt, as far as the study is concerned, that most of the groups under examination do employ emotionally and psychologically taxing techniques in the conversion of recruits. Many of their practices clearly are intended to make recruits doubt relationships and activities of their past and press them to accept new, radically different beliefs and life-styles. It also is readily apparent that the movements employing such techniques are highly effective; people do change radically and certainly not always to their own benefit.

However, this description also fits many a religious, social, political, psychotherapeutic, fraternal, or other organization whose practices never have been considered to be beyond the range of the acceptable. The adherents of these organizations can manifest fanatical attachment, resistance to alternative views, and hostility to criticism. Their speech can become studded with the cliches of their groups and their time and energies consumed in service to their causes or leaders.

Does that mean that we must accept coercive practices by some movements just because other organizations employ them? Certainly not. It does mean, though, that we must be prepared either to restrain all organizations equally or somehow identify legislatively definable ways to differentiate between what the movements do and what others do.

The study doubts that society is prepared to do the former. It would not tolerate the wholesale prohibition of fire-and-brimstone revivalism, rousing political oratory, encounter-based psychotherapy, religious retreat and asceticism, or other such emotionally and psychologically taxing techniques of persuasion and conversion.

Nor could the study currently see any way of doing the latter. Even the ardent anti-cultists interviewed by the study, could not draw substantial distinctions between, for example, cultic milieu control and the rigors of a remote, monastic retreat. It was argued that there was a difference. The movements employed pressure tactics in battery while other groups used fewer and used them less intensively. But the study did not envy those drafting legislation who might have to define the point where the coercive pressure of persuasive or conversion techniques becomes illegal.

Is Conversion Voluntary?

Even if it were possible to draft these kinds of legislative distinctions, though, another issue would put the legitimacy of the effort in doubt. There still would remain the vexing question of how far a recruit is brainwashed or hypnotized into conversion and how far he is acting on free will.

As Dr. Saul Levine suggests in the report on his sub-study, there is ample reason to believe that the movements are not required to use much persuasion in many, perhaps most, cases. In these instances, those who join the groups are well on their way to conversion to an undefined something before they come into contact with specific movements. In any attempt to apportion responsibility for a conversion, Dr.

Levine says:

> The confounding factor may be the initiate or convert him-
> self . . . . In all the cases we have examined, members before
> joining were characterized by having significant voids in their
> lives. They experienced alienation, demoralization and low
> self-esteem, and many were looking for answers to life's per-
> ennial dilemmas. A group which fills these voids and promises
> answers, attracts these particularly disposed individuals. But
> the crucial ingredient is the predisposition . . . . The conver-
> sion experience is a revelation to these individuals . . . .
> Because of their extreme need to believe and belong and to
> feel good about themselves, the group may have to do very
> little to convert new recruits. They almost do it themselves . . .
> that control is often self-generated.

Quite aside from questions of whether conversion is self-induced, opinions of clinicians interviewed by the study varied considerably about the extent, if any, to which the groups were capable of depriving recruits of their free will. Some believed the groups were fully capable of suspending the individual's capacity for critical judgment and free choice. Others believed the individual could never be robbed of his rationality and freedom of choice nor, by the same token, relieved of responsibility for what happened to him. Still others felt that at some indistinguishable point, which probably varies from one individual to another, some practices might have the effect of negating freedom of thought and action.

Are brainwashing and hypnosis facts in the movements, then? Or are they inappropriate images that a former member and his family might use to divest themselves of responsibility for an embarassing episode? The study has no conclusive answer to these questions, for there seems to be no firm consensus on them even among those schooled in the study of the mind.

For now, the study can acknowledge "brainwashing" only as a highly colorful and intriguing metaphor for what happens, not only in movements examined here, but in many other high-pressure organiza-tions with stirring causes and charismatic leadership. Even the parallels that Robert J. Lifton and others draw between classical brainwashing and the movements' practices fail to demonstrate that the two are anything more than analogous. As Dr. Levine notes, each characteristic of mind control established by Lifton is open to broad interpretation. "They do not lend to concise measurement," he adds, "and one is still left with a controversy as to whether brainwashing is being practised by the cult."

Same Problem with Hypnosis

The problem is much the same involving allegations that the groups practice hypnosis. Most movements in this study do engage in the induction of altered states of mind. That is, in fact, their professed goal; that is the transcendent state. Is it, however, a hypnotic state? Is it a trance in which an individual's free will can be bypassed and he can be made to act contrary to what he would normally perceive as his best interests? Given the predisposition of members to believe and do as their leaders tell them, could it not conceivably be a matter of self-hypnosis?

An indication of the current state of professional knowledge on this matter was contained in a paper prepared in 1979 for the Ontario Psychological Association by Dr. Frank Auld. Dr. Auld says:

> Leading researchers on hypnosis such as Ernest Hilgard have much to tell us about this mode of functioning. Hilgard's latest book on hypnosis . . . offers a theory of hypnosis — Hilgard's neodissociation theory — and a rich store of empirical findings. This book does not, unfortunately, give us definitive criteria for judging if what the cults and mind development groups do to their members is hypnosis.

But even if we were convinced that the groups practiced hypnosis — and it is alleged that at least one mind development group has — definition of the term for legislative purposes seems currently to be impossible. Ontario Ministry of Health officials said a sampling they took of medical opinion on a definition failed to produce a consensus. Even Dr. George Matheson's submission to the study implies a difficulty where it states that, using the "natural" approach, a hypnotist can work during a normal social contact without his subject knowing. Surely such approaches pose major problems in respect to legislative definition.

Is it possible, then, that the community will be assaulted by groups, operating beyond the pale of legislative restraint, and expanding their ranks in an orgy of brainwashing and hypnosis? Not likely. If, in fact, any of the movements do practice mind control, the evidence suggests that they are not effective at it. Research in many centers by investigators in a variety of disciplines has indicated that membership in a group is usually of brief duration — usually no more than a year and frequently much shorter. Although the study's own sampling was small and not formally constituted for such purposes, the experience of former group members, who were interviewed, was in line with the research findings. Of 28 former members interviewed, 8 had stayed in their movements less than six months, 10 for six months to a year, and only four for more than three years.

Although new legislative remedies may not seem likely in the foreseeable future, perhaps the courts can still be a recourse for those who feel they have suffered a loss of freedom through mind control. As Professor David Weisstub explains in detail in the paper he prepared for the study, existing common law remedies might be adapted for the purpose. He notes, for example:

> Over time, false imprisonment actions have been modified to accommodate diverse and subtle constraints on the quality of physical movement, and have also contained a psychological component. Defendants have been exonerated where a

reasonable means of escape was available to the plaintiff. If it could be shown that a reasonable person would have feared considerable humiliation or discomfort, then the courts have been sympathetic to find imprisonment.

At the same time, the current state of knowledge — and, hence, legislation — need not be accepted as an unchangeable status quo. It is clear that, in several of the movements, as well as many other areas of society, something is happening. Efforts must be made, with government assistance, by universities, individual scholars and others to demonstrate the legitimacy or emptiness of the brainwashing metaphor and to develop functional definitions of mind-manipulative practices.

HEALTH

In setting out the terms of reference for this study, the Attorney General said:

> The government has received particular expressions of concern in relation to the effects of mind development practices and the practices of sects and cults on the mental and physical health of group members . . . .

The study had just barely begun its review of complaints in government files and its interviews with anti-cultists when it became clear that the concern expressed to the Government was substantial. It also was clear that many of those who complained were certain in their own minds that many practices of the movements were serious threats to the mental or physical health of members — indeed, often were primary causes of mental or physical deterioration.

In the study's view, it seems highly likely that the experiences several former members reportedly underwent in various movements did contribute to health problems they suffered. The pivotal words here, though, are "contribute to." Many established and even broadly respected institutions — universities, traditional religions and social organizations — generate stresses that *contribute to* mental or physical ill health in some people. However, it is a long leap between acknowledging an organization's practices as a *factor in some* illnesses and flatly identifying them as *the cause* of illness. On the basis of the evidence involving the movements' practices, the study could not make that leap. The study could also not envisage any legislative forms beyond existing statutes that could effectively and fairly protect converts from the harm they might suffer if subjected to a group's practices.

The following eight observations, drawn from the study's own research and that of Dr. Saul Levine, were, in large part, the foundation upon which these conclusions were based:

* Relatively few of the people, who were studied by Dr. Levine and were or are in the groups under study, are known to have

deteriorated psychologically. Those who did break down — particularly in a mind development group known to have used confrontation techniques, verbal abuse and occasional physical abuse — were succumbing to situations they found too stressful. Others, however, survived those same experiences with no apparent ill effects. It is likely, as Dr. Levine notes, that the number of people who suffered psychological problems is greater than the number known to have sought psychiatric or medical care. Still, it would seem that something in the personality of the individual — a quality of unusual sensitivity or fragility, a toughness or a resiliency — is a major factor in whether he or she will be harmed by a particular experience.

* Only a small number of persons, who had been members but had left groups, related totally negative experiences. Most former members, even if strongly disenchanted with their movements on other grounds, were relatively healthy and admitted that their membership had some positive effects.

* Most of those who became casualities or experienced substantial psychological difficulty short of breakdown seem to have undergone personal crises in their lives prior to joining their movements. A few clearly had been unstable. Of the cases used by Dr. Levine in his sub-study, one-third actually had psychiatric histories that predated their involvement, although only a few of the study's own interviewees had such histories.

* A substantial proportion of the active group members interviewed by Dr. Levine said they had been ill and psychiatrically distressed before joining but their health had improved subsequently. Dr. Levine noted that many said they slept better, ate better, felt stronger, were far less anxious, and had given up drugs. As well, they no longer felt alienated or demoralized. He also found that they felt a sense of self-esteem and spiritual awakening that was both novel and exciting. These observations were echoed in the study's own interviews with 45 active members of various movements.

* Suggestions that regression, weight loss, alienation, inflexibility, and lack of adaptability, or deterioration of physical appearance were common among group members are challenged in Dr. Levine's report. These are not characteristics of most members of the various movements, he contends. Again, most active group members interviewed by the study seemed physically well and mentally alert. They were functioning well and, though doggedly supportive of their movements, could discuss issues coherently. Dr. Levine does, however, acknowledge that members do exhibit such symptoms of the so-called "cult syndrome" in some cases and cautions against minimizing that as a cause for concern. Here, too, the study's observations matched Dr. Levine's.

* Many of the 20 clinicians, mostly psychiatrists, interviewed by Dr. Levine were also questioned by the study. All, even the professed anti-cultists among them, agreed that many other institutions or organizations, which were accepted in society, engaged in practices that were assailed as dangerous when employed by various movements. Traditional denominations, faith healers, "respectable" psychotherapies, even fraternities and secret societies, had their casualties as well. And each year, some students who are unable to cope with pressures in universities — especially law or medical schools — suffer serious psychiatric breakdowns, even commit suicide.

* Evidence in support of claims that the practices of particular groups were the sole or even significant factors in psychiatric problems suffered by some members is highly inconclusive. There is no doubt that practices such as confrontation, meditation, ecstatic dancing or chanting, can yield disturbing experiences. Some, such as confrontation, are intended to be disturbing. Indeed, there is little doubt that, given the appropriate personality, some practices could exacerbate existing psychological problems. However, most clinicians Dr . Levine and the study interviewed argued that no clear and direct causal link had been forged between such practices and psychiatric disturbance. "The documentation," Dr. Levine says, "is not rigorous and conclusions regarding causation are certainly open to serious question."

* Since, for whatever reasons, the conversion to a movement is usually sudden and involves a change of lifestyle, the physical and mental health of some inevitably will be affected, at least at first. For example the adoption of a vegetarian diet might shock the systems of some people in a way that would have a severe impact on their health. Similarly, adapting to the rigorous sleep and work patterns of some groups inevitably would prove at least temporarily debilitating for many.

However, none of those who reportedly suffered from adopting these life-styles seemed to have been physically coerced into doing so. At the same time, large numbers of active members, who presumably were living under the same conditions, appeared to be suffering no ill effects.

In the light of such observations, the study concluded that no new government measures were warranted involving the groups' impact on their members' health. This was the study's view about therapeutically-oriented groups and movements of a more exclusively religious nature.

A central factor in that conclusion was that there seemed to be no way of tracing a direct causal relationship between any group's practices and the ill effects they allegedly inflicted. Most members seemed to have had no such experiences and many claimed, in fact, to have benefited from their participation. Additionally, there was no way of offsetting the force of claims that a casualty's pre-disposition to breakdown had made him an explosion waiting for something, anything, to set him off.

It is true with regard to at least one mind development group, that there was a strong enough circumstantial link between its practices and reported casualties that the case for legislative controls was arguable. However, whether in the case of this group or any other, the study doubted that there was any workable way to prohibit a particular group from employing any of its allegedly destructive techniques.

Assuming that the destructive practices could be defined for legislative purposes—a doubtful assumption in itself—it seemed to the study that neither of the two ways of achieving the objective was satisfactory.

On the one hand, legislators could attempt to prohibit the use of certain practices—perhaps confrontation, medication, and induction of altered states of consciousness—by cultic groups. Then, however, the problem would become one of defining a cult. For legislators to attempt to do so inevitably would involve determining what constitutes acceptable religious belief, a matter into which government traditionally has not intruded.

A second alternative might seem on the surface a more palatable approach. Again, assuming that dangerous practices could be defined, they would be prohibited unless undertaken by licensed, professionally-trained practitioners. In the course of its interviews, the study found that licensing was highly attractive to some of the persons interviewed. These people felt there was safety in professionalization because it would permit standards to be imposed on those who would undertake mind-affecting practices and would require them to screen out clients who were at risk.

However, it seemed to the study that this approach was unacceptable for many of the same reasons that resulted in the "Proposal for Legislation to Control the Practice of Psychologists in Ontario," (commonly known as "The Psychologists' Act, 1977"), being withdrawn. Many practices, employed by various groups to promote self-improvement and expand the mind, are generally the same as techniques employed by many non-professional, "respectable" organizations and individuals. Various clergymen, psychotherapists, community organizations, management training specialists and others, who qualify only as experienced laymen, also use the techniques. To restrict the practices in question exclusively to formally trained professionals would mean experienced laymen no longer could employ the techniques. Even the professionals consulted by the study agreed that to ban such non-professional counselling and therapies would unduly restrict the freedom of the individual to seek solace and assistance where he chooses. It would also make some highly effective practitioners unavailable to him.

The study also had some serious doubts about the effectiveness and legitimacy of any attempts that might be made to control the abusive use of certain techniques. It doubts whether these techniques should be controlled by requiring their practitioners to be licensed. It agreed with Dr. Levine's following observation:

> Various professional guilds have attempted to get around being lumped with the questionable practitioners of the art of psychotherapy by requiring licensure, as mandated by law. This has proven to be of limited benefit, if of any at all. Paradoxically, some evidence shows, that licensing maintains a structure that is in the self-interest of the service provider and may even oppose the public interest. Licensing may result in the institutionalization of a lack of accountability to the public. It may encourage elitism and higher fees, discourage innovation and progress, obfuscate malpractice, discriminate against the disadvantaged, and severely limit the contribution of paraprofessionals. Recently statutory regulations by licensure or certification have been burgeoning, but abuses do not appear to have been curtailed in any way. There is also some sentiment, albeit controversial, that psychotherapy has not yet reached the stage of definition of techniques and responsibilities that would merit licensure.

GENERAL CONCLUSIONS

In the light of the evidence at hand, there seems to be no area in which the people of Ontario would be served by the government implementing new legislative measures to control or otherwise affect the activities of cults, sects, mind development groups, new religions or deprogrammers. To the extent that the movements and deprogrammers foster problems that are susceptible to legal resolution, the criminal and civil law appear already to afford sufficient avenues of punishment and redress.

That is not to say current law is sufficient to cope with all vexing problems in this field. The study still is disturbed by questions surrounding the concepts of cultic brainwashing, mind control, mental coercion and hypnosis. It remains disquieted by the wanton use of confrontation techniques by some groups. It is convinced that some movements are, as their detractors say, corrupt, even pernicious. It has no doubt that some leaders are false prophets who lure bewildered people through a maze of absurdities, waste talents and abuse intellects for the sake of some self-gratification. All that and other unresolved problems leave the study feeling somewhat uneasy.

However, the study can conceive of no new laws that would be warranted under the criteria set out earlier in this section. One of those criteria required that legislation to restrict the movements' activities include clear definitions of the practices to be prohibited and, where necessary, the groups to be restrained. Yet, none of the sources the study consulted, including many psychiatrists, were able to define concepts such as brainwashing or mental coercion in legislatively functional terms. None could propose ways of distinguishing between qualified and unqualified users of mind development and other techniques that would not bar "respectable" practitioners from using them. They could not, for that matter, define a cult, sect or new religion for legislative purposes in a way that would satisfy the dictates of justice.

A second criterion, set by the study for new legislation in this area, required that the evil to be contained would have to be of such size and importance that any restraints, which statutes might impose on human rights and freedoms, would be acceptable. There were practices that clearly could be damaging to some who undertook them. There were beliefs that most people likely would find bizarre, even unsavory. And some people unquestionably had suffered as a consequence. Yet, to intervene in such matters would involve government as an arbiter in determining the appropriateness of personal choice and belief. The evil, the study had to conclude, was simply not of sufficient magnitude.

The study found support for its position in the final report of the Committee on the Healing Arts, which was submitted to the Ontario government in 1970. The committee, which had inquired into practices of several sectarian healers, faith healers, spiritualist groups and new religions, concluded:

> The possibility of producing harm does not in our view justify the prohibition of the practice; effecting of harm does. Where there is evidence of a minimal amount of harm the two interests, the right to freedom of choice on the one hand and the interests of society in preventing harm on the other, must be weighed. Where the harm is real, but on the whole, insignificant, and this is always a question of judgment, it is our view that the freedom of choice should not be sacrificed.

Furthermore, police, who were contacted by the study, did not envisage a need for new legislative action. Religious leaders, clinicians, educators and other professions most often warned against it. Even the more ardent anti-cultists found it impossible to propose statutory measures which would not unduly limit freedoms, not only of the groups and their members, but others in the society as well. Certainly the study could not devise any.

None of the 32 Ontario Crown Attorneys, who answered the study inquiry, indicated a concern that the groups were menacing society. Similarly, 47 U.S. Attorneys General, who responded to letters from the study, said their jurisdictions had not passed statutes to curb such groups.

Unfortunately, eternal vigilance is not the only price of liberty. Casualties also are a cost. The society that values its freedoms must accept that it cannot always protect those of its members who voluntarily relinquish their independence, devote their assets to empty causes or engage in practices that cause them harm. Where matters of faith and association are involved, the individual who is truly free is free not only to enjoy, but also to suffer from his choices.

None of this means, of course, that a free society is powerless against groups it perceives to be engaging in unacceptable activities that are beyond the reach of law. For example, even where governments may not intervene for fear of abrogating rights and freedoms, a free press and citizenry have a right to responsible inquiry. That right already has proved in Ontario to have been a potent weapon. A highly controversial religious commune examined in this study reportedly has succumbed to such pressure, sold its country property and disbanded. A mind development group, the subject of much press criticism, has suffered a drastic drop in membership and the defections of several key staff members who became disillusioned when the leadership's scandalous behavior was revealed.

Indeed, the conduct of this study, which was an undertaking designed simply to shed light on certain issues, appears to have had a sobering effect on some groups. There is reason to believe that even the non-coercive, informal approach of the study served to make some groups moderate their practices and led some of their stalwarts to question the groups' operations more rigorously. The evidence suggests, for example, that some of those who defected from a mind development group did so when the study, which seemed to them a fair-minded inquirer, was given patently untrue answers to questions it had asked of the group's leaders. During the 18 months the study was functioning, very few additional complaints of any significance involving the groups studied were received. All pertinent ministries and public and private agencies had been encouraged to contact the study about any developments or problems that might have been relevant to this project.

The exercise of responsible inquiry, the exposure of ideas and activities to public scrutiny, then, are themselves moderating influences on cultic and, for that matter, other groups. But in its attempts to protect itself against whatever threats may be posed by some such groups, a society also can forearm its members by forewarning them. Repeatedly, throughout its interviews and in many of its submissions the study was urged to promote public education in this field. What some parties envisaged as education, of course, amounted more to propaganda for one or another viewpoint. But the study concluded that there is profound and widespread public ignorance regarding cults, sects, mind development groups, new religions and even deprogramming. It works not only to the detriment of uninformed people, who are ensnared by predatory movements or deprogrammers to whom the image of predator is applied unjustly. Accordingly, some groups were among those urging a fair and balanced program of public education. Perhaps one of the best expressions of the need for public education was contained in the 1978 report on a study of cultic groups conducted by the Jewish Community Relations Council of Greater Philadelphia. The report says:

> The community as a whole needs to have a realistic picture of what is and is not going on with cults. . . . They need to know so that they will be aroused and ready to respond when support is needed for public action. They need to know so that irresponsible or inappropriate action may be effectively restrained. Young people in particular need to know more about the cults, their tactics, their beliefs, and the issue they raise. Since high school and college students are the "cults'

prime target population for recruiting, and since so much of this recruiting is done in a deceptive and manipulative manner, education about the cults and their methods can serve as a form of innoculation against entrapment.

Who should conduct such programs? In the study's view they should be undertaken by community groups and institutions, but *not* by government or with government involvement.

This is of course distinct from the role to be played by the Ministry of Consumer and Commercial Relations, and the Ministry of the Attorney General in educating the public about relevant existing legislation which they administer. Governments simply should not participate in efforts to resolve issues where questions of faith or belief may be involved. Elaborating on who should and should not undertake public education in this field, the report of the Jewish Community Relations Council continues:

> Programs of public education must be presented by authorities who are perceived as trustworthy and reliable by the community at large. Although former cult members and the parents of past and present cult members and parents of the most basic educational resource of such a program, we have observed that many former cult members and parents of cult members do more damage to their own credibility than they do to the credibility of the cults in making public presentations. Altogether too often these talks tend to be hysterical, hyperbolic, and factually inaccurate. Obviously the intense personal involvement that these people have makes it difficult for them to discuss the issue in a dispassionate and reflective manner. This is understandable, but it does mean that the main purveyors of public education in this area will have to come from elsewhere.

But while the study does not feel the government can appropriately participate in such public education programs, it does believe the schools, even though they are public institutions, do have a role in this area. The quest for spiritual certainty and salvation, whether in religious or secular movements, has been and still is too significant a fact of human existence to be ignored by educators. It has shaped history, it appears to be affecting the lives of many — especially the young — in the present and it promises to continue doing so in the future. Therefore, the study believes that schools would do well to educate their students about the historical, social and spiritual antecedents of the phenomenon and to describe its manifestations in today's society.

While it is acknowledged that the school's role is an ever-broadening one, it is nevertheless the study's view that the type of information described should be introduced at least into the optional World Religions courses available to secondary school students. At the same time, though, aspects of the subject also could be incorporated into core courses in history and social studies. The material should be prepared carefully to avoid bias and should be taught by historians or social scientists versed in the objective presentation of controversial materials. As the Mackay Commission cautioned in its 1969 report on religious education,

The greatest care must be taken in the provision of a program of religious information to avoid, either by implication through emphasis or otherwise, or explicitly by an attempt to indoctrinate a particular religion, the proselytization of a pupil.

Society, then is not without protection against the questionable activities of exploitative destructive movements. Existing laws are as extensive as currently feasible and likely give a good deal more protection than their use to date would suggest. At the same time, society has recourse outside the statutory realm which, if taken wisely and fairly, can curb excesses that laws cannot address.

That being the case, the study can identify no legitimate grounds on which to base substantive recommendations for government action. In the light of the evidence and the bulk of the advice at hand, none seems warranted.

CONGRESSIONAL HEARING ON RELIGIOUS "CULTS": A Testimony

REV. BARRY W. LYNN

Senator Dole and Members of the Committee:

My name is Barry W. Lynn. I am an ordained minister in the United Church of Christ, and a member of the District of Columbia Bar. Much of my theological training was in the area of the psychology of religion. I am speaking today on behalf of the Office for Church in Society of the United Church of Christ. I do not claim to speak for all of the 1.8 million members of our denomination.

The United Church of Christ and its predecessor denominations, however, have maintained a clear commitment to the protection of the guarantees of the First Amendment to the Constitution. In June of 1973, the Ninth General Synod, our most representative body, called upon our agency to offer legislative testimony in behalf of the preservation and protection of First Amendment rights, including those of speech, press, and religion.

The Eleventh General Synod in 1977, faced with the growth of many new forms of religious activity, affirmed as well that we should work to extend the precious heritage of religious freedom to new groups with which we are not in theological agreement.

This morning, I would like to discuss the restraints under which the Congress must act in the attempted regulation or even investigation of activities which are labelled by their participants to be religious in nature.

Regulation of Religious Activity

The First Amendment guarantees both that the Congress shall not establish religion and that it shall not abridge the free exercise thereof. Proponents of regulation of religious activity frequently allege that the Congress cannot limit beliefs, but may limit acts which are labelled "religious." This simplistic view does not reflect Constitutional

---

Rev. Barry W. Lynn is the Legislative Counsel of the Office for Church in Society, United Church of Christ.

standards. It is now clear that only the gravest abuses endangering paramount state interests give occasion for Constitutionally permissible limitations of religious activity. *Sherbert v. Verner* 374 U.S. 398 (1963).

Even such a worthy goal as compulsory high school education has been held to be insufficient to counterbalance the claim of religious freedom. *Wisconsin v. Yoder* 406 U.S. 205 (1972). Subsequently, courts have upheld the refusal of jury duty, use of certain otherwise illegal drugs, and rejection of life-saving therapy on "free exercise" grounds. *In Re Jenison* 267 Minn. 316, 125 N.W.2d 588 (1963), *People v. Woody* 61 Cal. 716, 394 P.2d 813 (1964), *In Re Estate of Brooks* 32 Ill.2d 361, 205 N.E.2d 435 (1965). Certainly legitimate state interests were involved in these cases, but they were not seen as sufficiently compelling to override the sincere practice of one's religious faith.

Congress must resist efforts to restrict the non-criminal acts of new religious groups or so-called "cults," although this is urged by many of the witnesses today. Professor Richard Delgado, for example, in his widely read article on this subject suggests that the government has an "interest in regulating the recruiting and indoctrinating practices of extremist religious groups" when they prove "harmful." *Religious Totalism: Gentle and Ungentle Persuasion,* 51 S.CAL. L.R. 1-98 (1977). His bases for demonstrating harm, however, do not rise to a compelling state interest which warrants restrictions.

Mr. Delgado and others allege harm through the precipitation of psychological problems in some members of such groups. To arrive at this conclusion they engage in an unsystematic chronicling of terrifying anecdotes and quasi-scientific reports which lead them to belief in a theory of "mind control" at least as dubious and incomprehensible as the theologies of the religious groups they attack.

There is no question that some members of such groups develop psychological problems. That, however, does not rise to the level of a compelling state interest to regulate religion. We do not even know if those psychological difficulties are solely or primarily related to their religious experience, or to earlier developmental problems. Furthermore, we are not a nation which legislates on the basis of possible damage to the most susceptible, gullible, or weak-willed persons. We do not restrict free speech merely because some sensitive persons are emotionally distressed by the words of Nazis or Communists. We should not attempt through law to infringe upon the proselytizing, instructing, praying, chanting or preaching of any religious group because some persons who hear it might become unreasonably influenced. Although I too find some of their educational methods distasteful, they are not as a legal matter different in quality than the tactics used by virtually every religious faith and secular institution in our society.

Mr. Delgado and others posit regulation on alleged social harms caused by "cults" as well. Most documented incidents, such as the rape of new converts, the physical abuse of infants by inadequate nutrition, and the forced use of drugs, should be vigorously controlled by existing criminal laws which find such practices so abhorrent that no serious "religious" claim can be entertained in their defense. Where funds are raised under false pretenses state and Federal criminal fraud statutes should be and are invoked.

Any further or special regulation seems unnecessary. Again, merely because the tactics of some groups seem offensive or bizarre they cannot be treated differently than conventional religious organizations without violating the neutrality required by the Establishment Clause. *Abington School District v.s Schempp* 374 U.S. 203 (1962).

It is also important to note that if recruiting practices were regulated it would not only violate the First Amendment rights of the religious organization to disseminate information, but also the First Amendment rights of the public to receive that informatiuon. *Red Lion Broadcasting Co. v. FCC* 395 U.S. 367 (1969); *Thomas v. Collins* 323 U.S. 516 (1945).

Defining the Truth or Falsity of Religious Claims

The first cornerstone of the law of religious liberty, then, is that religious practices may be regulated only upon a showing of a compelling state interest of the highest order. The second foundation is that it is not permissible for governments to define the truth or falsity of religious belief. The kcy case involved allegations of mail fraud against the "I AM" movement. *U.S. v. Ballard* 322 U.S. 78 (1944). Although the Supreme Court affirmed that the "good faith" of the mail soliciters could be evaluated, it refused to permit jury consideration of the "truth or falsity of the religious beliefs or doctrines" of those on trial.

Once it is determined that an individual legitimately holds a religious belief, it is not proper for government to evaluate the origin of that belief. Critics of new religions frequently allege that the groups use "psychological coercion" on potential converts. For the Congress to adopt this conclusion would place them in a Constitutionally forbidden zone. In a case involving conservatorship orders for several Unification Church members in California the court wisely noted, in rejecting such orders:

> Evidence was introduced of the actions of the proposed conservatees in changing their life styles. When the court is asked to determine whether that change was induced by faith or by coercive persuasion is it not in turn investigating and questioning the validity of the faith? *Katz v. Superior Court* 73 Cal. App. 3d 952, 141 Cal Rptr. 234, 255 (1977).

Faith is by nature totally subjective. One cannot measure its presence or absence in any way in which a legislature may take official notice. Neither does the recanting of some adherents call into question the faith of an entire group.

"Deprogramming"

"Deprogramming" raises serious questions about the right of individuals to practice their faith and associate with those they choose.

This cherished right is vital for adults, who are generally the targets of this authoritarian method, yet even minors are increasingly becoming entitled to serious protection of their First Amendment interests in private decision-making. *Planned Parenthood of Central Missouri v. Danforth* 96 S.Ct. 2831 (1976).

So far, this has largely been a state matter. Nevertheless, proposals have been made by practitioners of this tactic that a 'justification'' defense be explicitly added to the Federal Kidnapping Act. With it parents or their agents could legally "kidnap" their adult offspring if they had reason to believe it would prevent a larger harm. Such a defense, however, would invite a gigantic increase in the physical and emotional violence now done by "deprogrammers." Lest anyone feel that they will use great restraint, many of these charlatans now admit to the "deprogramming" of born-again Christians and even members of political groups with which they disagree. To explicitly add a "justification" defense would be an open invitation to bring back witch-hunting and the Inquisition.

Congressional Investigation of Religious Activity

There are limits to the investigative power Congress may exert in regard to religious activity. Constitutionally, it is not within the power of Congress to act as a judge of specific instances of alleged criminal activity or as a prosecutor or unpopular causes or groups. If there is substantial evidence of a pattern of illicit behavior — be it arson for hire or fraudulent fundraising by organizations which claim to be religious — investigations may be cautiously conducted. Fundamental fairness and equity, however, require that any organizations cited as involved in misconduct must be given the opportunity to reply.

Conclusion

Mr. Justice Douglas, in 1944, reviewed the Constitutional history which is implicitly on trial here today. He wrote: "The Fathers of the Constitution were not unaware of the varied and extreme views of religious sects....They fashioned a charter of government which envisaged the widest possible toleration of conflicting views." *Ballard*, at 87.

If the Congress or state governments end up making any mistakes in response to the phenomenon of new religious groups, let those mistakes be on the side of religious tolerance. When our nation's leaders have done otherwise, and erred on the side of intolerance or hysteria, they have always plunged us into the darkest periods of our history.

The United Church of Christ is a 1957 union of the Evangelical and Reformed Church and the Congregational Christian Churches. The Congregational Church was the established church in Salem,

Massachusetts in 1692, and a Congregational elder presided at the infamous witchcraft trials. With that sense of history we are particularly troubled at any hint of governmental scrutiny of religious faith.

PART IV

CONVERSION:
A THEOLOGICAL VIEW

CONVERSION AND HUMAN DEVELOPMENT

THOMAS McGOWAN

The phenomenon of recent and non-normative spiritual movements in our society should be a high priority for theological investigation. This topic offers the theologian the opportunity to be of service to the community by interpreting for a baffled public the contemporary interest in new religious groups. Since conversion is such a central category in the examination of even traditional religion, and especially since conversion to marginal religion has frequently and pejoratively been called "brainwashing," there is an evident need for theology to explore the dynamics of the conversion experience. The theologian has the duty to try to make understandable the apparently sudden turning of thousands of our best young people to seemingly bizarre beliefs and strange religious practices. A recent book has called this phenomenon "snapping,"[1] but theology must be open to the possibility that it is instead a faith experience, an election by God. How can we claim consistency if we acknowledge Paul's experience on the road to Damascus to be religious conversion but deny the same possibility to a young Krishna devotee? There is a danger if we always explain away in purely psychological or sociological terms conversion to a new religion because we then have difficulty holding onto the distinctively spiritual dimension of our own life. This paper will study this highly controversial question and hopefully offer some insights which may lessen the tension within religious and civil society concerning today's conversions. It will try to allow for both the faith of the believer which sees God's central role in conversion and the science of the psychologist which sees conversion as part of a process in human development.

TOWARDS A DEFINITION

Religious conversion can refer to many realities — joining a church, being "born again," having a change of moral behavior, accepting new

---

Thomas McGowan is Professor of Religious Studies at Manhattan College

theological doctrines. Sometimes conversion seems to be gradual growth to a new consciousness, and at other times as a sudden, discontinuous event, charged with highly emotional features. Conversion can be described as the completion of a journey of the spirit; or as an unexpected leap forward in the process of spiritual development; or as the unification of a divided self, as when a person is brought to a new integrity from a condition of brokenness and unhappiness; or as a sudden change of direction, a "metanoia," an unanticipated turning around and going towards God; or as enlightenment and awakening, much as when Siddhartha Gautama received light and became the Buddha; or as an act of surrender, a being grasped by ultimate concern, indeed a kind of falling in love with God.

It is quite evident, therefore, that the term "conversion" is rich in many meanings. Theology has traditionally fallen into two schools of thought as it had tried to describe this foundational experience. On the one hand it speaks of "formation" and being "once born," while on the other it speaks of "transformation" and being "twice born." It is this distinction which William James has in mind when he writes about the "religion of the sick soul." In general, the Catholic tradition has emphasized nurture and spiritual development through sacramental life and education, while the Reformed tradition is the belief that salvation is election by God. If this be so, then sacraments and other nurturing instruments are only the offer of salvation. Salvation itself cannot be effectively received until the conversion experience, which is God's election. As Reinhold Niebuhr writes:

> The self in this state of preoccupation with itself must be "broken" and "shattered" or, in the Pauline phrase, "crucified." It cannot be saved merely by being enlightened. It is a unity and therefore cannot be drawn out of itself merely by extending its perspective upon interests beyond itself. If it remains self-centered, it merely uses its wider perspective to bring more lives and interests under the dominion of its will-to-power. The necessity of its being shattered at the very center of its being gives perennial validity to the strategy of evangelistic sects, which seek to induce the crisis of conversion. [2]

But even Niebuhr denies any absolute necessity of a single crisis. He quickly adds in a footnote to the above quotation that "the shattering of the self is a perennial process and occurs in every spiritual experience in which the self is confronted with the claims of God, and becomes conscious of its self-centered state." [3]

Perhaps the best American proponent of the more Catholic view is not a Catholic at all but Horace Bushnell, a nineteenth century Congregationalist minister who wrote and preached extensively on Christian nurture. He argued that religious life is not something discontinuous and extraordinary, but rather the process of personal divinization. Conversion for Bushnell was only the beginning of the work of the gospel, and therefore the church should not direct itself exclusively to securing conversions. Nurture for him was not, however, an attempt to substitute natural development for the direct action of divine grace. He emphasized that man is not capable by himself of rectifying the dire consequences of sin but needs the converting and regenerating power of God. But, he warns, neither is regeneration a disruption by God of the normal laws of growth. Bushnell described man as having a religious nature which moves instinctively towards God. Man cannot satisfy this yearning by his own power, he acknowledges, but when God indwells him he can be regenerated in a process of spiritual development.[4]

My view of conversion is similar to Bushnell's. Conversion seems best defined as a spiritual journey towards self-realization in God. In any human experience which confronts the transcendent there exists the dynamics of conversion in the sense that there is at the same time a self-acceptance and a reaching beyond what we are now. There is the tension between maintaining the known self and moving forward freely into a relatively new identity. Conversion, as Niebuhr ably observed, is a never-ending process and occurs every time the self is confronted with the claims of God and so is moved off center. A person develops by becoming a new self that transcends the previous self. Conversion then is the marker event which announces the successful completion of the journey through a crisis to a higher spiritual life; even more fundamentally, it is the whole process of growth in the work of self-transcendence.

THE CONTRIBUTION OF
DEVELOPMENTAL PSYCHOLOGY

I will develop the thesis that conversion is the process of spiritual development by examining, first of all, the work done by William James at the turn of the century. James used the discipline of psychology to show that conversion is a recognizable natural phenomenon of growth with room for the believer's contention that God is its initiator. He defined conversion as "the process, gradual or sudden, by which a self hitherto divided, and consciously wrong, inferior and unhappy, becomes unified and consciously right, superior and happy, in consequence of its firmer hold upon religious realities."[5] This change he explains in terms of a person's mindset. It makes a great difference in a person's life if new ideas which were subconscious move to the level of consciousness. To say that someone is converted, James writes, means "that religious ideas, previously peripheral in his consciousness, now take a central place, and that religious aims form the habitual centre of his energy."[6] Ordinarily, radical personality changes are retarded by the person's well-formed patterns of ideas and mental habits, but if new information is acquired, and if the subject is one in whom the subconscious life is active, there may result what James calls "an element of marvel," or a sudden conversion, especially if some emotional occasion acts as a trigger.[7]

James concurs with E.D. Starbuck's conclusions that conversion serves as a passage in the human growth process. Starbuck had compared young evangelicals who had had conversion experiences with other young people who had grown more gradually into spiritual life. Each group was about the same age, between fourteen and seventeen. Each group showed the same previous symptoms — a feeling of incompleteness and imperfection, brooding, depression, morbid intro-spection, a sense of sin, anxiety about the hereafter, distress over doubts. Each group also manifested the same results after either the conversion or the more gradual growth — a happy relief and a new con-fidence in self. Starbuck argued from this evidence that the conversion experience serves only to intensify and shorten the period of develop-ment by bringing the person to a definite crisis. In agreement, James writes: "Conversion is in its essence a normal adolescent phenomenon, incidental to the passage from the child's small universe to the wider intellectual and spiritual life of maturity."[8] Although some later developmental psychologists might disagree with James' identification of adolescence as the norm for the conversion experience, his point is well made that conversion is a kind of intensification of a normal growth experience.

James distinguishes two types of conversion experience based on what he sees as two forms of human mental activity. The first he calls "volitional" and the second "self-surrender." In the volitional type the change is usually gradual and consists, he claims, "in the building up, piece by piece, of a new set of moral and spiritual habits."[9] As an example of "volitional" conversion, James cites Charles G. Finney, perhaps the most famous nineteenth century American revivalist, who saw salvation only as "an offer of something to be accepted." "All that was necessary on my part," Finney claimed, "was to get my own con-sent to give up my sins and accept Christ."[10] But even in this kind of volitional conversion there are critical points where the movement forward seems much more rapid and results in what appears to be a new plateau of consciousness or ability. To illustrate this, James quotes Starbuck's analogy of a musician who "may suddenly reach a point at which pleasure in the technique of the art entirely falls away, and in some moment of inspiration he becomes the instrument through which music flows."[11] Starbuck compares this to the convert who awakens to an appreciation of religion.

The "self-surrender" type of conversion finds relief in the abandon-ment of the struggle. James says this is analogous to the difficulty we sometimes have in recalling a forgotten name. The more we work at it the more likely our efforts are to fail, as if the name were jammed somewhere in our subconscious and our concentration only wedges it in more firmly. But if we give up the work the name will usually saunter into our consciousness, seemingly of its own will. James suggests that the conscious or volitional effort reflects the imperfect self because it is concerned only with the turning away from sin and not really with the striving towards righteousness. Subconsciously, however, the subject may be working towards the ideal even though this ideal may seem "jammed" by his voluntary efforts. If the subject yields, however, the new relationship to God which has been subconsciously maturing may have the opportunity to break forth. As James puts it, "When the new centre of personal evergy has been subconsciously incubated so long as to be just ready to open into flower, 'hands off' is the only word for us; it must burst forth unaided!"[12]

James is aware that these ideas might be interpreted by theists as a rejection of divine participation in the conversion experience, but he argues that psychology and religion are actually in some kind of harmony up to this point since both admit that salvation comes from forces outside the conscious individual. But, while psychology defines these forces as subconscious and therefore not transcendent, religion insists they are the direct operation of God. James maintains, however, that the insights of psychology can be reconciled to the beliefs of religion. He admits that it is understandable for those who have had a conversion experience, especially an instantaneous one, to believe it is a miracle rather than a natural process. After all, extraordinary phenomena occur — voices are heard, lights seen, a feeling of newness is experienced. But the suddenness of the conversion is not really the issue, he argues. The suddenness may reflect only the simple psychological peculiarity that one subject is more attuned to subliminal mental work than another. If the subject has a different personality, one not as open to this subconscious activity, then his conversion, if it occurs at all, would most likely be of the gradual kind. It must be recognized, James says, that the worth of a thing is not decided by its origin. The ultimate test is not how it happens but what is attained. And conversion according to James has very real results:

> What is attained is often an altogether new level of spiritual vitality, a relatively heroic level, in which impossible things have become possible, and new energies and endurances are shown. The personality is changed, the man *is* born anew, whether or not his psychological idiosyncrasies are what give the particular shape to his metamorphosis. "Sanctification" is the technical name of this result. [13]

James lists as the most fundamental effect of conversion the belief by the subject that he or she is now under the control of God. The feelings that result from this "state of assurance," as James labels this belief, are, first of all, the loss of worry and the sense that all is ultimately well with the world. For Christians this is expressed often in terms of God's "grace," "justification," or "salvation." The second feature of this new assurance state is the perception of truths not known before, a certain noetic quality which opens the subject to new intuitive modes of knowledge. A third peculiarity of this state is the objective change which the world often appears to undergo. There is usually the sense of clean and beautiful newness, not only within the person but also in the world outside.[14]

Concerning other external manifestations of conversion, such as unconsciousness, convulsions, visions, involuntary vocal utterances, and suffocation, James attributes these merely to nervous instability. Reports of lights, as for example St. Paul's blinding heavenly vision or Constantine's vision of a cross in the sky, James calls simply hallucinatory, luminous phenomena.[15]

There exists no conflict between psychology and religion for James because the psychological explanation of certain external phenomena in conversion and the notion of the subconscious self in no way exclude belief in a divine role. As he says, "If there be higher powers able to impress us, they may get access to us only through the subliminal door."16 God can indeed effect supernatural changes through natural means. And, most important in James' mind, the final test for authenticity lies not in the question of whether or not God uses the psychological processes to bring about conversion, but rather in the nature of the changes made in the converted person.

The developmental psychologists agree with but also move beyond James' views of human personality growth. Since development means essentially becoming a new self who transcends the self one had previously been, their work can be seen most fundamentally as an examination of the conversion experience. Conversion is intrinsic to the very notion of development since development to a higher stage of moral or cognitive consciousness necessarily means the transcendence of a previous stage. Development of this kind when expressed in the religious language of conversion is often called being "born again," "saved," "elected," "enlightened," etc. I will explore this close connection between the theology of conversion and developmental psychology by sketching in the models of personality growth given by Jean Piaget, Erik Erikson, and Abraham Maslow.

Jean Piaget

Jean Piaget works primarily at describing and explaining the structures of knowledge. He is a developmental psychologist in that he is concerned with uncovering the growth processes in cognitive functioning from birth through adolescence. Unlike many American psychologists of the behaviorist school who are more interested in stimulus-response relationships and the concept of reinforcement, Piaget infers the existence of internal mental processes. He distinguishes two aspects in the child's intellectual development — the psychosocial and the psychological. By psychosocial he means "everything the child receives from without and learns in general by family, school, educative transmission." By psychological he means spontaneous development, that is, "what the child learns by himself, what none can teach him and he must discover alone; and it is essentially this development which takes time."17 The notion of proportionality, for instance, can only be understood by a child about the age of eleven. It is not taught to the child; rather, the child comes to understand it. Problems dealing with proportionality can be taught only after the concept has spontaneously become part of the child's cognitive ability. According to Piaget, psychological development precedes psychosocial development and marks off the internal and spontaneous changes that are taking place in the cognitive and moral growth of a child.

Although Piaget does not claim that children move in some kind of discontinuous fashion from one discrete stage to another, he does distinguish four periods which are useful in conceptualizing the forward-flowing developmental process of cognition. First he identifies the period of sensorimotor intelligence, which he dates before about age eighteen months. At this time the child does have intelligence, which Piaget describes as the capacity to solve new problems, but the child does not yet have thought, which is interiorized intelligence not based on direct action but on symbolism. The second stage, which Piaget names preoperatory representation, begins with speech and lasts until about age seven or eight. At this time the child develops the capacity to represent something with something else, in other words, the ability to symbolize, especially to use speech symbols. The third stage, called by Piaget the stage of concrete operations, lasts from about ages seven to eleven. At about age seven a fundamental turning point is noted in the child's development. The child becomes capable of deductive reasoning on theories and propositions.[18]

The child's cognitive development will only be complete, Piaget asserts, when each stage has been gone through successively, because each is necessary to the achievement of the following one. Each stage builds on the old but moves forward to something new. These developments may indeed be seen as conversions, as for example when the child begins to have the notion of general space and to see himself or herself as only one object among others. As Piaget remarks, this involves "a total decentration in relation to the original egocentric space."[19] Such a new outlook on life is a kind of Copernican revolution, to use Piaget's own terminology, and may be quite as important and even earthshaking to a person as any religious conversion.

Erik Erikson

Erik Erikson has analyzed the course of human development in terms of eight stages of personality growth. He describes his own work as the effort to "present human growth from the point of view of the conflicts, inner and outer, which the vital personality weathers, re-emerging from each crisis with an increased sense of inner unity, with an increase of good judgment, and an increase in the capacity 'to do well' according to his own standards and to the standards of those who are significant to him."[20] Each step is a kind of conversion in the sense that it is a crisis of radical change in perspective. Erikson uses the term "crisis" in a developmental way to connote, as he says, "not a threat of catastrophe, but a turning point, a crucial period of increased vulnerability and heightened potential."[21] According to Erikson's scheme, each stage "comes to its ascendance, meets its crisis, and finds its lasting solution," which hopefully is positive personal growth.[22]

The first of Erikson's eight stages involves the development of the sense of basic trust during the very first years of life. The crisis which must be met and overcome is the impression of being deprived, divided, even abandoned. The second stage is the battle for autonomy in which the child comes to delineate the subjective from the objective, himself or herself from the outside world. The crisis here is to control the anal zone with its two contradictory modes of retention and elimination. This stage becomes decisive, writes Erikson, for establishing the "ratio between loving good will and hateful self-insistence, between cooperation and wilfulness, between self-expression and compulsive self-restraint or meek compliance."[23] The third stage is referred to as the sense of initiative and dated by Erikson as beginning at the end of the third year. The child at this time acts intrusively, crashing into other people's space, butting into conversations, endlessly asking questions, even at times physically attacking others. Erikson compares this stage to what Freud called the "latency" period, or that long delay between the time of emerging infantile sexuality and physical sexual maturity. The crisis of this third period concerns the contest for a favored position with one of the parents, even a favored sexual position. The inevitable and necessary failure, says Erikson, leads to guilt feelings and the fear of losing the penis, or on the part of the girl the conviction that she has lost it, as punishment for secret fantasies and deeds.[24]

Erikson describes the fourth stage as one of a developing sense of industry. A child begins to want to make things, to be a worker, even to be a potential provider in preparation for later becoming a biological parent. The crisis to be faced at this stage is the temptation to feel inferior and to expect failure. The fifth stage, and perhaps the most significant in terms of personality growth, is the search for identity. The developing person searches for an occupation at this time, but even more importantly, he or she searches for people and ideas to have faith in. Erikson labels the crisis of this stage as role confusion, the inability to settle on a self-identity.

The final three stages are called by Erikson those "beyond identity," by which he means those post-adolescent years which are characterized by the uses people make of their identity. The sixth stage concerns the crisis of intimacy, or, in Erikson's words, "the capacity to develop a true and mutual psychosocial intimacy with another person, be it in friendship, in erotic encounter, or in joint inspiration."[25] Someone who is still not sure of his or her identity usually shies away from interpersonal intimacy, or conversely becomes promiscuous, which is only another way of retaining a sense of isolation. The seventh stage is that of generativity, a concern for establishing and guiding the next generation. Where this urge for propagation is frustrated, there is danger of stagnation, boredom, and interpersonal impoverishment. The eighth and final of the stages is integrity, which Erikson describes as "the acceptance of one's one and only life cycle and of the people who have become significant to it as something that had to be and that, by necessity, permitted of no substitutions."[26] It is ultimately the acceptance of the fact that one's life is one's own responsibility. The crisis at this time is the danger of despair which comes with the realization that time is too short to attempt to start another life.

These "eight ages of man," as Erikson has called them, can be seen as conversion experiences.[27] According to Erikson, a person advances in psychosocial adaptation when a favorable solution is reached to a particular life crisis. At the right time the person is ready for a decisive encounter with his or her environment and the environment, in turn, is ready to call out from the person the qualities of trust, autonomy, initiative, industry, identity, intimacy, generativity, and integrity. Erickson says that there is definitely a sequence from one stage to the next, but there are variations in tempo and intensity. An individual or even a culture may linger over one or the other of the stages, or may on the other hand accelerate through certain stages. The work of each stage must be completed, however, before the next critical encounter can be entered into. The work of conversion is certainly akin to this work of personality development since it too involves a crisis situation which produces a new level of living.

Abraham Maslow

Abraham Maslow believes with Piaget and Erikson that the psychological characteristics that define humanness are innate and natural to the person and that environmental factors like education and culture only help what already exists in embryo to become real and actual. A person advances into fuller being, says Maslow, in a way similar to how an "acorn may be said to be 'pressing toward' being an oak tree."[28] Such growth involves a kind of "little death" as a person moves from one level of life to another. it is a conversion which is marked by pain but which results in new life. As Maslow expresses this idea:

> Growth has not only rewards and pleasures but also many intrinsic pains and always will have. Each step forward is a step into the unfamiliar and is possibly dangerous. It also means giving up something familiar and good and satisfying. It frequently means a parting and a separation, even a kind of death prior to rebirth, with consequent nostalgia, fear, loneliness and mourning. It also often means giving up a simpler and easier and less effortful life, in exchange for a more demanding, more responsible, more difficult life. Growth forward is in spite of these losses and therefore requires courage, will, choice, and strength in the individual, as well as protection, permission and encouragement from the environment, especially for the child. [29]

Perhaps Maslow comes closest to discussing in a formal way what theology has always meant by conversion when he writes about what he calls the "peak-experience" Although he never equates the two, the characteristics of the peak-experience which he cites are very similar to the characteristics of conversion given in the traditional religious literature. In describing the peak-experience Maslow lists these sixteen aspects:

> 1. The subject appears to become more integrated than at other times. By this Maslow means "more at peace with himself, less split between an experiencing-self and an observing-self." [30]

2. The subject has a new ability "to fuse with the world," as Maslow puts it, as for example when two lovers come closer to forming a unity instead of staying two discrete people. This new identification is a transcending of self, a going beyond and above selfhood. The effect on the person in the peak-experience, says Maslow, is to make him or her "relatively egoless." [31]

3. The subject seems to be operating at the highest level of power, "at concert pitch," in Maslow's words. [32]

4. The subject in the peak-experience acquires a new ease of action, or, as Maslow expresses it, "the look of grace that comes with smooth, easy, effortless fully-functioning, when everything 'clicks,' or 'is in the groove,' or is 'in over-drive.'"[33]

5. The subject in the peak-experience seems more responsible, more self-determined, more his or her own boss in making decisions.

6. The subject is free of the fears, doubts, self-criticisms that have frequently curtailed creative action in the past.

7. The subject is more spontaneous than at other times, more guileless, ingenuous, even childlike.

8. The subject is the recipient in the peak-experience of the gift of new birth, as it were, since the personality change is so radical that it reflects a newly emergent reality, a new creation. Maslow emphasizes what theologians would call the "election" aspect of the experience by using the phrases "created out of nothing," "unexpected," "novel," "untutored," "unhabitual," "unstriven for." [34]

9. The subject becomes more unique and idiosyncratic. The peak-experience causes the social identities or roles which have been assumed over the years to drop away and allows the person to be more authentically an individual.

10. The subject is liberated in the peak-experience from the tyranny of the past and the future. He or she is most "all there" at this time because there is no need to drag in expectations based on past solutions or on future plans.

11. The subject comes to a truer self-development by being freed from those external restraints or laws which restrict inner growth. This antinomian aspect of the peak-experience Maslow explains in terms of how a person begins to understand the non-self best by letting it be itself, by permitting it to live by its own laws. Similarly, he writes, "I become most purely myself when I emancipate myself from the non-me, re-

fusing to let it dominate me, refusing to live by its rules, and insisting on living only by the laws and rules intrinsic to me." 35

12. The subject takes on a character which seems to transcend ordinary needs and drives. Maslow calls such a person "godlike" because divinity has usually been associated with this kind of non-wanting.

13. The subject communicates in speech which tends to become more and more poetic and mythic.

14. The subject has such a sense of completion and fullness in the peak-experience that it can be compared to an orgasm or a total catharsis of emotions. Maslow finds it understandable that people have even compared it to death, as if any perfect completion is metaphorically a death.

15. The subject is moved to a kind of cosmic playfulness which delights in both the smallness and the largeness of the human being. It contains elements of triumph and perhaps also of relief; it is, says, Maslow, simultaneously mature and childlike.

16. The subject feels lucky, fortunate, graced. As a consequence, recipients of the peak-experience often need to express their thanks to God or others for this gift, and they have the impulse to do something good for the world by way of repayment.

Admittedly, Maslow intended with these sixteen characteristics to offer only an evaluation in the language of psychology of the human experience which he called the peak-experience. It seems legitimate, however, to recognize the similarity between his description and theology's account of religious conversion. Conversion, like the peak-experience, is said to make the broken person whole again, to bring about a mystical union with God and a consequent loss of ego, to raise the sinner from the "dark night of the soul" to new heights of spiritual power, to bring the person down to a childlike position before God. Conversion is also seen as God's election of the sinner and call to grace, as being "born again," as receiving forgiveness for past sins and deliverance from the "old man," as becoming free through the law of the gospel. Conversion is a divinizing experience, an ineffable encounter which can be imaged only in the mythic argot of religion, a spiritual catharsis, a celebration of intense joy and happiness, a call to help bring about the kingdom of God on earth. These parallels between Maslow's characterization of the peak-experience and religion's rhetoric concerning conversion are too close and too valuable to be ignored. What Maslow seems to have given us is the psychological equivalent of the religious understanding of conversion.36

CONVERSION STORIES

In order to examine further my thesis that conversion is an aspect of human growth, I will look at eight examples of christian conversion. Most of these have significantly modified the course of Western history; each has at least changed radically the course of the subject's own life. In every instance, however, there is evidence of developmental processes at work.

St. Paul

Probably the most famous conversion in Christian history is that of Paul, recorded in Acts 9: 1-22; in Galatians 1: 13-15; and in I Corinthians, 15:8. Paul is initially an enemy of the "new way" and does all in his power to destroy it. While on a journey to Damascus to ferret out and prosecute its members, he is struck by a flash of light, falls to the ground, and has an auditory experience of a voice identified as that of Jesus. He is left blinded but three days later recovers his sight with the help of Ananias, a follower of Jesus. He is then baptized, receives his new name, spends some time in training with the Christians, and finally goes forth as a defender of the new religion and preacher of its doctrines. The elements of Paul's conversion are not dissimilar to countless contemporary conversions: the initial hostility; the visionary and auditory phenomena; the guru or spiritual guide who leads the recruit out of darkness and into the new light; the period of initiation or novitiate which is marked by sacrifice, hard work, and above all the proving of one's new identity; and finally the evangelistic fervor which is released on the presumably waiting world.

Although Paul's change of heart might seem at first to be the classic example of a sudden and totally discontinuous personality change, it might better be interpreted in the light of William James' insights into the work of the subconscious. The personality of Paul found it necessary to adamantly resist this new "cult" and to stand fast in the old faith. He outwardly worked out this need by trying to destroy those who threatened his old belief system. He was, after all, comfortable and secure as Jew and Pharisee and consequently on guard to preserve this safe identity. But as he rationalized consciously against the Christians he may have come subconsciously to accept their claims. More contemporary psychologists might call his condition one of "cognitive dissonance," but William James would refer to it as the "self-surrender" type of conversion. Paul's new beliefs may have become "jammed" in his subconscious, to use James' phrase, and were only released after a sufficiently long period of incubation. The final collapse of "Saul" and the emergence of "Paul" might seem to have come on suddenly and without preparation, but if James' ideas can legitimately be applied to this case, the conversion might only indicate the sudden breakthrough of personality growth which had been taking place for some time. James says that it is sometimes only in self-surrender or the very abandonment of the struggle that this crisis of simultaneously holding two different worldviews can be resolved. [37]

St. Augustine

The story of Augustine is another example of gradual growth leading to an apparently sudden conversion. Even the most famous passage from the *Confessions* brings out this sense of journey: "Thou madest us for Thyself, and our heart is restless, until it repose in Thee." [38] And Augustine himself describes his conversion as a moral and intellectual development. Morally he grew to sanctity from such sins as "friendship of this world," lies, thefts, the love of stage plays, reliance on astrologers, and "carnal corruption." [39] But those who come to Augustine for prurient reasons are soon disappointed. Augustine does not ultimately see his conversion in terms of morality since he recognizes that God had given him innate qualities of truth and goodness, or as he puts it, "a trace of that mysterious Unity whence I was derived." [40] For Augustine the journey was essentially an intellectual quest for God as truth.

By the end of his twenties Augustine's intellectual journey had already taken him in and out of the Manichaean sect. When he discovered that even the great teacher Faustus was not able to answer his questions, Augustine became disillusioned with the Manichaeans but, interestingly enough, did not leave them abruptly since, as he tells us, "finding nothing better, I had settled to be content with what I had." [41] Augustine finally did turn inexorably towards the Christian faith when he came to realize that all things are good because they are the creation of God. Even things which have been corrupted had to have an essential goodness about them in order to be corruptible. [42] While this philosophical and theological insight freed Augustine from the last vestiges of Manichaeanism, it did leave him in a spiritually vulnerable position and caused him to adopt an agnostic stance, waiting "till something certain should dawn upon me, whither I might steer my course." [43] During this liminal period Augustine was fortunate enough to be supported emotionally and personally by two spiritual guides, the incomparable Monica and the bishop Ambrose. With their help and his own intellectual efforts he finally reached the preparatory stage for conversion in which he was, as he relates, "drawing nearer by little and little, and unconsciously." [44]

When Augustine was thirty-two the journey ended in the well-known scene in the garden with his friend Alypius. Augustine had been procrastinating over the decision for some time but finally prayed that some resolution would come that very day. At that moment he heard the voice of a boy or girl from a neighbor's house chanting "Take up and read." When he opened the scriptures he read Paul's admonition: "Not in rioting and drunkenness, not in chambering and wantonness, not in strife and envying; but put ye on the Lord Jesus Christ, and make not provision for the flesh, in concupiscence." This he interpreted as a reference to his own state and a sign from God of his election. Like

many other converts recounting their experience, Augustine uses the
metaphor of enlightenment to speak of the change which came over
him. He writes that at the moment of finishing the sentence "by a light
as it were of serenity infused into my heart, all the darkness of doubt
vanished away."[45]

Augustine's conversion, like Paul's, can be interpreted in terms of
William James' theory as occurring over a long period of time on the
subconscious level before breaking through in one climactic moment
into the consciousness. It can also be seen as illustrative of Piaget's and
Erikson's models of the developmental character of human growth.
Augustine himself admits that much of his progress was made "subconsciously,"[46] and he describes his conversion as the culmination of a
series of growth experiences. Each step is marked by a painful but
creative leaving behind and a moving forward — leaving behind his
former teachers for new ones, rhetoric for Christian doctrine, Manichaeanism for Christianity. The extraordinary experience in the garden
was for Augustine the point at which he finally gave up his efforts to rationally control his spiritual life and instead prayed to God for help in
resolving his life crisis. This moment of self-surrender became the
marker event of his new and mature personality.

Martin Luther

In *Young Man Luther* Erik Erikson offers an interpretation in the categories of developmental psychology of another conversion that
radically affected the history of the Western Christian Church. His thesis is that Martin Luther grew into his role of reformer by successfully
resolving over the period of his youth his identity crisis, that critical
transition which is like a "second birth." For some people, Erikson
says, this crisis is "apt to be aggravated either by widespread
neuroticisms or by pervasive ideological unrest."[47] Luther's conversion was of this violent kind and was worked out in terms of his relationships with his father and his church. He denied his father's wish
that he should become a secular leader by choosing monastic silence;
he denied his church's expectation that he be a quiet monk by speaking
out vigorously as a reformer.

At the age of twenty-one Martin Luther entered the Augustinian
monastery as the result of a vow he had taken when a bolt of lightning
struck the ground near him during a violent storm. His life in the monastery became one of complete absorption with the question of justification and the practice of penance. During this time, according to
Erikson, Luther manifested those psychological characteristics which
are usually associated with such religious obsession — suspiciousness,
scrupulosity, moral sadism, and a preoccupation with dirtying and in-
fectious thoughts and substances.[48] But the underlying conflict, argues
Erikson, was the fear of failure as a son to his father and, I think it is
legitimate to add, as a son to his church. These two elements were
joined together in the person of Dr. Staupitz, who as Luther's mentor
represented a benevolent parental presence but as a religious superior

also represented church authority. Staupitz was an ambivalent father figure, therefore, who both loved and punished, much the same way as Jesus was understood at this time by Luther.

According to Erikson's model, Luther's conversion involved 'the forging for himself of an ideology or total perspective which gave him a mature identity and moved him beyond these conflicts of youth. The moment which marked off this growth process probably occurred in the toilet, appropriately enough, because, Erikson argues, this is the place where the human condition of retention and elimination takes place, and it is here where Luther changes from being a restrained to an explosive person. [49] Erikson's reconstruction of the scene has Luther working on an exegesis of Psalm 71: 2, "Deliver me in thy righteousness," by applying as a touchstone the text of Romans 1:17, "For therein is the righteousness of God revealed from faith to faith: as it is written, 'The just shall live by faith.'" Luther's great catharsis in the "tower" or toilet came with the realization that Christ's faith is God's righteousness. Luther saw that God's justice is not consigned to a future day of judgment based on our earthly deeds but is identified with the faith in which we live here and now. Not only did this theology give Luther a way to understand his role as a son of God the Father, says Erikson, but it offered in the Bible a maternal element which he could acknowledge in order to be "at last a mother's son." [50]

Luther had his conversion experience in 1512 at the age of twenty-eight. History records the mighty deeds which followed: the nailing of the ninety-five theses against indulgences on the door of the Castle Church in Wittenberg, the burning of the Pope's bull of excommunication, the publication of the New Testament in German, and the defiant "Here I Stand!" speech delivered before the Diet in Worms. These are the actions of a man who has transcended his former self and arrived at an identity capable of facing ostracism and death because of personal convictions arrived at through creative stages of inner growth.

John Bunyan

The spiritual autobiography of John Bunyan, *Grace Abounding to the Chief of Sinners*, gives another example of conversion, this time that of a man struggling for most of his life with feelings of doubt and despondency and only gradually arriving at some sense of salvation. Bunyan's conversion can best be understood as an agonizing growth beyond the pathological to the positive and creative aspects of Puritan theology. His early years were marked by the sins of cursing, swearing, lying, blasphemy, and by the horrors of visions of devils. He tells us that by the age of nine or ten he was "so overcome with despair of Life and Heaven" that he even wished to be a devil himself. [51] At one time while playing a child's game on the Sabbath he heard a voice from heaven challenging him to give up his sinful life, but, after reflecting that he was already damned anyway and so had nothing to lose, he continued his game. Only after he was publicly reproached by a woman did he stop his habit of swearing, but even this was not for religious reasons, he says, because he did not yet "know Jesus Christ." [52]

Bunyan began to advance spiritually when he overheard some women in the town of Bedford talking about the work God had done on their hearts through a "new birth." This consoling idea appealed to him and he placed himself under the instruction of the minister of the Bedford congregation, John Gifford. From this teacher Bunyan learned the methodology he was to use for many years on his spiritual journey. Gifford admonished Bunyan never to accept "any truth upon trust, as from this or that or another man or men, but to cry mightily to God that he would convince us of the reality thereof." [53] Since Bunyan believed that scripture was the way God spoke the truth to him, scripture became the source of proof-texts for the resolution of his spiritual crises. Laboriously and indeed compulsively he searched the Bible in order to interpret and validate each little step of progress or regression.

Bunyan experienced periods of doubt, as when he wrestled with questions of God's existence, the divinity of Christ, the truth of scripture, and even such a contemporary concern as the relationship of world religions to Christianity. [54] He also had periods of scrupulosity, as when he was tormented at meals by a nagging voice exhorting him to leave the table and go off to pray. When he stayed to eat he felt guilty; when he left to pray he felt hungry. [55] At times his suffering was so severe that he wished he were a dog or a horse with no soul to lose.[56] For a period of at least four and a half years he was convinced that he was damned because in a moment of frustration he said of Christ, "Let him go if he will." This he feared was the "unpardonable sin." As Bunyan describes the agony of this crisis, "Down I fell, as a Bird that is shot from the top of a Tree, into great guilt and fearful despair; . . . I was like a man bereft of life, and as now past all recovery, and bound over to eternal punishment." [57]

Relief for Bunyan did not come in one cataclysmic moment of conversion but in long arid periods of searching set off by occasional events akin to Maslow's peak-experiences. One day about two years after his supposed rejection of Christ, for example, he felt a rush of wind which "brought light with it" and showed "that Jesus Christ had yet a work of Grace and Mercy for me, that he had not, as I had feared, quite forsaken and cast off my Soul." [58] This hope lasted for about three or four days before despair set in again. On another occasion he heard a voice saying, "This sin is not unto death," and on the following day, "I have loved thee with an everlasting love."[59] Again he was filled with consolation, but after several weeks the despair returned and lasted an amazing two and a half years more. During this time Bunyan tried to rationalize his way through his spiritual sickness — arguing for instance that the unforgiveable sin would have to be public and his was not — but was never able to satisfy himself. He did make a step forward, however, when he decided to pray even though he believed his salvation hopeless, to act rather than merely to agonize. But his freedom finally came from a passage which spontaneously came into his head: "Thy righteousness is in Heaven." He had a vision of

Jesus Christ at God's right hand and realized that his salvation came from heaven and not from himself. Bunyan apparently had to experience existentially this central Reformation doctrine in order to make it real for himself. His years of anguish, searching the scriptures, rationalizing, and praying reached fruition at a moment of passivity when he gave up the effort and allowed the answer to break through. It was much like the experience Luther had in the tower and which William James calls the conversion of self-surrender. Bunyan tells us that as a result of this grace he was released from the chains that bound him and from "those dreadful Scriptures of God" which had troubled him with their dire predictions of damnation.[60] He was left with feelings of "sweet and blessed comfort." [61]

Jonathan Edwards

In order to understand the significance of conversion for another Puritan, Jonathan Edwards, it is necessary to realize that the heart of Puritan doctrine consisted in the belief that God would choose Saints to people the kingdom on earth. This election would be manifested by a significant spiritual experience which could be verified before the whole church membership. The difficulty was to distinguish those religious experiences which were brought about by human efforts from the free and sovereign election by God. Modern psychology might see a developmental chain from religious event to religious event, but Puritan theology acknowledged only the discontinuous act of God as true conversion. An examination of Edwards' life, however, shows a pattern of growth events and not one, totally unconnected conversion moment.

Edwards had a series of religious "awakenings" in his youth. The first came as a child when there was a stirring in his father's congregation. He was so affected that he began to pray five times a day and with some of his schoolmates built a booth in a swamp to be used as a secret place of prayer. At another time when he was sick with pleurisy he had his first encounter with the same kind of horror Bunyan had faced almost a century before. God "brought me nigh to the grace," he writes, "and shook me over the pit of hell."[62] As a result he made his chief purpose in life the effort to avoid sin and practice his religious duties. But this seeking of salvation in fear was not true conversion, he acknowledges, because it was done in a "miserable manner" and never "issued in that which was saving." His concern to live the religiously good life continued, he says, but it never again "seemed to be proper to express that concern by the name of terror."[63]

Edwards tells us that for many years he had intellectually wrestled with what he called the "horrible" doctrine of God's sovereignty, especially as it concerned predestination. When he stopped rationalizing and let his reason rest, there occurred, much in the way William James describes this phenomenon, a "wonderful alteration" in his mind so that since that day he had "quite another kind of sense of God's sovereignty." He now had a "delightful" conviction and the doctrine appeared "exceedingly pleasant, bright, and sweet."[64] In fact, he progressed from his initial negative feelings to the acceptance of absolute sovereignty as God's most loveable attribute. Edwards at first thought this change of attitude came from some advance his reason had made in seeing the justice and sense of the doctrine, but he later recognized that his new understanding was a gift from God.

As a result of this spiritual growth which was gradually taking place, Edwards was able to change his type of prayer to that of simple enjoyment of God. Likewise, his approach to Christ began to shift from analyzing the work of Christ to "meditating on Christ, on the beauty and excellency of his person."[65] Sometimes this new, more mystical, relationship with Christ produced in him "a kind of vision," as he calls the experience, "of being alone in the mountains, or some solitary wilderness, far from all mankind, sweetly conversing with Christ, and wrapt and swallowed up in God." This new sense that he had of divine things, he writes, "would often of a sudden kindle up, as it were, a sweet burning in my heart, an ardour of soul that I know not how to express."[66] But these new affections were not yet identified in Edwards' theological judgment as election by God. He says that it had not occured to him that these feelings could be spiritual and salvific. In the context of William James' psychological judgment, however, it can be argued that the developmental process was indeed operating subconsciously and spiritual growth was taking place on a direct plane leading towards a new and in some ways final breakthrough to a higher level of Christian life.

This breakthrough came to Edwards as he was walking along in a pasture after having finished a conversation with his father concerning his spiritual state. As he records the scene, there suddenly came into his mind "so sweet a sense of the glorious majesty and grace of God, as I know not how to express."[67] This was an experience so intense and so productive of spiritual results that Edwards took it to be the moment of God's election. The world became filled with God's glory, and prayer became as natural as breathing.[68] Like the subjects of the peak-experience in Maslow's study, Edwards had feelings of inexpressible joy and peace, of new spiritual powers, and participation in a graced and holy world.

The experience in the pasture caused Edwards to want to become a "complete" Christian, and he formalized this wish in a solemn dedication of himself to God on January 12, 1723. But this did not end his spiritual journey. Fourteen years later, in 1737, again alone and at prayer in a secluded country spot, Edwards had another deeply felt religious experience which he describes as a "view" of the glory of the Son of God. "The person of Christ appeared ineffably excellent," he writes, and affected him in such a way that he wished to be "emptied and annihilated, to lie in the dust and to be full of Christ alone."[69] He adds that he had similar experiences of Christ several other times, as well as sensations of the sanctifying power of the Holy Spirit and the scriptures. Although he admits that after his first conversion he felt more immediate feelings of joy in the Christian life, he realizes that his spiritual development has progressed since then, and he has reached a stage in later years where he has a more "full and constant" delight in God.[70] This shows a recognition by Edwards of not just one but a series of conversions and a keen understanding of the maturing of his own spiritual life.

John Henry Newman

The conversion of John Henry Newman was unlike the Puritan experiences of election found in Bunyan and Edwards, but not dissimilar to the change of affiliation gone through by Paul or the rational route travelled by Augustine. Newman tells us in the *Apologia* that his conversion was basically an intellectual development involving the painful recognition of the inadequacy of the Anglican communion and the rightness of the Roman Catholic claims. His journey began in the Oxford Movement, which he saw as a "second Reformation" whose purpose was to uphold primitive Christianity. When he studied the Fathers, however, he was led to the painful conclusion that the Anglican community had indeed left the ancient faith. When he tried to find the catholic roots in the Anglican Church in his famous Tract 90, he succeeded only in alienating his orthodox colleagues and bringing himself a step closer to union with Rome.

Newman grew intellectually towards conversion by gradually coming to a new understanding of three propositions on which he had built his spiritual life. The first of these was the principle of dogma. Religion as a "mere sentiment," he says, "is to me a dream and a mockery."[71] On this level he felt that his joining the Church of Rome involved no rejection of past beliefs but rather a new fullness of faith. The second proposition affirmed the claim in a visible church with sacraments and rites. Here again he experienced no challenge to long-held beliefs. But the third principle, which identified the Church of Rome as evil and the Pope as antichrist, had to be radically rejected. He admits that this change was not easy "even when my reason so ordered me," and so a gradual and largely unconscious process was needed before he could come finally to give up in his "deliberate judgment" his past prejudices. [72]

Newman's special anguish involved being for many years without a firm religious base, in a "state of moral sickness," as he describes it, "neither able to acquiesce in Anglicanism, nor able to go to Rome."[73] Since his Anglicanism at this time consisted mainly in arguments against Rome and since he could not yet accept Roman Catholic doctrine, he was peculiarly without a theology to support himself. He resolved to meet this crisis of spiritual ambivalence by reason alone but soon discovered that this need to rationalize seemed only to clog his mental processes and to delay his final conversion. Only when he recalled the story of Samuel, who showed trust in God by lying down to sleep while awaiting God's instructions, did he accept a more passive role and allow time to help answer his questions.[74]

During the last few months before his conversion Newman worked through a final question which concerned the nature of truth itself. He feared that if he could give up now what had in the past been true to him, he could never be sure that he would not do the same thing again in the future. He answered this dilemma by writing an essay on doctrinal development to show that the church in coming to a clearer understanding of doctrine does not mean to declare false a previous and less perfect understanding. A living church can grow and develop without changing its divine deposit of faith, he argued, and doctrinal development does take place, in fact, as a process in which later formulations of the truth build on previous ones. Newman implies that such development has also been happening in his own life.

Finally Newman was ready for the "revolution of mind" which would lead him from his old home to a new one. [75] Although it was a momentous occasion, he avoided any fanfare and simply asked a priest for admission into the Roman Catholic Church. The act of conversion resulted in no great intellectual change, or firmer faith, or even more fervor, Newman reports, but it did bring about an end of doubt. It was "like coming into port after a rough sea." [76]

Thomas Merton

The journey of a twentieth century convert, Thomas Merton, was from modern secularism to ancient Trappist asceticism. Merton tells us in his popular autobiography, *The Seven Storey Mountain*, that in his childhood he received no formal religious or moral instructions and was left with the general attitude that all religions were more or less praiseworthy. As a youth studying in England he developed what he calls a "natural faith," but this was not sufficient to make sense out of the problem of suffering and death when his father developed and eventually died from a brain tumor. Because of this lack of a vital faith he became "the complete twentieth-century man," he writes, someone who belongs to the world and who exists "on the doorsill of the Apocalypse, a man with veins full of poison, living in death." [77] In his younger years he reveled in these secularist feelings because they appeared to free him from authority and make him a great rebel. As he writes, "I fancied that I had suddenly risen above all the errors and stupidities and mistakes of modern society." [78] When his schoolmates stood to recite the creed, he remembers keeping his lips shut and deliberately declaring his new found atheism with the words, "I believe in nothing." [79] Even when he almost died from blood poisoning he recalls no fear but only apathy. [80]

While on a school holiday in Rome, Merton was at least temporarily lifted out of his spiritual torpor in rather startling fashion when he had a vivid experience of his dead father. His father was as present, Merton writes, "as if he had touched my arm or spoken to me." [81] Although the experience passed in a moment, he was deeply affected because of the insight it gave him into his own sorry state and because it moved him to pray for the first time not just with lips and intellect but "out of the very roots" of his own being. [82] His soul felt "broken and clean, painful but sanitary like a lanced abscess, like a bone broken and re-set." [83] This "great grace," as he calls it, was like "a capitulation, a surrender, a conversion," and left him with the sensation of having been reborn. [84] He even briefly entertained the notion of joining the Trappists, he remembers, but had no real idea at that time who they were. When he returned to the United States he made tentative approaches to the Episcopal and Quaker churches in his neighborhood and even briefly investigated the Mormons while at the Chicago World's Fair. Soon his newborn religious enthusiasm abated, however, and by the time he returned to Cambridge he was again spiritually dried out and ready to take up a rather dissolute life as an undergraduate. Merton himself recognizes the growth process at work in these deaths and rebirths, which he sees as the age-old dynamics of Christian spirituality. It is simply "the crucifixion of Christ," he says, "in which He dies again and again in the individuals who were made to share the joy and the freedom of His grace, and who deny Him." [85]

The next time Merton returned from England he was in the throes of another conversion, this one leading to communism. At least this conversion was the acknowledgment of his selfishness, he conceded, and reflected his desire to foster a social conscience. But this utopian dream also faded and Merton found himself, like Augustine, "beaten by this futile search for satisfaction where it could not be found." [86] Paradoxically it was the very helplessness of his position which led to what William James might call his self-surrender. "I had come very far to find myself in this blind-alley," Merton writes, "and it was my defeat that was to be the occasion of my rescue." [87]

Perhaps the person who came closest to being an intellectual guru for Merton was Mark van Doren of Columbia University, whom he credits with having taught him to think. Other powerful influences on his intellectual journey towards conversion were Etienne Gilson and Jacques Maritain, and especially William Blake, from whom he learned the need for a vital faith to reveal the world as charged with the reality and presence of God. These people brought Merton beyond atheism to a position of wanting religion and in fact doing something about it. He began to go to Mass and discovered a new inner peace and contentment. In a scene reminiscent of Augustine's conversion, while reading he was stirred by something like a voice which asked him, "What are you waiting for?" After only a few moments of hesitation he went to the priest at the local rectory to ask admission into the Catholic Church.

But for Merton true spiritual transformation meant not only conversion of the intellect but also of the will. It is not enough to believe in God or in the teachings of the church, he says, or even "to sit up all night arguing about them with all comers." [88] What is also needed is a change of heart. Merton recounts an extraordinary experience he had which led to this conversion of the will. It occurred in a church in New York City when it became suddenly clear to him that his whole life was at a crisis. He felt that he had been brought to the church "to answer a question that had been preparing, not in my mind, but in the infinite depths of an eternal Providence." [89] This revelatory experience left him with the conviction that he was called to be a priest. As a final sign of his vocation he had the sensation one evening of hearing the bell of Gethsemani Abbey ringing and in fact summoning him to become a Trappist monk. "The bell seemed to be telling me where I belonged," he writes, "as if it were calling me home." [90]At the time he wrote this Merton could only imagine the further growth events which would eventually lead him out of the monastery and into dialogue with the Eastern religions.

Merton's account of his spiritual life illustrates very well the developmental nature of conversion. In his own words, "We are not converted only once in our lives, but many times; and this endless series of large and small conversions, inner revolutions, leads to our transformation in Christ." [91] Merton set as his goal nothing less than becoming a saint. [92] He made progress towards this goal by negotiating his way from the sterile despair of a secularist and atheist to the creative hope of a Christian and monk.

Charles Colson

The conversion of Charles Colson offers a good example of the contemporary phenomenon of "born again" Christianity. Colson's autobiographical account shows how he changed from Watergate criminal to evangelist, or, as the jacket of his best seller provocatively expresses it, "How Nixon's hatchet man found spiritual rebirth." Colson's story begins with feelings of emptiness and meaninglessness and ends with physical and spiritual healings. Along the way there are people who support him and crisis events which call forth creative and developmental responses.

The person who first awakened Colson from his spiritual lassitude was a "born again" Christian businessman named Tom Phillips, who encouraged him to pray in a personal fashion. This new form of charismatic prayer quickly brought Colson to his knees crying but with the wonderful feeling of being renewed through his tears in a kind of spiritual baptism. There came, he writes, "the strange sensation that water was not only running down my cheeks, but surging through my whole body as well, cleansing and cooling as it went." [93] This emotional catharsis was followed up by an intellectual quest for the truth in the reading of C. S. Lewis' *Mere Christianity*. Although this study took place during only one week on the Maine coast, it was for Colson like a "journey of thousands of miles," as he says, and resulted in his surrender to Jesus: "Lord Jesus, I believe in You. I accept You. Please come into my life. I commit it to you." [94] This conversion gave Colson a new confidence and a new view of himself and the world, effects quite similar to Maslow's characteristics of peak-experience. As Colson describes the event:

> With these few words that morning, while the briny sea churned, came a sureness of mind that matched the depth of feeling in my heart. There came something more: strength

and serenity, a wonderful new assurance about life, a fresh perception of myself and the world around me. In the process, I felt old fears, tensions, and animosities draining away. I was coming alive to things I'd never seen before; as if God was filling the barren void I'd known for many months, filling it to with a whole new kind of awareness. 95

Although there was some negative reaction to his conversion when it was first reported in the press — some even calling it another "dirty trick" — Colson found that his newborn spiritual life was nurtured by the support he received from a network of new evangelical friends. This fellowship cut across political party lines and formed what he terms "a veritable underground of Christ's men all through the government." 96 But in order to grow spiritually he felt it necessary to free himself from the past and therefore pleaded guilty to his part in the Watergate crimes. The punishment of prison was helpful, he says, in working to destroy his pride and giving him the opportunity to witness about Christ to the other prisoners. It was in prison that his conversion was completed with baptism in the Spirit. This occurred during a Bible study class and felt like a "most curious effervescent sensation" rushing through his body.97 Colson describes it as a second conversion which resulted in more understanding for prison officials and more love for his fellow inmates.

The power of the Spirit was manifested for Colson in an extraordinary way shortly after his pentecostal experience. The event was the healing through prayer of a prisoner who had been close to death. Colson interpreted this as a victory for Christ over Satan and as a sign of God's approval of his evangelical work in prison. Shortly after this he took a further step in his conversion, one which he describes as a "total surrender," completing what had begun only eighteen months earlier. "Lord, if this is what it is all about," he prayed, "then I thank You." With these words he felt a final release which was what he calls "the real mountaintop experience" which truly set him free. 98

Colson grew spiritually by replacing his need for politically powerful friends with a new Christian fellowship, and his desire for personal dominance with a new identity based on surrender to Christ. His previous spiritual malaise, perhaps best epitomized by Watergate, gave way during his conversion to a sense of new direction and purpose. His was a conversion of nurture according to the models of Piaget and Erikson, with quite discernible steps along the way — the first prayer, the reading of an influential book, the acceptance of guidance from more spiritually advanced people, the submission to Christ as personal savior, the baptism in the Spirit, the evangelical mission. And Colson himself admits that the journey is not yet over. Even the title of his book, *Born Again,* he warns, is not to be taken as suggesting that he has arrived at some state of spiritual superiority but only at a fresh start at putting his life in order.99

ISSUES RELATED TO CONVERSION TO
THE NEW RELIGIONS

There are several key points which I believe must be considered when speaking of conversion to the new religions, especially in the American context. First of all, the conversion experience is not new. Conversion was such an essential element of Puritan theology, for example, that church membership was reserved to those who could testify to their election. In addition, the long history of revivals in America, led by such forceful evangelists as Jonathan Edwards, George McGready, Charles Finney, Dwight Moody, Billy Sunday and Billy Graham, is most fundamentally a story of religious renewal and conversion. It is also instructive to realize that the marginal religions, or the "cults" as they have been pejoratively called, are not something brand new but have an important place in American religious history. Puritanism itself was for all purposes considered a "cult" by many seventeenth century European Protestants, and Puritans in turn did not hesitate to ostracize from their commonwealth such religious mavericks as Quakers and Baptists. Far from being a unique product of the last couple of decades, forms of unusual spirituality have been a part of American religion for a long time. So also has been the tension between these marginal groups and the larger environing religious and civil communities.

American history has seen the growth and frequently the decline of such eccentric communities as the Shakers, the Oneida commune, the Rappites, and the Transcendentalist communitarian experiments at Hopedale and Brook Farm. Sometimes such groups have survived to become rather accepted religions, like the Mormons, the Seventh Day Adventists, and the Jehovah's Witnesses. One wonders what the future holds for today's odd religionists — the Moonies, Scientologists, Krishnas. Indeed, few of the current "cults" could surpass Mormons in doctrinal creativity with their beliefs in baptism for the dead, marriage for eternity, and polygamy. Nor could many of today's new religions succeed in claiming that their occasionally novel religious rituals are more inventive than the Shaker dance. And no matter how financially astute some of the modern-day prophets are, it is doubtful that they could outdo Father Divine and Sweet Daddy Grace in amassing riches. In other words, it's all been done before! The new religionists may truly believe that their insight, their methods, their theology is unique, but it is closer to the truth to say that America has long been a spawning ground for radical forms of spirituality.

But the fact that religious experimentation has had a long life on the American scene doe not explain why so many idealistic young men and women are converting to the new religions today. What is the attraction which causes highly qualified people to engage in such an extreme lifestyle change? One explanation may concern the way young people view time. Young people, who probably have plenty of time, paradoxically feel and act as if they have very little. They are impetuous to produce immediate remediation of the world's ills and are heartened, therefore, when the new religions similarly seem to take time seriously by offering their recruits the chance to have a real impact on their environment within a very short time. Erikson describes how a young person may work through his or her identity crisis by waiting for some event or some person to come along and give meaning to time. The young person is promised in this encounter, says Erikson, "instead of the reassuring routine and practice of most men's time, a vast utopian view that would make the very disposition of time worthwhile."[100]This kind of importance is given to time when a person, regardless of his or her youth, is invited to a direct participation in the work of building whatever form of the kingdom of God the new religion's particular theology envisions — a participation not usually found in the more traditional religions. While in most mainline religions fairly advanced age seems to be a prerequisite for leadership roles, this is not usually the case in new religions. I have interviewed members of the Unification Church, for example, who are only in their twenties but already statewide church leaders or administrators of rather sophisticated church-related business ventures. It is not surprising that in a society where young people often feel left out, the new religions would appeal by the very fact that they invite the young to participate fully and hold out to them immediate and seemingly attainable goals.

Another reason why young people join the new religions may be the opportunity they offer to grow personally within new associations or "families." At a time in personality development when the young adult is expected to leave home, he or she may find it advantageous to seek out a new family based on theology rather than biology. Erikson says that potentially creative people sometimes build the personal foundations for their later career during what he calls "a self-decreed moratorium, during which they often starve themselves, socially, erotically, and, last but not least, nutritionally, in order to let the grosser weeds die out, and make way for the growth of their inner garden."[101] This hiatus is declared, he says, in order to avoid the danger of success without a well-formed identity. Perhaps for some young recruits membership in the new religions offers this period of pause for continued self-development and the chance to work out life goals in the company of similarly creative and dedicated people.

This question of family is a particularly sensitive one since it involves young, apparently vulnerable people abandoning the biological group in order to follow their religious impulses in a new kind of association. The Unification Church, for example, is faced squarely with this dilemma because on the one hand it speaks of families as the way to salvation but on the other it seemingly breaks up families. To young people who have perhaps never experienced a tight-knit family, the Unification doctrine of the restored family through "True Parents" may contribute the strong yet loving figures who have been missing in their lives. And, strange as it may seem to Western romantic sensibilities, even the "arranged marriage" doctrine may satisfy real needs and yearnings found among many young men and women concerning the setting up of their families. As for those young people who have had strong, loving family relationships, they may have gained in the nurturing environment of the home the very maturity, strength, and courage which allows them to leave that home. If critics of the new religions refuse to accept the explanation that such family breakups are necessary during the formative, pre-kingdom years of the "cult," what meaning can be given to Jesus' invitation to leave father and mother to follow him? A spiritual counselor in a traditional religion would surely advise a novice to stay away from badgering parents if it were a choice between the old and the new family.102 Of course, for any religion to isolate its members from legitimate and creative family ties is reprehensible. If this abuse has occurred in traditional religions it is to be condemned; if it now occurs in the new religions, it is equally blameworthy. The fact remains, however, that the new religions seem to fulfill some people's search for human friendship and to offer their initiates an appealing, communal, familial way of life.

Other reasons may also be given for the current popularity of the new religions. In the decade of the 1960's, and even into the 1970's, for example, many young people tried drugs as a quick route to some kind of personal fulfillment. Recently there has been a reaction against such "artificial" techniques, however, and so some of today's youth may have turned to the new religions which are usually rigorously conservative in the use of drugs and make their appeal along much different lines, like following some charismatic leader or joining some satisfying community.

There has also been a growing awareness and acceptance of Eastern spirituality which has both influenced innovative practices within traditional religions and has led to the founding of new religions. Harvey Cox traces this development very well in his book *Turning East.* 103 He recounts his own journey concerning Tibetan meditation from a position of objective study, to some participation, to full participation and states that this Eastern prayer practice met a deep, previously unrecognized need in his own life. Many people are joining new religions with an Eastern orientation because they experience there a sense of religious fulfillment that they did not find in their orthodox Western religion.

A final suggestion for the recent upsurge in conversions to the new religions concerns the present religious climate in the United States. In the past, new religious groups often emerged from periods of revival. The Mormons, for example, were founded in 1830 after decades of intense revivalism which swept back and forth over the area around Palmyra, where Joseph Smith grew up. America now seems to be in a similar time of revival and as a result people affected by new religious impulses are rejecting the old ways of practicing religion and are seeking out new forms of religious expression. The new religions, often with strong leaders and "revealed" doctrine, claim to offer a kind of religious certainty and stability in a time of flux.

Critics of the new religions may admit that conversion to marginal groups is not a new phenomenon in America, but they ususally argue that at least the techniques being used are new and that is the reason why so many young people are leaving the faith of their fathers for the new "cults." For example, John Clark, a psychiatrist and outspoken critic of the new religions, identifies as the "central activity" of these groups "the sudden conversion through aggressive and skillful manipulation of a naive or deceived subject." 104This sudden conversion is brought about, he says, by highly programmed behavioral control techniques which narrow the subject's attention and focus it to the point of becoming a trance. These techniques he lists as loss of privacy and sleep, creation of a bizarre new atmosphere, change of language, continuous control of the excitement level, and an onslaught of new information. He claims these maintain the state of dissociation and result in the convert's becoming dependent on the new group for his or her identity.

This method of behavior control, rather infelicitously called "brainwashing," has been studied over the last twenty-five years, especially in connection with the system of Chinese thought reform practiced on prisoners during the Korean War. Joost Meerloo, for example, has identified a three-part pattern of deconditioning, identification with the enemy, and reconstruction of the ego. The deconditioning or ego-destruction comes about when the subject loses the power to resist as the result of intimidation, humiliation, isolation, and interrogation; the identification with the enemy or the conversion, when the self-pitying subject turns to the enemy for comfort; the rebuilding of the ego or the new identity, when the subject comes to rationalize and justify the new ideology. 105 William Sargant has noted the similarity between the techniques described by Meerloo, which are used for political conversion, and the techniques used in religious conversion. He also makes the point that the subject most susceptible to either brainwashing or religious conversion may be the simple, healthy extrovert.106 Robert Jay Lifton, another critic of brainwashing, offers an even more elaborate model to explain the process. He says eight conditions are present in the course of the deliberate destruction of the old ego and the programmed formation of a new one. The subject is isolated from the outside world; is told of the plans the group has to better the world; is made to feel guilty for his or her pre-conversion ignorance; is encouraged to confess publicly inner fears and anxieties; is taught that the new beliefs are based on scientific truth; is given a new vocabulary which has special meaning within the group; is practiced in the importance of the group over the individual; and is led to believe that the world is now divided between those saved and those doomed, between divine and satanic forces.107

The sociological patterns involved in conversion to the new religions have also been investigated. In a 1965 study, for example, Lofland and Stark trace the development of a convert to "DP" (Lofland's pseudonym for the Unification Church) through various stages: the sense of frustration and dissatisfaction with the way one's life is being lived; the seeking of new answers to the problem of identity; the loss of one's former religious beliefs and the more gradual curtailing of former religious practices; the meeting of members of the new religion and the development of bonds with them, along with the corresponding weakening of ties with people outside the group; and finally intensive interaction with the group, often involving living with them and joining in their work.[108]

In a follow-up 1977 study John Lofland claims that the Unification Church has elaborated over the years "incredible nuances" in their conversion techniques. He lists five steps in their method of recruiting: the "picking-up," or the initial contact by means of a street encounter or some small request like a donation; the "hooking," or the holding onto the subject by an invitation to dinner or even to an indoctrination camp in the country; the "encapsulating," or the further involvement of the prospect by some kind of weekend workshop which focuses on the groups's ideology by means of lectures and enhances the identification process by group meals, group exercises, fatigue, and even some mild sexual excitement brought on by frequent patting and hugging across the sexes; the "loving," or the projection of the feeling of being loved and the desire to melt together into the loving, enveloping embrace of the collective (frequently called "love bombing"); the "committing," or the drawing of the "blissed out" prospect into full working membership, involving street peddling and believing participation.[109]

Rosabeth Moss Kanter presents a similar model to explain the sociological factors at work in building commitment to a new group. The process begins, she says, with sacrifice, which involves abstinence and austerity. This makes membership seem more valuable since a high price has been paid. The second factor is investment, which provides the recruit with a stake in the fate of the community. If this investment is irreversible there is even more of a chance that the person will stay. The third factor is communion, which is the sense of connectedness, belonging, participation in the whole, mingling of the self in the group. This is fostered by shared work, ritual, and especially persecution. The fourth factor is mortification, which strips away aspects of the individual's previous identity and makes him or her dependent on authority for direction. This frequently includes confession and mutual criticisms and sanctions. The last factor is transcendence, which is the awe associated with the group leader, as well as the sense of rightness and even divinity in the subject's own life.[110]

Some critics of the new religions argue from these kinds of psychological and sociological studies that manipulation is used to force conversion on susceptible young people. They cite the exhausting workshops, long lectures, periods of isolation, food deprivation, and "love-bombing" as evidence of sinister motives. Indeed, my own research on Unification Church members has verified the use of some of these practices. It must be remembered, however, that these techniques are really not new. They may be dangerous but they have been used before in many traditional religions. Spiritual directors have long recognized a kind of death-resurrection pattern in the process of conversion and, consequently, have seen the need for partial breakdown of the "old man" in order to form the new one. They have used techniques quite similar to the ones being criticized in order to bring about this renovation. Erikson speaks of such methods, for example, when he describes Luther's initiation into the monk's life. The subject of such an initiation must be separated from the world long enough so that new convictions might be able to replace much of what was learned in childhood and practiced in youth. Erikson points out that such training may be a kind of "shock treatment," for it is expected to replace very quickly what has developed over many formative years. It must bring the subject to the point of "identity-diffusion," he says, "but short of psychotic dissociation." Eventually it must try to send the individual back into the world "with his convictions so strongly anchored in his unconscious that he almost hallucinates them as being the will of a godhead or the course of all history." Erikson adds that late adolescence is the favorable period for such indoctrination because in adolescence "an ideological realignment is by necessity in process."[111] All this is very dangerous business, of course, and any abuse should be vigorously identified and condemned, whether it is found among mainline or marginal religions.

A few critics of the new religions are themselves practicing a controversial form of behavior modification called "deprogramming." This is the process through which a person who has been converted to one of today's "cults" is subjected to a coercive program of behavior intervention aimed at destroying the social hold of the marginal group and faith in its doctrines in order to re-establish those values, attitudes, and beliefs which apparently were held previously. Those who engage in deprogramming justify their actions on the claim that since the marginal religions gain converts through brainwashing, the subject did not make a valid and voluntary commitment in the first place. The ersatz conversion only left the person psychologically enslaved and unable to act independently of the group's directives. What is needed, therefore, is a conversion reversal if free will and rational choice are to be restored to the victim. Since freedom is such an American value, this rationale gives to deprogramming the semblance of not only therapeutic but even moral legitimacy. As one anti-cult writer describes it, "Deprogramming aims at breaking the chains of fear, guilt, and repetitive thought, and at forcing evaluation of the unexamined beliefs that were injected into the victim's unresisting mind by the cult leaders after the behavioral chains were originally established."[112]

Deprogrammers claim that their goal is not education to a new ideology but rather the liberation of the individual. Therefore, even if the deprogramming succeeds in removing the subject from the new religion, there still remains the question of a substitute for the faith that appeared to be so meaningful. Frequently the young adults who are deprogrammed have left forever the faith of their childhood but are offered only a negative viewpoint to fill the gap. J. Stillson Judah surmises that this is the reason why some deprogrammed people become deprogrammers themselves and why others return to their former lives of alcoholism and drug abuse.[113]

Since deprogrammers view themselves as liberators, it is evident that they equate brainwashing with a kind of demonic possession. Deprogramming then becomes the religious act of exorcism and so is beyond criticism.[114] It also follows that the object of their attack is not the individual but the "cult." This shows a willingness to distinguish legitimate from illegitimate religion, a distinction most difficult to make without endangering Constitutional guarantees of religious liberty.

Deprogramming has been condemned by some because it employs the same methods as brainwashing and in fact adds the physical coercion factor. While there seem to be few verified cases of abduction for proselytizing purposes in the new religions, forcible restraint and kidnappping are rampant in deprogramming. It is ironic that parents and concerned critics of the new religions sometimes use methods as bad as or even worse than those used by the groups they profess to despise. Deprogramming raises all kinds of ethical questions because it involves long periods of confinement; cursing and other forms of verbal abuse; lack of any kind of informed consent; sometimes deceit to entice the subject away from the group; the use of people who are not trained physicians or psychiatrists, with the resulting danger that profound psychological damage may be inflicted on the subject; and the probability of the permanent destruction of trust within the family. In addition, since the whole deprogramming effort aims at inculcating "right thinking," there is of course the threat that certain groups will have the power to decide for others what is normal and acceptible. Such social engineering could have far-reaching consequences for all forms of religion. As George Kieffer warns, "To allow one group to decide for another what constitutes correct thoughts is a dangerous precedent to be tolerated in a democratic society."[115]

It should also be recalled that there is a long history of bigoted attacks against conversion to strange religious groups. To cite just one example from the thirteenth century, the family of Thomas Aquinas did all in their power to contradict his conversion to an odd collection of mendicant Friars called Dominicans. They engaged in what today would be called deprogramming efforts — locking him up in the family estate and enticing him to give up his vocation with threats and bribes. From our twentieth century vantage point it is easy to cheer Thomas' steadfastness and berate his family's selfishness, but do we react in similar fashion to stories of contemporary deprogramming? There are many legal, psychological, and indeed theological concerns that are not adequately faced if our society condones the involuntary deprogramming of converts to religious groups.

CONVERSION IN THE UNIFICATION CHURCH

During the summer of 1979 I distributed to members of the Unification Church in the New York City area a questionnaire which was intended to gather information about the types of persons who joined this new religion, the circumstances of their conversion, their reasons for staying, and their expectations for the future. I received answers from seventy-four people. In addition to these written responses I have orally interviewed eight members of the church between October 1978 and June 1980. I offer here a summary of the written questionnaires and the oral interviews because one of the main concerns of this paper is the question of conversion as it applies to members of the new religions in America. The eleven questions and the summaries of the responses are as follows:

Name

Sixty-five (88%) of the seventy-four answering the written questionnaire identified themselves, even though this was optional. All those being orally interviewed were known to me by name. The willingness to be identified has significance in view of the threat some members feel about deprogramming efforts.

Age

Sixty-seven (82%) were between the ages of 25 and 30; the youngest respondent was 25, the oldest 50.

Sex

Fifty (61%) were male, 32 (39%) female.

Geographical Background

Sixty-one (74%) were United States citizens, 21 (26%) citizens of other countries. The foreign countries represented were: Japan (6), Canada (3), Australia (3), West Germany (3), Spain (1), Dominican Republic (1), England (1), Korea (1), New Zealand (1), and France (1). The American members came from twenty-six states. The largest number were from New York (10).

Educational Background

Seventy-nine (96%) have at least a bachelor's degree. Five respondents have a master's degree or some other higher degree (J.D. annd C.P.A.). Fine Arts had the highest number of undergraduate majors (8), but almost every area of study was represented by at least one respondent. Thirty-two different colleges were mentioned as degree granting institutions, even though this was not specifically asked. One explanation for the high percentage of college graduates in this sample is the fact that most of my respondents were candidates for the graduate theology program at the Unification Seminary in Barrytown, New York.

Religious Background

Thirty-two (39%) came from Protestant families; 31 (38%) Catholic; 9 (11%) Buddhist; 7 (9%) Jewish; 3 (4%) agnostic. Concerning the religion of the respondents themselves before their conversion, 23 (28%) were either agnostic or non-practicing members of a mainline church; 16 (20%) practicing Protestants; 15 (18%) practicing Catholics; 9 (11%) Westerners practicing some form of Eastern religion; 5 (6%) Buddhists; 4 (5%) theists, but with no church affiliation; 3 (4%)

practicing Jews; 7 (9%) no clear response.

Mystical Experiences

The question asked was "Since your association with the Unification Church, have you ever had 'mystical' experiences, such as visions, dreams, etc., which you interpret as being revelatory? If so, please describe your experiences." I asked this because in conversations with members I had become intrigued by the frequent references to such experiences. Sixty (73%) replied that they had had such mystical experiences, while 22 (27%) said they had not. Those who admitted to the experiences described them in terms of the following categories:

1. Experiences of Rev. Moon. By far the largest number, twenty-six out of the eighty-two respondents and interviewees (32%), recounted this kind of experience. Some typical descriptions were:

> "I saw the figure of Sun Myung Moon hanging on the cross. As I looked at his face, he was nodding, saying, 'Yes, it's me,' with such a feeling of love pouring out to me I knew the vision meant Sun Myung Moon had some relationship with Jesus."

> "He is very sad and many times crying unlike the way he is when he speaks to us."

> "I saw the face of the founder very small and at a distance. Also it began to move closer and closer, enlarging as it did so, with a cheerful, warm smile, until this vision (I was awake) was up to my nose, then vanished."

> "A large picture of Rev. Moon became very animated, winking and smiling at me. The voice of Heavenly Father told me, 'You are forgiven.' "

> "Rev. Moon was sitting in a car in a parking lot late at night and he donated two dollars to me when I fundraised to him. I had hoped it would be more but I became ecstatically happy at his heart and love for me."

2. Experiences of Jesus.

> "Jesus Christ appeared in a vision in the prayer room and told me to join the Unification Church."

> "I have seen Jesus in spirit forty or fifty times. I have also seen Moses and Rev. Moon."

3. Experiences of the presence of God.

> "Suddenly I felt a warm presence come over me and a hand patting me on the back consoling me. I felt cleansed inside and I felt and saw the presence of God in everything. After this I joined the church."

4. Experiences concerning the Unification Church.

> One respondent described an elaborate dream he had had repeatedly before joining the church. He was always climbing the sheer face of a cliff and then falling. "About three months after I joined I had the same dream," he wrote, "but the cliff

became covered with thick vines of ivy and I made it to the top." He attributed his new ability to his membership in the church.

Another respondent referred to an important church belief concerning the unification of the world when he told of a vision in which the faces of people of various cultures appeared to him. "I realized that God was revealing to me what he sees constantly," he wrote.

Another recounted a dream in which he was working with Rev. Moon pulling up dead trees, and he saw a beautiful house with an intricate floor design. He interpreted his dream as indicating the church's work of building a spiritual home.

5. Experiences concerning messages from the dead.

"I have met my dead uncle three times and discussed my conversion and future."

Another respondent wrote of "feeling the presence of my dead grandfather consenting to my joining the Unification Church."

Another had a vision of his grandfather three days after his death. "I spoke to him a long time," he wrote, "and taught him the first chapter of Divine Principle."

6. Experiences concerning America.

One respondent told how on July 4, 1978, while attending a morning prayer service, she was visited by "several attractive 'high-level spirits' " who sat next to her. She said they claimed to be "people who had worked in the early days of America" and were now disappointed in the direction the country was taking. They asked her to continue working to build up America again.

7. Experiences which foretell events.

One respondent recalled a dream which anticipated the rally held by the church in Madison Square Garden on September 18, 1974.

8. Experiences concerning conflict in the world.
One respondent described a dream relating to the story of Cain and Abel, which serves as an important model in Unification theology to explain the tension between good and evil. He wrote, "I saw a man killing another man with a primitive weapon and then a historical repetition of the same act using more and more sophisticated weapons. I related this to the story of Cain and Abel."

9. Experiences which indicate a heightened self-awareness.

"I have had my sense of smell change so that certain places, such as gay people areas and immoral streets have become very terrible smelling."

"I am a very 'nuts and bolts' kind of person. I like baseball, golf, spaghetti, good music, etc., and I intend to remain so. But my experiences in a life of faith have put me in situations (sometimes difficult) where God has blessed me with many visions of people (spiritual), voices, physical contact with spirits, spiritual smell, visual awareness, and sensual awareness, revelation, and intuition."

The Conversion Experience

For this information I simply directed the respondents to narrate how they joined the Unification Church. In answering this, most indicated the way in which they first met the church. Some made their initial contact through meeting church members, usually in a street encounter (26%); some through a lecture or workshop (23%); some through a friend already in the church (13%); some through studying the Divine Principle (12%); some through a dinner invitation to a church center (12%); some through an organization which was not at first identified with the church, such as the Collegiate Association for the Research of Principles (CARP) or the Creative Community Project (7%); some through a newspaper advertisement (4%); some through a public talk by Rev. Moon (4%).

Many respondents indicated their feelings or their personal life circumstances just before joining. Some said they had just graduated from college, were in the last year of college, or were looking for a job (23%). A significant number used words like "searching" and "seeking" in their accounts (22%). Three joined after elaborate prayer retreats — one after praying for forty days in the California desert, another after praying during an entire Christmas vacation, and the third after praying for two weeks alone in his apartment (4%). Two joined right after the death of a close family member (2%). One respondent followed his girl friend into the church.

For some the period of time between first encountering the church and definitely joining was very short, that is, under three weeks (21%). But contrary to many claims made in the press of the immediate "brainwashing" of recruits, the vast majority of the respondents joined after a significant lapse of time, between three weeks and seven years (79%). However, supporting the opinion that the so-called "Oakland Family" of the church, which until very recently had been directed by the husband and wife team of Mose and Soo Lim Durst, is especially successful in recruitment, one out of every four respondents (24%) joined in California.

In general, two ideological or theological reasons were given by the respondents for their conversion: the seeking of answers to questions concerning the meaning of life and the desire to improve the world or at least themselves through this new community. Here are some typical responses:

1. Seeking answers.

    "During the weekend I was 'love bombed' and also 'truth bombed.' After that I wanted to stay and discover the source of all that love and truth so that I too could give love and truth."

    "I joined the Unification Church because my reasons for rejecting religious faith were answered in its teachings."

    "At the conclusion of the final lecture I exclaimed, 'That's the most logical thing I've ever heard!' Then prayers and tears and overpowering feelings of love sealed my conversion experience."

2. Seeking social and personal improvement.

    "All my life I had a kind of dream or hope that the world could be a better place."

    "Even when I was ten years old I was inspired (especially by Martin Luther King) by an inexhaustible desire to help make an ideal world where people could look at each other as true brothers and sisters. I had been turned off by religion because it seemed all words and no action."

    "I saw the lifestyle and heart of the kind of person I wanted to become."

    "I had been searching to find God more completely in my life and specifically to find a religious commitment so that I could grow spiritually."

    "I felt the Unification Church was the pot of gold at the end of the rainbow."

I offer here some additional accounts of conversion given by members of the Unification Church. The first four are responses to the 1979 questionaire and the last two are summaries of stories told to me in personal conversations.

(K. H., female, age 27) I was working on a college campus. I had just moved back to Cincinnati after college and traveling. I was spending my free time with friends from the past and a few people I knew from college. It seemed like we were always doing the same thing — getting high and looking for something to do. I found out a guy I was dating was engaged. I didn't see much in that. People seem to accept any morality these days. I was thinking I'd like a change in my life, so I thought it must come from making new friends. I realized what an effort it took to make a friend from a huge campus full of strangers on your lunch hour. But I sank back in my self-improvement book and decided that next week I would make the effort. Five minutes later, a girl came and sat next to me and asked how I was doing and if she could talk to me for a few minutes. I told her I was amazed at what she had just done (come up and speak to a stranger). It all happened from there. I heard the Divine Principle workshop the next weekend. Back at work on Monday I knew I had become a different person.

(G. S., male, 28) After graduating Pratt with honors, my desire to find God became the most important thing in my life. Besides design, I had become increasingly interested in "perfection." So I tasted metaphysics, existentialism, meditation. By graduating, I had fulfilled my responsibility to my parents. Yet I hadn't found my life work. I was convinced that God knew my life work, and so I determined to find a way to meet Him. In college, I had fellowshipped with three major Hindu spiritual groups and done much reading. (I had lost respect for Christianity.) When I heard the Divine Principle, I was impressed by its comprehensiveness, its logic, and its implications. So I determined to study it and examine it until I could prove its veracity or falsity. I moved in physically and really joined about eight months later. By that time my major questions had been answered.

(D. J., female, age 30) I was finishing my first year of graduate work at Boston University. Much of my studies directly confronted personal, religious, historical questions. While studying in a lounge of the theological department I met a member of Unification Church. We discussed issues of career, family, marriage, world affairs, religion, the existence of God, etc. I accepted an invitation to attend the seminars at Boston Center. I was very interested in finding deeper answers to the purpose of life and the way to realize love in human relationships. I had experienced many things in my life already — through relationships, work and travel. I was very concerned with the lack of true love, true morals, and the emphasis on material life in America. I often felt very pained by the evil and selfish base in the events of the world and my own experience of life. I wanted to find a true culture and hope for future life.

(J. K., male, age 37) Externally, I was studying for the bar exam in San Francisco in January 1974, heard Rev. Moon speak on January 20, took the bar exam in February, visited the church center March 20, moved in April 23. Internally, I began searching for the truth in the form of a lifestyle meaningful for the individual and the entire world at age seventeen, just before senior year in high school. I tried most of the options our society offers during the next fourteen years — school, jobs, marriage, travel, drugs, etc. — but did not find what I was looking for until I was thirty-one. I've been here ever since, no longer searching, but *living*.

(C. D., female) I was born an only child in Germany and was raised by a very loving and open mother. I was aware from an early age that all was not right with the world and so joined many activist groups, especially while in college, in order to help bring about some social reform. But none of these activities seemed to satisfy my. It was not until I met K., a Unification Church member, that I felt the search was over. I received instructions from him and joined the church in a short time.

(T. S., female) While I was a Catholic nun I was considered to be happy and successful. But after many years as a nun I realized that what had formerly held meaning for me no longer did. I would go to Mass in the morning and feel nothing. I was aware of my searching for answers when I first met the Unification Church members and began to spend time with them. In fact, I became a member of the Unification Church even before I left my former community. When I told the nuns that I had become a "Moonie" they thought I had had some kind of breakdown, but I know that I have found meaning and happiness in my new life.

Family Reaction

I asked the question, "How has your family reacted to your conversion?" Fifty-one respondents (62%) said they had a good relationship with their family. Of this number, sixteen said the relationship was positive or at least trusting; thirty-five described it as having been strained in the beginning but now working out in better fashion. Twenty-three (28%) reported some degree of animosity on the part of their family. Seventeen of these described their relationship as "negative" and six as "very negative." Some of the six who said "very negative" pointed out that their parents belonged to organizations which are actively working against the so-called "cults," and five said they had personally been subjected to deprogramming efforts. Four respondents (5%) said their parents liked the church but not Rev. Moon; another four (5%) said their parents had in fact joined the church or were "associate members."

Many respondents blamed the news media for causing their parents' negative attitudes. Some criticized their parents for trying to impose their own "material" goals on their children. A few referred to the difficulty their families had in trying to deal with the negative feelings of friends and neighbors towards the Unification Church.

Maintenance of Commitment

I asked the respondents to describe why they remain members of the Unification Church. The reasons given were many and most respondents gave more than one. I have indicated in the following list the number of times each reason was given and the percentage of the eighty-two respondents who gave it. I have also included in most cases one or more typical responses.

1. Thirty-five (43%) referred to the church's role in helping them form a deeper personal relationship with God.

> "I've seen God work in my life. I found out He is real and I think He wants me to be here."

2. Twenty-five (30%) found truth in the Divine Principle.

> "Having fiddled with college philosophy courses for four years, I was delighted with the logic and content of Divine Principle."

> "I know through personal experience in prayer and everyday church activities of fundraising and witnessing that Divine Principle is the completed truth for the modern age we are living in. A combined understanding of the scientific and religious approaches to explain the purpose of life, the existence of God and the spirit world, who is man, can best be answered according to the Divine Principle teachings."

3. Twenty-one (26%) stayed because of Rev. Moon.

> "I personally recognize the revelation of Sun Myung Moon to be universally true and desire to follow his standard of becoming a God-centered individual."

4. Twenty (24%) said they wanted to solve world problems and build the Kingdom of God on Earth.

> "I want to solve the problems and miseries of mankind, and I know we have the only solution."

> "This movement is 1000% determined and mobilized and working around the clock each day to bring revolution to the Kingdom of God on earth."

5. Fourteen (17%) spoke of self-growth and fulfillment in the church.

> "I realize that this is the only lifestyle I can live to really accomplish my internal goal and become the kind of person I strive to be."

6. Ten (12%) stay because of the friendship, love and dedication of the other members.

> "My friends in the Unification Church are the joy of my life. Their standard of love and friendship is unprecedented in my life."

> "[I remain] because the faith and dedication of the members

is strong; they are determined to be the forerunners/pioneers of a new world — and are making sacrificial effort daily to achieve that."

7. Five (6%) gave as the reason for staying the chance for personal involvement and action.

"Instead of just watching this renewal taking place, I want to be an active part of it."

8. Two (3%) cited as the reason for their perseverance the fact that they had recently been matched for marriage by Rev. Moon.

9. One (1%) wrote of self-sacrifice as a motive for remaining in the church.

"I remain a member of the Unification Church because this work is my destiny. I want to fulfill my destiny by giving my life to God for the perfection of myself, my family, my society, nation, and world."

10. One (1%) said he stayed in order to help defeat communism.

The Future

I asked the respondents to describe how they see their future life as members of the Unification Church. Most listed more than one contribution they expect to make. I include here the goals that were set out, the statistics of the responses for each goal, and some typical responses.

1. Forty-five (55%) mentioned the prospect of marriage and parenting. In order to properly interpret the fact that a majority of the respondents gave this answer, it is necessary to appreciate the centrality of the doctrine of marriage in Unification theology. It also helps to know that in May 1979, just three months before the written survey was taken, 705 couples participated in a "matching," or engagement ceremony, presided over by Rev. and Mrs. Moon in the church's World Mission Center in New York City.

"Within a few years I will marry and begin raising a family. When my life is done I know this will be my single most important accomplishment."

"I want to raise a big family of happy, healthy, strong, righteous children who love God and all the people of the world and who can make big changes, and who can be an inspiration to this world."

2. Eighteen (22%) envisioned some form of teaching as their future role. Most seemed to refer to the evangelical work of teaching the Divine Principle, but three intended to, get Ph.D. degrees and six specifically expressed their hope to teach academic disciplines on the college level.

3. Sixteen (20%) indicated their immediate goal of attending the Unification Seminary in Barrytown.

4. Fifteen (18%) expected some form of leadership role in the church, either religious or business.

> "I see my future as a leader! Contrary to general belief, members are given free channels to education, program design, and participation in the society's projects at large."

> "I sincerely hope that I can accomplish my goals in the realm of leadership on some level, whether it be in art, politics, science, or religion."

5. Ten (12%) said they were open to God's will concerning the future.

> "I hope to someday teach Divine Principle to many people, but if I end up cleaning tables, that's great too."

> "I want to be versatile so that I can leave off managing a newspaper one day and take up something entirely different — like fishing, retail sales, farming, anything — without losing a stride. However visible or inconspicuous my work may be, I see it as having historical significance."

6. Seven (9%) referred to doing missionary work.

> "Sometimes I envision myself as a foreign missionary working to fight against the strife in underdeveloped countries."

7. Seven (9%) said that their ambition was simply to become a better person.

> "I don't see my future much in terms of positions or doing a certain type of thing, but rather in terms of personal character and achievement."

8. Five (6%) said they looked forward to the creation of the ideal world.

> "I see the clear possibility that we can build up the ideal world which all mankind has been looking for throughout history with God's hope and desire. It sounds like a dream, but this is true."

> "The church itself may dissolve but the family will grow. As in any family there are both good times and hard times. We're

trying to take responsibility for the entire world situation so there will be some tears but someone has to do the work. Our children will be grateful."

"I sincerely hope that I can accomplish God's will by working to save America and help its global responsibility to serve the world under God's direction."

9. Four (5%) spoke of overcoming communism.

10. There were also a couple of unique responses. One mentioned the need for the church to "wage war on Satan," while another expressed the desire to become a midwife.

The members of the Unification Church whom I surveyed and interviewed are relatively young, well-educated, idealistic, highly motivated people. Although there do seem to be techniques used by the church to attract new members and hold onto old ones, there is no evidence of so-called "brainwashing" in either the written replies or the oral interviews. Most seem to be relatively independent young men and women who had in many cases already rejected the religion of their childhood long before accepting this new religion. At the same time there is the fact that many joined during some liminal period during which they may have been most vulnerable — right after college, for example, or while traveling on their own, or after some personal disappointment, or after the loss of a job, or even after the death of a loved one.

It is possible that, for some, membership in the church offers what Erikson spoke of as a pause for identity completion before beginning life's real work. In fact, some members acknowledge the church to be only a temporary condition which might dissolve as the "Unification Movement" succeeds. The work these members see as the ultimate goals of their chiliastic expectations is nothing less than the restoration of an originally perfect world.

The responses also touch on many theological beliefs within the church: the role of the second messiah, the place of the family in the new society, the struggle with communism, the making of indemnity or sacrifice for the sins of the world. The prevalence of visions, revelatory dreams, and other forms of mystical experience is difficult to explain. Some of it may be connected to the church's theory about the proximity of the spirit world and the possibility of human interaction with it; some of it may have its origin in the spiritualism practiced by some of the early Korean members.

The conversion stories these respondents tell jibe quite well with the conclusions of Piaget and Erikson concerning the developmental processes at work. Very few indicated any kind of impetuous conversion: most spoke of months or years characterized by feelings of malaise, incompleteness, and searching. For most, deliverance came gradually, and the conversion experience marked an intellectual breakthrough with the discovery of truth in the Divine Principle or an emotional catharsis with the discovery of love, acceptance, and friendship in the new community. Their conversion experience produced the feelings of peace, new energy, and sense of achievement associated with Maslow's description of the peak-experience.

I have accepted for the purposes of this paper the insight of developmental psychologists that there is an innate quality or ability in human nature that can be developed. This has allowed me to define conversion in terms of the self-transcendence which manifests itself, sometimes suddenly, sometimes gradually, in those marker events which set off the various stages of personality growth. I have attempted to illustrate this developmental aspect of conversion in the eight examples which I chose from the history of Western Christianity. Conversion to the new religions has raised special problems for Christian theology, but I believe the Christian response should be to evaluate this form of religious commitment from the strength of the gospel as it has been lived and interpreted for centuries within the orthodox tradition, while at the same time judging the Christian commitment in the light of the new religions' ideas of truth. Christian theology should be alert to unmask any false religious claims which could lead to loss of human dignity or even human life, but it should also be open to learn from the new religions and to respect the faith of their converts.

NOTES

[1] Flo Conway and Jim Siegelman, *Snapping: America's Epidemic of Sudden PersonalityChange* (New York: J.P. Lippincott Co., 1978).

[2] Reinhold Niebuhr, "Grace as Power in, and as Mercy towards, Man," in *Conversion,* William E. Conn, ed. (New York: Alba House, 1978), 28-29.

[3] *Ibid.,* 34.

[4] Horace Bushnell, *Discourses on Christian Nurture* (New Haven: Yale University Press, 1960).

[5] William James, *The Varieties of Religious Experience* (New York: The New American Library, 1958), 157.

[6]*Ibid.,* 162.

[7]*Ibid.,* 163.

[8]*Ibid., 164.*

[9]*Ibid.,* 169.

[10]*Ibid.,* 170.

[11]*Ibid.,* 169.

[12]*Ibid.,* 172.

[13]*Ibid.,* 194.

[14]*Ibid.,* 198-199.

[15]*Ibid.,* 201.

[16]*Ibid.,* 195.

[17]Jean Piaget, *The Child and Reality,* Arnold Rosin, trans. (New York: Penguin Books, 1976), 2.

[18]*Ibid.,* 10-30.

[19]*Ibid.,* 16.

[20]Erik Erikson, *Identity: Youth and Crisis* (New York: W.W. Norton and Co., 1968), 91-92.

[21]*Ibid.,* 96.

[22]*Ibid.,* 95.

[23]*Ibid.,* 109.

[24]*Ibid.,* 119.

[25]*Ibid.,* 135.

[26]*Ibid.,* 139.

[27]Erik Erikson, *Childhood and Society* (New York: W.W. Norton and Co., 1963.

[28]Abraham Maslow, *Toward a Psychology of Being* (New York: Van Nostrand Reinhold Co., 1968), 160.

[29]*Ibid.,* 204.

[30]*Ibid.,* 104.

[31]*Ibid.,* 106.

[32]*Ibid.,* 106.

[33]*Ibid.*

[34]*Ibid.,* 108.

[35]*Ibid.,* 109.

[36]For a recent and popular account of the developmental stages of adult life, see Gail Sheehy, *Passages: Predictable Crises of Adult Life* (New York: E.P. Dutton, 1974).

[37]For a similar interpretation of Paul's conversion, see Robert H. Thouless, "The Psychology of Conversion," in *Conversion,* William E. Conn, ed., 137-147.

[38]*The Confessions of Saint Augustine,* Edward B. Pusey, trans. (New York: Random House, 1949), 3.

[39]*Ibid.,* 16, 22, 29, 37, 55.

[40]*Ibid.,* 23.

[41]*Ibid.,* 83.

[42]*Ibid.,* 134.

[43]*Ibid.,* 94.

[44]*Ibid.,* 93.

[45]*Ibid.,* 167.

[46]*Ibid.,* 93.

[47]Erik Erikson, *Young Man Luther* (New York: W.W. Norton and Co., 1962), 14.

[48]*Ibid.,* 61.

[49]*Ibid.,* 204-205.

[50]*Ibid.,* 208.

[51]John Bunyan, *Grace Abounding to the Chief of Sinners* and *The Pilgrim's Progress,* Roger Sharrock, ed. (London: Oxford University Press, 1966), 8.

[52]*Ibid.,* 14.

[53]*Ibid.,* 39.

54*Ibid.,* 33.

55*Ibid.,* 45-46.

56*Ibid.,* 35.

57*Ibid.,* 45.

58*Ibid.,* 55.

59*Ibid.,* 61-62.

60*Ibid.,* 74.

61*Ibid.,* 76. It must have been a bit disconcerting for Bunyan when he tried to find the passage which had freed him only to discover that it was not in the Bible. He accomodates I Cor. 1:30 to mean the same thing, however.

62Jonathan Edwards, "Personal Narrative," in *Basic Writings of Jonathan Edwards* (New York: The New American Library, 1966), 82.

63*Ibid.* Although Edwards is perhaps most popularly known for his sermon "Sinners in the Hands of an Angry God," his rejection of terror here as the way to true conversion is more consistent with his theology.

64*Ibid.,* 83.

65*Ibid.,* 84.

66*Ibid.*

67*Ibid.*

68*Ibid.,* 84-85.

69*Ibid.,* 93.

70*Ibid.,* 95.

71John Henry Newman, *Apologia Pro Vita Sua* New York: Random House, 1950), 75.

72*Ibid.,* 79.

73*Ibid.,* 91.

74*Ibid.,* 137.

75*Ibid.,* 113.

76*Ibid.,* 237.

77Thomas Merton, *The Seven Storey Mountain* (New York: The New American Library, 1963), 89.

78*Ibid.,* 97.

79*Ibid.,* 101.

80*Ibid.,* 100-101.

81*Ibid.,* 114.

82*Ibid.*

83*Ibid.,* 115.

84*Ibid.,* 115-116.

85*Ibid.,* 123.

86*Ibid.,* 165.

87*Ibid.*

88*Ibid.,* 227.

89*Ibid.,* 250.

90*Ibid.,* 357.

91Thomas Merton, Letter published in *Informations Catholiques Internationales* (April 1973), quoted by Mark Searle, "Journey of Conversion," in *Worship* 54 (1980), 48-49.

92Merton, *The Seven Storey Mountain,* 234.

93Charles W. Colson, *Born Again* (New York: Bantam Books, 1976), 128.

94*Ibid.,* 144.

95*Ibid.*

96*Ibid.,* 151.

97*Ibid.,* 363.

98*Ibid.,* 392.

99*Ibid.,* 4.

100Erikson, *Young Man Luther,* 101.

101*Ibid.,* 44.

102See Richard DeMaria, "A Psycho-Social Analysis of Religious Conversion," in *A Time for Consideration: A Scholarly Appraisal of the Unification Church,* M. Darrol Bryant and Herbert Richardson, eds. (New York: The Edwin Mellen Press, 1978), 82-130.

103Harvey Cox, *Turning East: The Promise and Peril of the New Orientalism* (New York: Simon and Shuster, 1977).

104John Clark, "Cults," *Journal of the American Medical Association* (1979) 242:3, 280.

105Joost Meerloo, *The Rape of the Mind* (New York: Grosset and Dunlop, 1956).

106William Sargant, *Battle for the Mind* (New York: Doubleday and Co., 1957), 81.

107Robert Jay Lifton, *Thought Reform and the Psychology of Totalism* (New York: Norton and Co., 1961).

108J. Lofland and R. Stark, "Becoming a World-Saver: A Theory of Conversion to a Deviant Perspective," *American Sociological Review* (1965) 30, 862-874.

109John Lofland, " 'Becoming a World-Saver' Revisited," *American Behavioral Scientist* (1977) 20:6, 805-838.

110Rosabeth Moss Kanter, *Commitment and Community: Communes and Utopias in Sociological Perspective* (Cambridge: Harvard University Press, 1972), 75-125.

111Erikson, *Young Man Luther,* 134.

112W. West, "In Defense of Deprogramming," pamphlet (Arlington, TX: International Foundation for Individual Freedom, 1975), quoted in Anson D. Shupe, *et al.*, "Deprogramming: The New Exorcism," *American Behavioral Scientist* (July-August 1977) 20:6, 947.

113J. Stillson Judah, "New Religions and Religious Liberty," in *Understanding the New Religions,* Jacob Needleman and George Baker, eds. (New York: Seabury Press, 1978), 206.

114See Shupe, *et al.*, "Deprogramming: The New Exorcism," 941-956.

115George H. Kieffer, *Bioethics: A Textbook of Issues* (Reading, MA: Addison-Wesley Co., 1979), 311.

116See Thomas McGowan, "The Unification Church," *The Ecumenist* 17:2 (1979) 21—25.

THEOLOGICAL STUDIES
ON CONVERSION:
A Bibliography

LEWIS R. RAMBO

Renewed theological interest in conversion is best evident in the excellent collection of essays edited by Walter E. Conn, *Conversion*. This book is a collection of 25 essays or portions of books by 23 different authors. The book is divided into five major sections: (1) setting the theological question: (2) historical and biblical perspectives; (3) psychological perspectives; (4) theological perspectives; and (5) personal conversion and the transformation of social structures. One of the major joys of this book is that it covers a wide range of theological and psychological territory. The overall thrust of the book is the orchestration of arguments that conversion is a progressive, integrative process which has consequences in the community — not merely the spiritual benefaction of the individual.

Theological reflections are derived from such people as Lonergan, Barth, Rahner, Kung, Baum and Guiterrez. The editor has demonstrated the importance of conversion to contemporary theology; and he shows that conversion or turning to God is a vital process in the life of the Christian, not a mere emotional experience relegated to the so-called "born again" religion. Indeed, conversion is not a single event, but an ongoing process in which the totality of a person's life is transformed. This position is a realization that the modification of an entire life takes time; and while there may be an immediate ontological change in a person's spiritual life, the consequences of that change often emerge only slowly and painfully in the life experience of the individual. The book is a manifestation of the new and vital role of the concept of conversion within contemporary theology, especially the theology inspired by Bernard Lonergan within the Catholic theological community.

One of the most penetrating selections in the book is from Gregory Baum. Based upon his serious reading of the sociological literature, Baum argues that theologicans must take upon themselves the responsibility for the analysis and rectification of the unintended conse-

---

Lewis R. Rambo is Professor of Pastoral Psychology at San Francisco Theological Seminary

quences of theological positions and practices. In this case, he selects the doctrine and practice of penance in the Roman Catholic Church. Sin is seen as primarily conscious, individual, moral (often sexual) evils. As a result, the social sins are virtually ignored, thus allowing for such attitudes as racism, sexism, etc. Conversion, in such a context, is merely the moral reform of the individual and her/his bad habits. Baum believes that a contemporary theology of conversion must include a more radical, fundamental alteration of the person's orientation to life, both personal and social. Likewise, Baum sees that the conservative Protestant emphasis on a "personal relationship to Jesus Christ" can have the unintended, but nevertheless destructive, consequence of reinforcing or ignoring social evils.

The psychological perspective in Conn's volume is represented by William James, Seward Hitner, Wayne Oates, Robert Thouless, Paul Johnson, and Jacques Pasquier. The psychological selections of the book may be characterized as being Jamesian and Freudian; that is to say, conversion is seen as a means by which conflict is resolved, dilemmas transcended, and wholeness achieved through the commitment to a higher set of values than personal gratification. The psychological selection may also be characterized as being theoretical rather than empirical. The tone of many of the psychological portions is pastoral. For instance, Hiltner sees every crisis in life as having the possibility of conversion — that is, a turning to God in a more fundamental manner. The minister is urged by Hiltner to see her/his vocation as facilitating such a radical reorientation in every facet of his/her work.

Conn, a professor at Villanova University, has made a significant contribution to scholarship with his fine selections, excellent introduction, bibliography, and organization. The book well represents the diversity, complexity, and significance of the conversion process.

Donald Gelpi's two books are fine illustrations of the way in which theological perspectives on conversion have been expanded. Gelpi builds on the work of Lonergan. Lonergan see three types of conversion: moral, intellectual and religious. Gelpi adds the affective (or emotional) dimension as being a salient part of the conversion process. Another important feature of Gelpi's thought is that he sees conversion as integrally related to the rest of theology. In other words, conversion is part of the total Christian message — thus, placing the topic within the proper context — not merely an emotional experience or a doctrine which asserts the superiority of one group over another. The encounter with God and the constant process of turning one's life to God over and over again is the theme which emerges in Gelpi's work and also in the book edited by Walter E. Conn mentioned above.

The reader is also directed to the excellent articles by Gabriel Fackre and S. McFague. The first combines biblical and theological insights in a very readable way. The second utilizes the recent studies of parables and asserts that the purpose of the parables is to force people to be vulnerable to God and thus conversion is a process of adventure and risk and not merely an emotional experience which confronts an individual.

Baillie, J., *Baptism and Conversion.* New York: Charles Scribners' Sons, 1963.

Barclay, W., *Turning to God: A Study of Conversion in the Book of Acts and Today.* Philadelphia: Westminster, 1964.

Barth, Christoph, "Notes on 'Return' in the Old Testament." *The Ecumenical Review,* 19 (1967) 310-312.

Castro, Emilio, "Conversion and Social Transformation." In John C. Bennett, ed., *Christian SocialEthics in a ChangingWorld.* New York: Association Press, 1966, 348-366.

Conn, Walter E. ed., *Conversion: Perspectives on Personal and Social Transformation.* Staten Island, NY: Alba House, 1978.

Dijkstra, Oswald, "Metanoia: The Moral Principle of the Christian Revolution." *The Clergy Monthly,* 30 (1966) 457-467.

Fackre, Gabriel. "Conversion." *Andover Newton Quarterly,* 14 (1974) 171-189.

Gelpi, D.L., *Charism and Sacrament: A Theology of Christian Conversion.* New York: Paulist Press, 1976.

Gelpi, D.L., *Experiencing God: A Theology of Human Experience.* New York: Paulist Press, 1978.

Gillespie, V. Bailey, *Religious Conversion and Personal Identity.* Birmingham, AL: Religious Education Press, 1979.

Goodwin, Johnnie C., *What It Means To Be Born Again.* Nashville, TN: Broadman Press, 1977.

Graham, William F., "Conversion — A Personal Revolution." *The Ecumenical Review,* 19 (1967) 271-284.

Haughton, R., *The Transformation of Man: A Study of Conversion and Community.* New York: Paulist Press, 1967.

Heikkinen, Jacob, W., "Conversion: A Biblical Study." *Mid-Stream,* 8 (1969) 92-114.

Heikkinen, J.W., "Notes on *epistrepho* and *metanoeo.*" *The Ecumenical Review,* 19 (1967) 313-316.
Hiltner, S., "Toward a Theology of Conversion in the Light of Psychology." *Pastoral Psychology* 17 (1966) 35-42.

Huberman, Steven, *New Jews: The Dynamics of Religious Conversion.* New York: Union of American Hebrew Congregations, 1979.

Hulsbosch, A., *The Bible on Conversion.* Trans. by F. Vander Heijden. De Pere, WI: St. Norbert Abbey Press, 1966.

Hwang, C.H., "Conversion in the Perspective of Three Generations." *The Ecumenical Review*, 19 (1967) 285-290.

Ingle, Clifford, ed., *Children and Conversion*. Nashville, TN: Broadman Press, 1970.

Jones, E.E., *Conversion*. Nashville, TN: Abingdon, 1959.

Katoppo, Marianne, "Conversion: An Asian Woman's Experience." *International Review of Mission*, 68 (1979) 156-160.

Krass, Alfred C., "Conversion in the United States Today." *International Review of Mission*, 68 (1979) 156-60.

Kurewa, N.N. Zvomunondita, "Conversion in the African Context." *International Review of Mission*, 68 (1979) 161-166.

Leininger, C. Earl, "The Dynamics of Conversion: Toward a Working Model." *Perspectives in Religious Studies*, 2 (1975) 191-202.

Loffler, Paul, "The Biblical Concept of Conversion." *Study Encounter*, 1, (1965) 93-101.

Loffler, Paul, "Conversion in a Ecumenical Context." *The Ecumenical Review*, 19 (1967) 252-260.

Lloyd-Jones, D.M., *Conversions: Psychological and Spiritual*. London: Inter-Varsity Press, 1959.

McFague, S., "Conversion: Life on the Edge of the Raft." *Interpretation*, 32 (1978) 255-268.

Mott, S.C., "Greek Ethics and Christian Conversion." *Novum Testamentum*, 20 (1978) 22-48.

Newbigin, Lesslie, "Context and Conversion." *International Review of Mission*, 68 (1979) 301-312.

Newbigin, Lesslie, *The Finality of Christ*. Richmond, VA: John Knox Press, 1969. See chapter on conversion, 88-116.

Nissiotis, Nikos A. "Conversion and the Church." *The Ecumenical Review*, 19 (1967) 261-270.

Olson, C. Gordon, "What about People-Movement Conversion?" *Evangelical Missions Quarterly*, 15 (1979) 133-142.

Pasquier, J. "Experience and Conversion." *The Way*, 17 (1977) 114-122.

Pauwells, C.F., "Theological Problems of Conversion." *The Thomist*, 11 (1948) 409-423.

Poling, David, *To Be Born Again: The Conversion Phenomenon*. Garden City, NY: Doubleday, 1979.